Accounting for Mismatch in
Low- and Middle-Income Countries

DIRECTIONS IN DEVELOPMENT
Human Development

Accounting for Mismatch in Low- and Middle-Income Countries

Measurement, Magnitudes, and Explanations

Michael J. Handel, Alexandria Valerio, and Maria Laura Sánchez Puerta

© 2016 International Bank for Reconstruction and Development / The World Bank
1818 H Street NW, Washington DC 20433
Telephone: 202-473-1000; Internet: www.worldbank.org

Some rights reserved

1 2 3 4   19 18 17 16

This work is a product of the staff of The World Bank with external contributions. The findings, interpretations, and conclusions expressed in this work do not necessarily reflect the views of The World Bank, its Board of Executive Directors, or the governments they represent. The World Bank does not guarantee the accuracy of the data included in this work. The boundaries, colors, denominations, and other information shown on any map in this work do not imply any judgment on the part of The World Bank concerning the legal status of any territory or the endorsement or acceptance of such boundaries.

Nothing herein shall constitute or be considered to be a limitation upon or waiver of the privileges and immunities of The World Bank, all of which are specifically reserved.

Rights and Permissions

This work is available under the Creative Commons Attribution 3.0 IGO license (CC BY 3.0 IGO) http://creativecommons.org/licenses/by/3.0/igo. Under the Creative Commons Attribution license, you are free to copy, distribute, transmit, and adapt this work, including for commercial purposes, under the following conditions:

Attribution—Please cite the work as follows: Handel, Michael J., Alexandria Valerio, and Maria Laura Sanchez Puerta. 2016. *Accounting for Mismatch in Low- and Middle-Income Countries: Measurement, Magnitudes, and Explanations.* Directions in Development. Washington, DC: World Bank. doi: 10.1596/978-1-4648-0908-8. License: Creative Commons Attribution CC BY 3.0 IGO

Translations—If you create a translation of this work, please add the following disclaimer along with the attribution: *This translation was not created by The World Bank and should not be considered an official World Bank translation. The World Bank shall not be liable for any content or error in this translation.*

Adaptations—If you create an adaptation of this work, please add the following disclaimer along with the attribution: *This is an adaptation of an original work by The World Bank. Views and opinions expressed in the adaptation are the sole responsibility of the author or authors of the adaptation and are not endorsed by The World Bank.*

Third-party content—The World Bank does not necessarily own each component of the content contained within the work. The World Bank therefore does not warrant that the use of any third-party-owned individual component or part contained in the work will not infringe on the rights of those third parties. The risk of claims resulting from such infringement rests solely with you. If you wish to re-use a component of the work, it is your responsibility to determine whether permission is needed for that re-use and to obtain permission from the copyright owner. Examples of components can include, but are not limited to, tables, figures, or images.

All queries on rights and licenses should be addressed to the Publishing and Knowledge Division, The World Bank, 1818 H Street NW, Washington, DC 20433, USA; fax: 202-522-2625; e-mail: pubrights@worldbank.org.

ISBN (paper): 978-1-4648-0908-8
ISBN (electronic): 978-1-4648-0909-5
DOI: 10.1596/978-1-4648-0908-8

Cover photo: © Thomas Vogel / Getty Images. Used with permission. Further permission required for reuse.

Library of Congress Cataloging-in-Publication Data has been requested.

Contents

Acknowledgments   xi
About the Authors   xiii
Executive Summary   xv
Abbreviations   xxix

	Introduction	1
	References	3
Chapter 1	**Defining and Measuring Skills and Mismatch**	**5**
	Defining Skills	5
	Defining Mismatch	13
	Notes	19
	References	19
Chapter 2	**Conceptual Framework**	**21**
	Explaining Mismatch: Standard Variables	21
	Using Skill Measures to Investigate Unobserved Heterogeneity	23
	Role of Structural Economic Conditions and Informality	29
	Notes	31
	References	31
Chapter 3	**About STEP**	**33**
	Introduction	33
	Notes	35
	References	36
Chapter 4	**Findings: Country Context**	**37**
	National Income and Employment Rates	37
	Educational Attainment, Achievement Levels, and Fields of Study	40
	Selection into Employment by Education and Achievement Level	46

	Quality of Employment	47
	The Task Content of Jobs	49
	Implications for Analyses	60
	Notes	60
Chapter 5	**Patterns of Educational Mismatch: Findings**	**61**
	Introduction	61
	Aggregate Distributions: Workers' Education and Job Education Requirements	62
	Aggregate Imbalances and Individual-Level Mismatch	64
	Joint Distributions of Personal and Job-Required Education	70
	Summary of Descriptive Mismatch Results	76
	Note	78
Chapter 6	**Explaining Education Mismatch**	**79**
	Introduction	79
	Predictors of Mismatch among Tertiary Graduates	79
	Models of Mismatch among All Workers	83
	Do Mismatched Tertiary Graduates Perform Tasks Reflecting Their *Education* or Their *Jobs*?	102
	Note	108
	References	109
Chapter 7	**Conclusion**	**111**
	References	115
Appendix A	Conditional Distributions of Worker and Required Education	119
Appendix B	Conditional Distributions of Job Education by Worker Education for Workers with Less than Upper Secondary Education	125
Appendix C	Summary of Logistic Regression Results with Country Labels	127

Boxes

1.1	Human Capital Theory	10
1.2	Mismatch and Wages	14
2.1	Policies to Change Educational Attainment	22
5.1	Discussion: Joint Distributions of Worker Education by Job Education	73

Figures

ES.1	Types of Mismatch	xviii
ES.2	Cross-Classification of Workers by Personal and Job-Required Education	xix
ES.3	STEP Survey Countries	xx
ES.4	Individual (Actual) Match Rates between Worker Education and Job-Required Education, by Country	xxi
2.1	Distributions of Worker Skills and Job Skill Requirements by Education Group	25
2.2	Distributions of Worker Skills by Worker Education, Overlapping Job-Required Education Levels	27
2.3	Distributions of Job Skill Requirements by Job Education, Overlapping Worker Education Levels	27
4.1	GDP per Capita, by Country, 2003 and 2013	38
4.2	Employment to Population Ratios, by Country, 2012	39
4.3	Reading Score Distributions, by Country	43
4.4	Reading Score Distributions for Upper Secondary and Tertiary Levels, by Country	44
5.1	Educational Distribution of Employed Persons, by STEP Country	62
5.2	Employed Mean Years of Education, by STEP Country	63
5.3	Distribution of Jobs by Job-Required Education Levels, by STEP Country	64
5.4	Education Match Rates, by Country	67
5.5	Rates of Over-Education, by Country	68
5.6	Rates of Under-Education, by Country	68
5.7	Rates of Over- and Under-Education, by Country	69
5.8	Joint Distribution of Worker Education by Job Education, by STEP Country	70
5.9	Conditional Distributions of Job Education by Worker Education, by Country	75
A.1	Lao PDR Row and Column Percentages	119
A.2	Ghana Row and Column Percentages	120
A.3	Kenya Row and Column Percentages	120
A.4	Bolivia Row and Column Percentages	121
A.5	Vietnam Row and Column Percentages	121
A.6	Sri Lanka Row and Column Percentages	122
A.7	Yunnan Province Row and Column Percentages	122
A.8	Armenia Row and Column Percentages	123
A.9	Macedonia, FYR, Row and Column Percentages	123
A.10	Georgia Row and Column Percentages	124
A.11	Ukraine Row and Column Percentages	124
B.1	Distribution of Job-Required Education for Workers with Less than Primary Education	125

| B.2 | Distribution of Job-Required Education for Workers with Primary Education | 126 |
| B.3 | Distribution of Job-Required Education for Workers with Low Secondary Education | 126 |

Tables

ES.1	The Cognitive Skills Domain	xvii
1.1	The Cognitive Skills Domain	6
1.2	Conceptual Map of Cognitive Skills: Three Levels and Four Kinds, Varying Applicability, and Numerous Sources	7
1.3	Cross-Classification of Workers by Personal and Job-Required Education	15
4.1	Labor Force Status of STEP Respondents and Selected Reasons for Inactivity	39
4.2	ISCED Levels and Mean Years of Education, by Country	40
4.3	Distribution of Years of Education among Tertiary Graduates, by Country	42
4.4	Mean Literacy Score by ISCED Level and Secondary-Tertiary Gap, by Country	45
4.5	Broad Fields of Study, by Country	45
4.6	Employment Rates by ISCED Level, by Country	46
4.7	Mean Literacy Score by Employment Status, by Country	47
4.8	Employment by Public/Private and Formal/Informal Sectors	48
4.9	Cognitive Skills Domain	50
4.10	Level of Reading Complexity at Work, by Worker ISCED Level, by Country	51
4.11	Level of Writing at Work, by Worker ISCED Level, by Country	52
4.12	Levels of Math Use and Problem Solving at Work, by Worker ISCED Level, by Country	54
4.13	Correlations of Job Tasks and Job-Required Education, by STEP Country	57
5.1	Aggregate Match Rates between Worker Education and Job-Required Education, by Country	65
5.2	Individual-Level (Actual) Match Rates, by STEP Country	67
5.3	Summary of Country Results	77
6.1	Hypothetical Rates of Tertiary Over-Education by Test Score Decile	80
6.2	Actual Rates of Over-Education among Tertiary Graduates by Test Score Decile	80
6.3	Rates of Over-Education among Tertiary Graduates by Employer Type and Sector, by Country	82
6.4	Over-Education Rates among Tertiary Graduates by Years of Education and Field of Study, by Country	82
6.5	Coverage of Regression Models, by Country	83

6.6	Summary of Significant Logistic Regression Results, Under-Education	84
6.7	Summary of Logistic Regression Results, Over-Education	85
6.8	Logistic Regressions Predicting Mismatch, by Country—Bolivia	86
6.9	Logistic Regressions Predicting Mismatch, by Country—Colombia	87
6.10	Logistic Regressions Predicting Mismatch, by Country—Ghana	89
6.11	Logistic Regressions Predicting Mismatch, by Country—Kenya	91
6.12	Logistic Regressions Predicting Mismatch, by Country—Vietnam	92
6.13	Logistic Regressions Predicting Mismatch, by Country—Sri Lanka, Lao PDR, and Yunnan Province	94
6.14	Logistic Regressions Predicting Mismatch, by Country—Armenia and Georgia (Over-Education Only)	96
6.15	Logistic Regressions Predicting Mismatch, by Country—Ukraine and FYR Macedonia (Over-Education Only)	97
6.16	Rates of Reading Complexity, by Match Group and Country	105
6.17	Rates of Writing and Math Complexity, by Match Group and Country	106
6.18	Rates of Problem-Solving Complexity, by Match Group and Country	107
6.19	Gap Ratios for All Task Measures and Means, by Country and Task	108
C.1	Summary of Logistic Regression Results with Country Labels	127

Acknowledgments

This report was prepared by a team comprised of Michael J. Handel from Northeastern University and Alexandria Valerio and Maria Laura Sánchez Puerta from the World Bank. Claire Miller provided research and editorial support. The team appreciates the strategic guidance and overall support received from Claudia Costin (Senior Director, Education Global Practice), Amit Dar (Director, Education Global Practice), and Luis Benveniste (Practice Manager, Global Engagements and Education Global Practice).

Helpful peer review comments were received from Roberta Gatti (Lead Economist), Margo A. Hoftijzer (Senior Economist), and Omar Arias (Lead Economist) from the World Bank and Glenda Quintini (Senior Economist) from the Organisation for Economic Co-operation and Development (OECD).

The team appreciates the overall assistance received from Lorelei Lacdao from the World Bank. The written pieces contained within this review were edited by Marc DeFrancis (DeFrancis Writing & Editing).

The report received financial support from the Skills and Information, Communication and Technology (ICT) Trust Fund received from the government of the Republic of Korea.

About the Authors

Michael J. Handel is associate professor of sociology at Northeastern University in Boston, Massachusetts, USA. He studies trends in labor market inequality and job skill requirements, particularly the impacts of changes in technology, work roles, organizational structure, and labor market institutions. His research has examined questions of skills mismatch and the impact of computers and employee involvement practices on wages, skills, and employment.

Michael has conducted the survey of Skills, Technology, and Management Practices (STAMP), a national panel survey of the skills and technology used by employees on their jobs in the United States and the management practices used by their organizations. Sections of that survey were used for the World Bank's STEP survey, the focus of the present report. Elements of his survey were incorporated into the Program for the International Assessment of Adult Competencies (PIAAC), conducted by the Organisation for Economic Co-operation and Development (OECD). He is advising the United States' Bureau of Labor Statistics on a new survey of skills and job requirements. He has also conducted research for the OECD comparing trends in job skill requirements across all advanced economies.

Michael received a PhD in sociology from Harvard University.

Alexandria Valerio has over 20 years of experience leading and managing large-scale research projects, multidisciplinary teams, and senior-level client relationships, with a policy focus on education reform (early, primary, and tertiary education), entrepreneurship, skills, and training in diverse country contexts. She has led multidisciplinary teams in the analysis, design, implementation, and evaluation of investment operations. Alexandria is currently leading global research agendas focused on measuring adult skills using large-scale household and employer surveys in 17 countries, analyzing the impact of different types of education and skill sets on employment and development outcomes, and identifying the characteristics of effective entrepreneurship education and training programs.

Prior to joining the Global Engagement and Knowledge unit in the Education Global Practice, she was responsible for the World Bank's education policy dialogue and lending portfolios in Latin America and the Caribbean (Argentina, Brazil, Chile, Nicaragua, Paraguay, and Panama), as well as in Angola and Mozambique.

Alexandria's work extends beyond the education sector, covering a wide range of issues, including social protection and labor, jobs, growth and competitiveness, child development, and school health. Her published work includes peer-reviewed books and papers on workforce development policy, technical and vocational training, entrepreneurship training, tools to measure skills in adult populations, cost and financing of early childhood education, social impact analysis of school fees, and school health programs to prevent HIV/AIDS in school-age populations. She is currently a Global Lead for the World Bank's Skills Global Solutions Group and serves as a core member of the global interagency group on Technical Vocational Education and Training/Skills and the technical working group on Human Resource Development for the G20.

Alexandria holds a PhD in comparative education and economics of education from Columbia University and a master's degree in public administration in economic development policy from the Maxwell School at Syracuse University.

Maria Laura Sánchez Puerta is a senior economist in the Jobs Group of the Social Protection and Labor Global Practice at the World Bank, where she specializes in the intersection of labor and development economics. She currently leads the jobs and skills agenda and coleads the global STEP initiative, including household and employer surveys measuring adult skills in 17 countries. She prepared one of the first job diagnostics at the country level and contributed to an innovative, multisector work program on jobs in Kenya.

Maria Laura's research includes cognitive and noncognitive skills and labor outcomes; design, implementation, and evaluation of active labor market programs; income mobility in Latin America; informality and labor market segmentation; and the effects of globalization on working conditions. Maria Laura has also supported analytical and operational work in Argentina, Brazil, Cambodia, Colombia, El Salvador, Indonesia, Kenya, Lebanon, Rwanda, and Tunisia.

Maria Laura holds a PhD in economics from Cornell University and joined the Institute for the Study of Labor (IZA) as a research fellow in 2007.

Executive Summary

Why Study Mismatch?

To stimulate economic advancement, low- and middle-income economies need educated, well-trained workforces to fill the types of highly skilled jobs that drive economic growth. Thus, improving educational attainment and quality and providing better training are all rightly put forth as policy recommendations for economic development. However, new findings based on data from the World Bank's STEP (Skills Toward Employment and Productivity) Skills Survey suggest that even in lower-income contexts, many workers are over-qualified for their jobs and unable to take full advantage of their skills. Quality education and training interventions are vital, but governments must also acknowledge the role that labor market health plays in education mismatch.

The term "mismatch" is used to describe scenarios in which workers are either over-skilled/over-educated or under-skilled/under-educated for their jobs. Most of the literature on mismatch focuses on higher-income countries and concerns rates of over-education among tertiary graduates. This publication seeks to expand on that research by employing data from the World Bank's STEP Skills Survey—which provides new data from 12 low- and middle-income countries that represent a range of economic and educational climates—to better understand the scope and patterns of education mismatch in the developing world. STEP collects information not only on workers' level of education and employment status, but also on the types, frequency, and durations of tasks they carry out at their jobs as well as some of the cognitive skills they use. The study also utilizes control variables to attempt to understand additional factors like gender, health, career stage, and participation in the informal labor sector, all of which may help explain the degree of mismatch.

The findings here indicate that over-education is common in diverse low- and middle-income country contexts, both those where tertiary graduates are relatively plentiful and those with much lower rates of educational attainment. The study also finds evidence that over-educated tertiary workers do not use all of their skills, potentially wasting valuable human capital and educational resources.

This publication is intended primarily for a policy-making audience. At the same time, because the findings suggest that job growth must go hand-in-hand with investments in education and training, they are relevant not only to policy makers but to business and education leaders and employers as well.

> **What Is STEP?**
> The World Bank's STEP Skills Measurement Program (STEP) is the first-ever initiative to measure skills in low- and middle-income countries. It is conducted as a household survey of working-age adults (ages 15–64) residing in urban areas, and provides new and detailed information on education, employment, and related topics.
> The program includes three modules: a direct assessment of reading, self-reported information on personal characteristics, and a survey of job-relevant skills.

What Do We Mean by "Skills," and How Does STEP Measure Them?

As research on job mismatch has expanded, so have the methods and systems for defining skills. Common distinctions among skills include those defined as *interpersonal*, those defined as *manual*, and those known as *cognitive* skills. It is the last type that is the focus of this research.

One way to understand the broad domain of cognitive skills is to distinguish them by levels and kinds of knowledge, degrees of generality or specificity across jobs, and the means by which they are acquired by workers (table ES.1).

There are a variety of ways to measure the skills a particular job requires. The traditional starting point has been to measure *job-required education or qualifications*, because it is the most straightforward information to define and collect. But even using education as a proxy for skills can be challenging, as one must be careful to avoid conflating the education of the job holder with the actual level of education required for a job. To address this, researchers employ various methods, including the following.

- **Statistical methods**—which typically measure the mean or modal education of workers within occupations and are the methods most frequently used for estimating job-required education. However, these methods blur the distinction between workers' actual education and job-required education, and they cannot distinguish between situations in which levels of worker education represent technical job requirements from situations of pervasive credential inflation.
- **Researcher judgment**—which has been used in a few studies but requires a high level of occupational aggregation and subjective decisions by the researchers who assign education levels to broad occupations.
- **Job-holder surveys**—which is the method STEP employs and involves collecting data at the job level by asking workers *themselves* what skills are required for their jobs. This is a reliable, easily implemented strategy that many international surveys have adopted.

Of course, determining the types of skills a job requires is far more complex than measuring basic credentials and levels of schooling needed. Skills can be

Table ES.1 The Cognitive Skills Domain

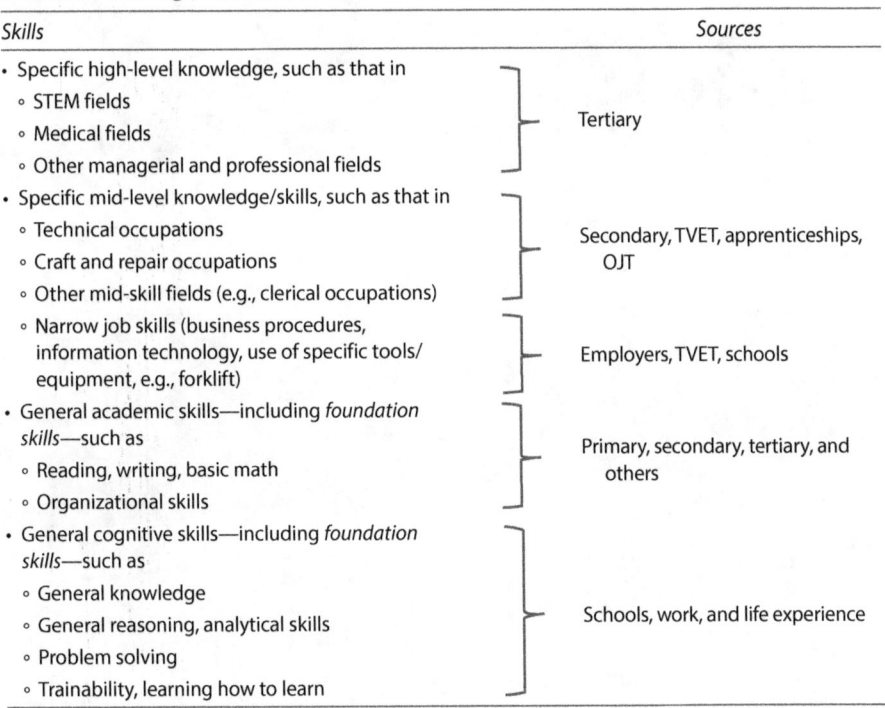

Note: STEM = science, technology, engineering, math; TVET = technical and vocational education and training; OJT = on-the-job training; primary, secondary, and tertiary refer to levels of formal education.

defined and categorized in almost limitless detail at the occupational and even job level, but for practicality of measurement and comparison, a balance must be struck. One feature that makes STEP unique is the survey's ability to capture detailed information not only on job holders' level of education, but also on

… **their fields of study.** STEP captures survey information on fields of study, which applies primarily to workers with tertiary and/or specific vocational education.

… **their jobs' required cognitive tasks.** STEP uses a system of explicit scaling to measure the reading, writing, numeracy, and problem-solving skills workers use both in their jobs and in their daily lives. The survey captures the complexity of tasks workers perform on the job.

… **their own cognitive skills.** STEP also contains a reading assessment, which can help determine how education translates into jobs with varying cognitive demands.

What Do We Mean by "Mismatch?"

In the context of work, mismatch can refer to education or skills—and usually refers to some combination of both (see figure ES.1). Mismatch occurs when workers' education and skills do not align with those required by their jobs.

Figure ES.1 Types of Mismatch

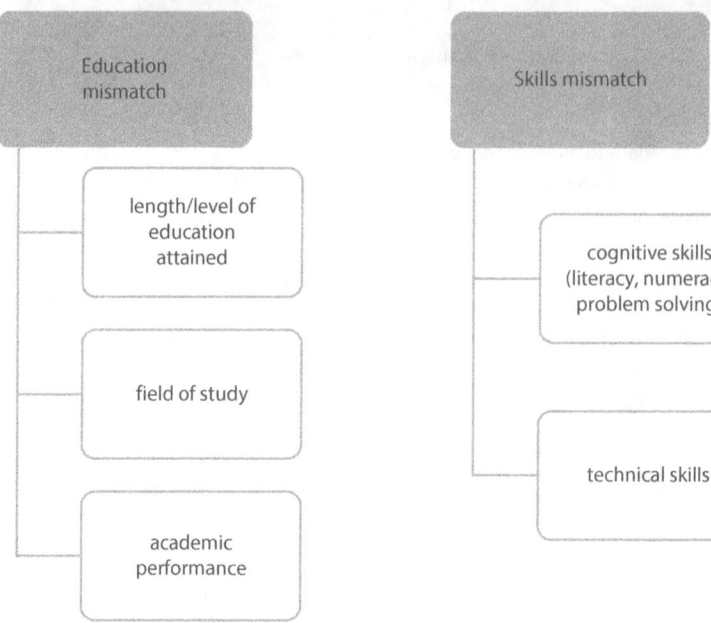

Education mismatch includes mismatch by the level of education attained (such as when a worker who has completed secondary school holds a job that requires only a primary education), mismatch by field of study (as when a worker with a tertiary degree in engineering manages a general import/export business), and mismatch by academic performance[1] (as when a worker who has strong literacy and numeracy skills holds a job that involves little reading and math). An important question is whether some of the mismatch by education level or field of study can be explained by usually unobserved differences in academic performance within levels or fields, as opposed to job market conditions that are outside the individual's control.

For the sake of simplicity, if we look only at education mismatch in terms of education level (identified here as "high," "medium," and "low"), the model illustrated in figure ES.2 emerges. Workers who are well-matched—whose own education aligns with the level required by their jobs—are indicated in orange. Ideally, healthy economies need as many people as possible to be *both* highly skilled *and* matched to jobs that require those high-level skills, rather than having many low-skilled workers in low-skill jobs even though such workers would technically be well-matched. In the figure, workers who would be considered over-educated are represented by green icons and those considered under-educated by blue icons. Key gaps in knowledge include the distribution of workers across these different conditions and the reasons workers end up well-matched or mismatched.

Executive Summary

Figure ES.2 Cross-Classification of Workers by Personal and Job-Required Education

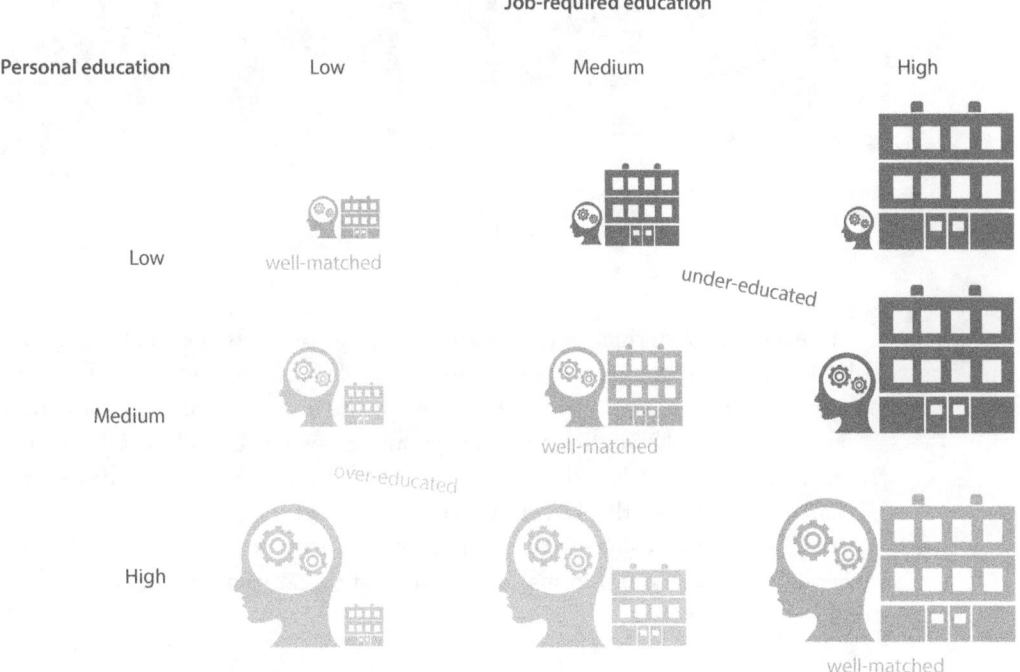

Source: Icons from The Noun Project.

What Countries Make Up the STEP Sample?

Twelve countries, representing four major regions and diverse national incomes, participated in the STEP survey, as illustrated in figure ES.3.

These 12 countries represent a range of average educational levels and performance, unemployment rates, and types of economy (such as economies with larger and smaller informal sectors and those with different rates of public/private employment). In terms of GDP, they range from lower income, such as Kenya and Ghana, to middle income, such as Colombia.

Employment rates vary greatly among the countries as well. To take the extreme cases, in the Lao People's Democratic Republic and Bolivia about 85 percent of the working-age population are employed, while in Armenia and Georgia the rates are closer to 35 percent. Employment rates provide important context for this study on mismatch because high unemployment rates among well-educated workers will result in an underestimate of mismatch prevalence (if we consider involuntary joblessness to be its own form of mismatch). In particular, the high unemployment and nonparticipation rates for tertiary graduates in the countries of Europe and Central Asia mean that while these countries might present lower mismatch rates, they still face serious problems matching people to jobs.

Figure ES.3 STEP Survey Countries

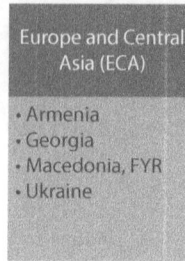
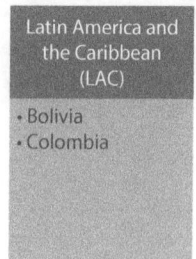

Educational performance ranges greatly across countries, both in the amount of education completed and as measured by academic performance. The four countries in Europe and Central Asia present the highest mean years of education—more than 12 years for all four countries—while Lao PDR, Ghana, and Kenya, each averages less than nine years. As expected, average reading scores (available for eight of the 12 countries) follow a similar pattern.

Last, this study explores employment patterns across the 12 countries by sector: public, private, and informal, which also vary greatly and have strong effects on levels of mismatch.

How Prevalent Is Education Mismatch in the Developing World?

The simplest way to define mismatch is to compare workers' personal education to their job-required education. At the individual level, this study finds mismatch to be a widespread problem across all 12 STEP countries, with over-education proving to be more common than under-education.[2] Among the highlights:

- *Vietnam* had the lowest match rate between worker education and job-required education, with just 26 percent of workers' jobs requiring education that matched their own. Seventy percent of Vietnamese workers held a job that required less education than they had personally attained (they were "over-educated") and just 4 percent held a job requiring more education than they had achieved (under-educated).
- *The Former Yugoslav Republic of Macedonia* had the highest individual-level match rate, with 73 percent of workers holding well-matched jobs. Twenty-two percent of Macedonian workers were over-educated, and 5 percent were under-educated.
- Overall, the mean job-education match rate for all 12 countries was 52 percent well-matched. The average over-education rate was 36 percent and the average under-education rate was 12 percent. Match rates for all countries are provided in figure ES.4.

Improving worker skills, whether through education or through other training, is one of the most common recommendations for promoting economic development.

Figure ES.4 Individual (Actual) Match Rates between Worker Education and Job-Required Education, by Country

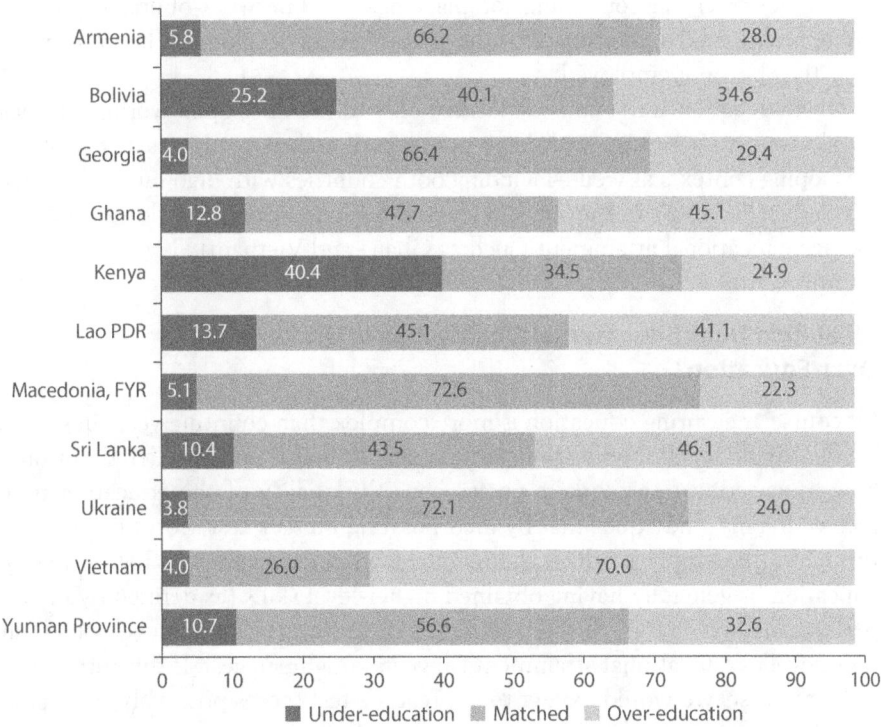

Source: World Bank STEP Skills Measurement Program.

However, the findings in this paper suggest that a large portion of worker skills in developing countries are *already* underutilized in the workplace, and that it is the skills *required by jobs*—not the skills workers themselves possess—that tend to lag behind. At the country level, it is clear that economic growth cannot take place through skills development alone; it is also necessary to foster the expansion of higher-skilled jobs to ensure that the capabilities of higher-skilled workers do not go underutilized.

It is also important to note that the above rates of *individual* (actual) mismatch differ from rates of *aggregate* mismatch, which are calculated by comparing the number of total jobs requiring specific levels of education to the total number of workers who possess each of those levels of education. Differences in the distributions of personal education and job-required education give an upper-bound estimate of the shares of workers and jobs that can be well-matched. For example, aggregate rates range from 66 percent well-matched in Vietnam to 89 percent well-matched in Macedonia, FYR. This indicates that education mismatch is not simply an issue of training an ideal number of workers to correspond with an ideal number of jobs at the same education level. If that were the case, actual and aggregate rates would be identical. Instead, the lower actual match rates indicate that there is also a need to help workers find the jobs that most effectively utilize their skills and match their educational backgrounds. Programs that seek to expand worker skills would be wise to also consider investing in efforts such as career counseling, job placement, and network-building activities like apprenticeships to ensure that the skills workers develop can be maximized once they become employed.

Over-education is not an issue limited only to the developed world, nor does it only concern countries with large numbers of college graduates. It persists in developing contexts as well—including both countries with high rates of tertiary education (like those in Europe and Central Asia) and those with lower levels of average educational attainment (such as Ghana and Vietnam).

What Role Does Educational Quality Play in Under- and Over-Education?

Of course, measuring education is more complex than counting years in school or identifying level of educational attainment. What if we considered not only how much education workers possess, but the quality of the education they received? This study does that by incorporating literacy test scores for eight of the 12 STEP countries, which shed light on whether receiving a better-quality education or generally having obtained higher-level skills (as defined by higher performance on literacy tasks) can help workers access higher-level jobs than their level of educational attainment (in years) might suggest. If this turned out to be the case, we would expect to see reading test scores positively associated with being categorized as "under-educated." Similarly, it would make sense to see low test scores associated with being over-educated for one's job, especially at the tertiary level.

And yet, findings from this study indicate that test scores do *not* play a major role in explaining under-education. Test scores do play some role in explaining rates of over-education, but it is not a large one.

- Five countries—*Bolivia, Colombia, Ghana, Kenya,* and *Vietnam*—had adequate data to predict rates of under-education relative to test scores. In none of these countries did the addition of literacy test scores significantly change the patterns of mismatch observed. It does not appear that better performance on literacy tests increases the likelihood of holding a job requiring greater education controlling for workers' education level and other covariates.
- Eight countries—*Armenia, Bolivia, Colombia, Georgia, Ghana, Kenya, Ukraine,* and *Vietnam*—had adequate data to predict rates of over-education relative to test scores. In four of the eight countries, when controlling for additional variables (see below), the odds of being over-educated rather than well-matched decreased as test scores increased.[3] However, the effect size was small, and other educational factors—such as level of tertiary education and field of study—were more strongly associated with likelihood of over-education, as were job characteristics, such as informality.

Overall, it appears that while low test scores (such as poorer academic performance) may play some role in workers' being forced to take jobs whose required education is below their attainment, high test scores (such as stronger academic performance) do not seem to explain under-education. Rather, it could be that to explain rates of under-education one must look at skills not measured by the STEP literacy test, including access to nonformal training, noncognitive skills, personal relationships, or other factors.

How Much of the Observed Mismatch Rates Can Be Explained by Other Variables?

Educational attainment is only one determinant of the jobs workers hold. Clearly, there are numerous personal, societal, and economic factors that may explain why individuals end up in jobs for which they are under- or over-qualified. Because little research exists on education mismatch in developing countries, it is particularly useful to include these variables in this study's model. The STEP Skills Survey includes background questions on areas like work history, household details, and health, which provide a number of additional control variables.

Past research (Sloane 2003; Jones et al. 2014) has explored several explanations for patterns of mismatch that go beyond aggregate skill and educational imbalances. First, observed over-education may be due to transitory labor market frictions. For example, young, well-educated workers may enter the job market lacking job experience, search skills, or effective networks and end up in jobs for which they are technically over-qualified, but eventually they may find their way to well-matched jobs as they gain career experience. Observed over-education may also be explained by individual preferences that make some workers (like students or women with small children) likely to accept jobs with lower educational requirements in exchange for benefits such as flexible schedules. Next, health-related limitations may make it more difficult for some workers to find jobs that match their qualifications. When using educational attainment as a measure of job matching, it is also important to account for the fact that some occupations in some contexts provide valid, alternative pathways for acquiring necessary skills, such as on-the-job training and years of job experience. In some cases, experience can substitute for education, so more experienced workers might be more likely to report being under-educated. In other cases, credential requirements may have risen in the period after more senior workers entered their occupation.

Last, although it is less recognized in the literature, gender, ethnic, or socioeconomic discrimination may play a role in some countries and occupations. Examining demographic variables for such patterns could shed light on their contribution to over-education. Which, if any, of these factors help explain the patterns of mismatch observed across the STEP sample?

- *Transitory labor market factors?* Only in two of the eight countries with available data were workers more than 10 years out of school more likely to be under-educated than workers less than 10 years out of school, indicating that workers may be able to replace education with skills learned on the job as they move through their careers. In no countries were young workers more likely to be over-educated than more experienced workers, indicating that workers may not be more likely to find better-matched jobs as they progress through their careers (although longitudinal data would be needed to confirm this).

- *Individual preferences?* Some people may accept a job requiring lower skills than they possess for the convenience of working fewer hours. However, contrary to expectation, working part-time is associated with under-education in two countries and is not generally associated with over-education.

- *Gender?* Only in Ghana were women more likely to be under-educated for their jobs than men, indicating that in all other countries women may, in fact, be just as able as men to substitute experience for formal education or use other alternative paths to occupational achievement. In terms of over-education, in some countries women with young children have higher odds of being over-educated than men.

- *Health limitations?* These do not explain either under- or over-education in participating countries.

- *Formal vs. informal sector?* Employment in the informal sector is negatively associated with under-education, which is logical since informality is typically a response to a shortage of other job opportunities. Employment in the formal sector, it follows, is one of the only variables that helps explain under-education relatively consistently. Public sector employment, which is generally associated with formality, is strongly associated with jobs that are better matched to worker education, whereas employment in the informal and formal private sectors and self-employment are associated with over-education.

- *Years of tertiary education?* Among workers who have some tertiary education, there is a strong relationship between years of tertiary education and likelihood of being well-matched (that is, holding a job that requires tertiary study). In all countries, workers with the fewest years of tertiary education faced a much greater risk of holding a nontertiary job and thus falling in the over-educated category.

- *Field of study?* Among tertiary graduates, the relationship between field of study and over-education varies between fields. For example, rates of over-education for graduates in the humanities and social sciences, health, and law tend to be below country averages, whereas rates for business graduates tend to be above country averages. Graduates of STEM/technical fields tend to be over-educated at rates similar to their country averages.

Overall, most of the control variables this study employs account for only a small part of the mismatch observed in STEP countries. Thus, much of the observed under- and over-education in these countries may indeed reflect genuine issues of education-job mismatch in their economies. The fact that the strongest indicators of over-education are employment in informal jobs of various kinds supports the conclusion that skill underutilization is a serious problem in developing contexts. There is a great deal of underemployment in developing countries relative to the measured skills of workers.

Do Workers with More Education Perform Higher-Level Tasks?

It is clear from these findings that over-education is prevalent across the 12 STEP countries. However, what is not clear is whether or not over-educated workers are actually performing the same types of tasks at work as their well-matched, less-educated coworkers. After all, individual jobs, even in the same industry or organization, are rarely identical. A worker with tertiary education may hold a job that officially requires only secondary education, but she may use additional skills in her everyday work that a colleague with a secondary education may not possess. If tertiary-educated workers perform high-skill tasks even in lower-skilled jobs, the observed rates of over-education may be more apparent than genuine.

STEP collects data not only on worker education and job-required education, but also on the types and complexity of tasks workers perform at their jobs and outside of work, including complexity of reading, writing, numeracy, and problem-solving tasks. This study uses this information on job task complexity to compare three categories of workers: well-matched workers with upper-secondary education, well-matched workers with tertiary education, and over-educated workers with tertiary education. Analyses examine the extent to which the tasks performed by over-educated tertiary workers are similar to those performed by well-matched upper secondary graduates as opposed to well-matched tertiary graduates. Among the findings:

- Overall, measured by what people actually do at work, tertiary workers in jobs requiring less than tertiary education have more highly skilled jobs than workers with upper secondary education in the same jobs. But this generally closes only about one-quarter of the skill gap between well-matched upper secondary workers and well-matched tertiary workers.
- *In almost all countries,* over-educated tertiary graduates perform tasks more similar to those performed by well-matched secondary graduates than to the substantially more complex tasks performed by well-matched tertiary graduates, which we might expect the mismatched tertiary graduates to be able to perform given their test scores.
- *Ghana* is the only country in which over-educated tertiary graduates fall squarely midway between well-matched secondary and tertiary graduates.

These results strongly suggest that measured over-education among tertiary graduates involves considerable genuine underutilization of skills. The nature of these graduates' work is determined more by their jobs than by their own educational level; their on-the-job tasks are much closer to the tasks of their (less-educated) coworkers than to those of their well-matched tertiary classmates.

Again, this supports the overall finding that skill underutilization is a challenge across diverse developing countries. STEP data provide evidence that, even in countries with high proportions of tertiary graduates, *a lack of higher-skilled jobs contributes to mismatch between workers' personal and job-required education, not simply a lack of workers with the skills needed for such jobs*. The benefits of investing in education and training programs will be dampened significantly as long as the growth in high-skilled jobs fails to keep pace with the output of education systems.

Take-Aways for Policy Makers

- **Over-education is prevalent not only in the higher-income world, but also in low- and middle-income contexts.**
  Eleven of the 12 STEP countries had higher rates of over-education than under-education, with an overall average of 36 percent of workers classified as over-educated. The fact that this includes both countries with higher levels and those with lower levels of average educational attainment suggests that over-education is not simply a matter of high-income countries producing too many college graduates. The problem is significant across countries with a range of educational and skill levels.

- **Academic performance, as measured by literacy scores, is not strongly associated with mismatch rates.**
  It appears that educational credentials and years of education are much greater determinants of over-education than test scores. Rather than suggesting that educational quality and academic skills are unimportant, this finding may suggest a widespread use of educational attainment as a signaling or screening mechanism by employers.

- **Mismatch rates cannot be attributed generally to gender, health limitations, individual preferences, or worker career stage.**
  Job sector (formal/informal, public/private) seems to be the variable that matters most in explaining over- and under-education patterns, suggesting that much of the mismatch observed in this study may be genuine.

- **Findings suggest that over-educated tertiary workers do not fully utilize their skills.**
  It is vital that expansion of education and training not take place in a vacuum; policy makers should consider accompanying such investments with policies to support the growth of high-skilled jobs.

Notes

1. This report uses the term "academic performance" in reference to what a student has actually learned through formal education (as opposed to "seat time"). In practice, this is typically measured through grade point average and (in the case of STEP) test scores.
2. See chapter 5, table 5.2, for job-education match rates for all 12 countries.
3. Significant at a 0.05 alpha-level.

References

Jones, Melanie K., Kostas G. Mavromaras, Peter J. Sloane, and Zhang Wei. 2014. "Disability and Job Mismatches in the Australian Labour Market." *Cambridge Journal of Economics* 38: 1221–46.

Sloane, Peter J. 2003. "Much Ado About Nothing? What Does the Overeducation Literature Really Tell Us?" In *Overeducation in Europe*, edited by Felix Büchel, Andries de Grip, and Antje Merten, 11–48. Northampton, MA: Edward Elgar.

Abbreviations

ECA	Europe and Central Asia
ETS	Educational Testing Services
GDP	gross domestic product
IO	industrial/organizational
ISCED	International Standard Classification of Education
ISCO	International Standard Classification of Occupations
IT	information technology
O*NET	Occupational Information Network
OECD	Organisation for Economic Co-operation and Development
PIAAC	Programme for the International Assessment of Adult Competencies
STAMP	Survey of Skills, Technology, and Management Practices
STEM	science, technology, engineering, and mathematics
STEP	Skills Toward Employment and Productivity
TVET	technical and vocational education and training
WDI	World Development Indicators

Introduction

A common prescription for improving jobs and living standards is increasing workers' education and skills, qualifying them for higher-valued-added tasks. However, the relationship between education and employment is not necessarily straightforward. A growing body of research has focused on understanding the patterns and causes of *mismatch* between workers' actual education and skills, on the one hand, and those required by their jobs, on the other.

Why is understanding mismatch—and its drivers—so important? For policy makers, it is necessary to make informed decisions about education, training, and job creation in their specific economic contexts. On both a societal scale and for individual workers, high rates of mismatch (in particular, high rates of over-education) can impact wages and worker morale. Some studies find that over-qualified workers are less likely to be satisfied with their jobs than well-matched workers with the same educational background (Tsang 1987; Battu, Belfield, and Sloane 2000; Verhaest and Omey 2006; and Verhofstadt, De Witte, and Omey 2007). While the literature on the relationship between mismatch (especially the *persistence* of mismatch) and wages is mixed, some research suggests a negative association. Guvenen et al. (2015) found that while mismatch declines over a worker's career, starting out in a poorly matched job can have a long-term impact on a worker's wages, even for those workers who go on to find a better-matched job in a different occupation.

Most of what we know about defining, measuring, and understanding mismatch comes from research on over-education in higher-income countries. Beginning in the 1970s, concerns about a surplus of college-educated workers and the diminishing returns of higher education sparked an interest in over-education. Freeman (1976) predicted in his much-discussed book, *The Overeducated American*, an ongoing decline in wage premiums for college- and high-school-educated workers. Smith and Welch's subsequent research (1978), which indicated that wage declines may not have been as large as initially feared, tempered some concerns. Duncan and Hoffman (1981) introduced research on over-education at the individual rather than the aggregate level that has informed much of the research since.

However, even as these early models have been changed and improved upon, other research has sought to make a distinction between workers who are over-educated and workers who are over-*skilled*. Studies like that by Allen and van der Velden (2001) have posited that over-educated workers are not necessarily over-skilled, meaning that they may still be appropriately matched to their jobs. Correcting for this omitted variable bias has proved challenging.

Overall, over-education common in the developed world and its prevalence range widely. A 2011 OECD meta-analysis found that when using qualification as a proxy for mismatch, up to a quarter of workers in OECD countries could meet the definition of being over-qualified, and one in three may be under-qualified (Quintini 2011). Most OECD countries fall between the two extremes of Sweden (where over 35 percent are over-qualified) and Finland (about 10 percent over-qualified). More recent research has confirmed these trends and even suggested that in parts of the world over-education may be increasing. The 2014 European Skills and Jobs Survey found that in the European Union (EU), about 25 percent of highly qualified young adult workers were over-qualified for their jobs. Moreover, those who graduated after 2008 were almost twice as likely to be over-qualified for their first jobs than those who had graduated between 1991 and 2000. Forty-two percent of EU employees felt they had "few opportunities to find a job matching their skills and qualifications" (Cedefop 2015).

Even with a rich literature to draw from, it is challenging to draw broad, global conclusions about rates of over-education, because different studies (even within the same country) often use different measurements for job-required education. Leuven and Oosterbeek (2011) found in their review of worldwide mismatch research that the overall mean rate for over-education was 30 percent of workers, while the overall mean for under-education stood at 26 percent. Breaking this down by continent (Asia, Australia, Europe, Latin America, and U.S./Canada), they found that the share of over-educated workers was, on average, largest in the U.S. and Canada and smallest in Asia.

But what does education mismatch look like, more specifically, in the *developing* world? Only a modest amount of research has addressed mismatch in these contexts, mostly due to lack of data on the years of education required for specific jobs. Mehta et al. (2011) used labor force surveys from four countries to observe over-education, which they measured based on rising education levels for low-return jobs with little technological change. They found evidence of over-education in low-skill jobs in the Philippines, mild evidence of the same in Mexico, and no evidence of it in India or Thailand. Other studies have looked at the relationship between education and jobs in individual countries or regions, such as Quinn and Rubb (2006) in Mexico and Herrera and Merceron (2013) in Sub-Saharan Africa.

However, little research exists on broader trends in mismatch across larger numbers of low- and middle-income countries. Is over-education prevalent in these contexts as well, or is under-education more widespread? Finally, are there factors specific to these contexts—such as gender dynamics, health limitations, and the presence of large informal sectors—that can help explain these patterns of mismatch?

The World Bank's STEP Household Skills Survey seeks to fill these gaps by providing new, detailed information on workers' education, skill, and job backgrounds in low- and middle-income countries. Unlike past skill surveys, STEP is particularly suited to address questions of mismatch because it contains parallel measures for workers *and* jobs, permitting more direct linkage between skills and education levels.

What do the STEP data tell us? Results from data on urban workers from a diverse group of 12 low- and middle-income countries show that mismatch is indeed common. As in most of the higher-income countries studied in previous research, in the developing world over-education is the most prevalent type of mismatch observed. When models include additional controls, it appears that mismatch does *not* reflect personal job preferences, search frictions associated with youth and inexperience, or health limitations. Both academic performance (test scores) and gender are associated with the probability of being over-educated, but the relationships are not as strong or consistent across countries as might be expected. Stronger associations are found between over-education and both working at an informal job and in a job outside the public sector.

This report is divided into three parts. Part 1 (Chapters 1 and 2) provides background and discusses the conceptual basis for understanding skills and mismatch. Part 2 (Chapters 3 and 4) explains the STEP samples and measures as well as the descriptive statistics for predictors used in analyses. Part 3 (Chapters 5 and 6) summarizes the mismatch rates found through the STEP surveys and analyses, controlling for detailed measures of worker skills and other worker characteristics as well as structural labor market characteristics relevant to alternative explanations of mismatch.

References

Allen, J., and R. van der Velden. 2001. "Educational Mismatches versus Skill Mismatches: Effects on Wages, Job Satisfaction, and On-the-Job Search." *Oxford Economic Papers* 53: 434–52.

Battu, H., C. Belfield, and P. Sloane. 2000. "How Well Can We Measure Graduate Over-Education and Its Effects?" *National Institute Economic Review* 171: 82–93.

Cedefop. 2015. *Skills, Qualifications and Jobs in the EU: The Making of a Perfect Match? Evidence from Cedefop's European Skills and Jobs Survey*. Cedefop reference series 103. Luxembourg: Publications Office of the European Union. http://dx.doi.org/10.2801/606129.

Duncan, G., and S. Hoffman. 1981. "The Incidence and Wage Effects of Overeducation." *Economics of Education Review* 1: 57–68.

Freeman, Richard B. 1976. *The Overeducated American*. New York: Academic Press.

Guvenen, Faith, Burhan Kuruscu, Satoshi Tanaka, and David Wiczer. 2015. "Multidimensional Skills Mismatch." Federal Reserve Bank of Minneapolis Research Department Working Paper 729, Federal Reserve Bank of Minneapolis, Minneapolis, MN. https://www.minneapolisfed.org/research/wp/wp729.pdf.

Herrera, J., and S. Merceron. 2013. "Underemployment and Job Mismatch in Sub-Saharan Africa." In *Urban Labor Markets in Sub-Saharan Africa*, edited by Philippe De Vreyer and François Roubaud, 83–108. Washington, DC: World Bank.

Jones, Melanie K., Kostas G. Mavromaras, Peter J. Sloane, and Zhang Wei. 2014. "Disability and Job Mismatches in the Australian Labour Market." *Cambridge Journal of Economics* 38: 1221–46.

Leuven, E., and H. Oosterbeek. 2011. "Overeducation and Mismatch in the Labor Market." In *Handbook of the Economics of Education*, edited by E. Hanushek and F. Welch, 283–326. Philadelphia: Elsevier Science.

Mehta, A., J. Felipe, P. Quising, and S. Camingue. 2011. "Overeducation in Developing Economies: How Can We Test for It, and What Does It Mean?" *Economics of Education Review* 30: 1334–47.

Quinn, Michael A., and Stephen Rubb. 2006. "Mexico's Labor Market: The Importance of Education-Occupation Matching on Wages and Productivity in Developing Countries." *Economics of Education Review* 25: 147–56.

Quintini, Glenda. 2011. "Over-Qualified or Under-Skilled: A Review of Existing Literature." OECD Social, Employment and Migration Working Papers 121, OECD Publishing. http://dx.doi.org/10.1787/5kg58j9d7b6d-en.

Sloane, Peter J. 2003. "Much Ado about Nothing? What Does the Overeducation Literature Really Tell Us?" In *Overeducation in Europe*, edited by Felix Büchel, Andries Grip, and Antje Merten, 11–48. Northampton, MA: Edward Elgar.

Smith, J., and F. Welch. 1978. "The Overeducated American: A Review Article." RAND P-6253, RAND, Santa Monica, CA.

Tsang, M. 1987. "The Impact of Underutilisation of Education on Productivity: A Case Study of the US Bell Companies." *Economics of Education Review* 6: 239–54.

Verhaest, D., and E. Omey. 2006. "The Impact of Overeducation and Its Measurement." *Social Indicators Research* 77: 419–48.

Verhofstadt, E., H. De Witte, and E. Omey. 2007. "The Impact of Education on Job Satisfaction in the First Job." *International Journal of Manpower* 28: 135–51.

CHAPTER 1

Defining and Measuring Skills and Mismatch

Defining Skills

Understanding a complex construct like "skills" requires systematically specifying its dimensions or facets and finding ways to effectively measure them. A skill can be defined as any capability that satisfies some practical requirement of work. That is, skill is not simply some knowledge, credential, status, or other personal characteristic; the quality or capacity must be directly relevant to job performance. A commonly used scheme distinguishes among types of skills that are *cognitive, interpersonal*, and *manual*.[1]

STEP (Skills Toward Employment and Productivity) contains information on each dimension, but cognitive skills are the focus in this report given their importance for most discussions of mismatch and given scope and complexity considerations. Of course, in recent years, research has elucidated the important role noncognitive skills (often called socioemotional or soft skills) play in cognitive performance, educational attainment, and labor market outcomes (Heckman, Sitxrud, and Urzua 2006; Carneiro, Crawford, and Goodman 2007), and such skills will be important to address in a future publication on the socioemotional dimension.

Even cognitive skills alone cover a wide range, which can be conceptualized systematically, roughly hierarchically, and by source, as in table 1.1, which divides cognitive skills into four categories, as follows.

Specific high-level, formal knowledge. This is usually acquired through tertiary education and is required for a number of highly skilled managerial and professional jobs.

Specific mid-level knowledge and skills. These skills usually require shorter formal education or training than the preceding and are common in technical, craft, and certain clerical jobs. This category also includes skills needed for different discrete, mid-skill tasks found across the occupational spectrum requiring brief training. Notable in this category are information technology skills, but the category also includes myriad other skills of varying generality or specificity

Table 1.1 The Cognitive Skills Domain

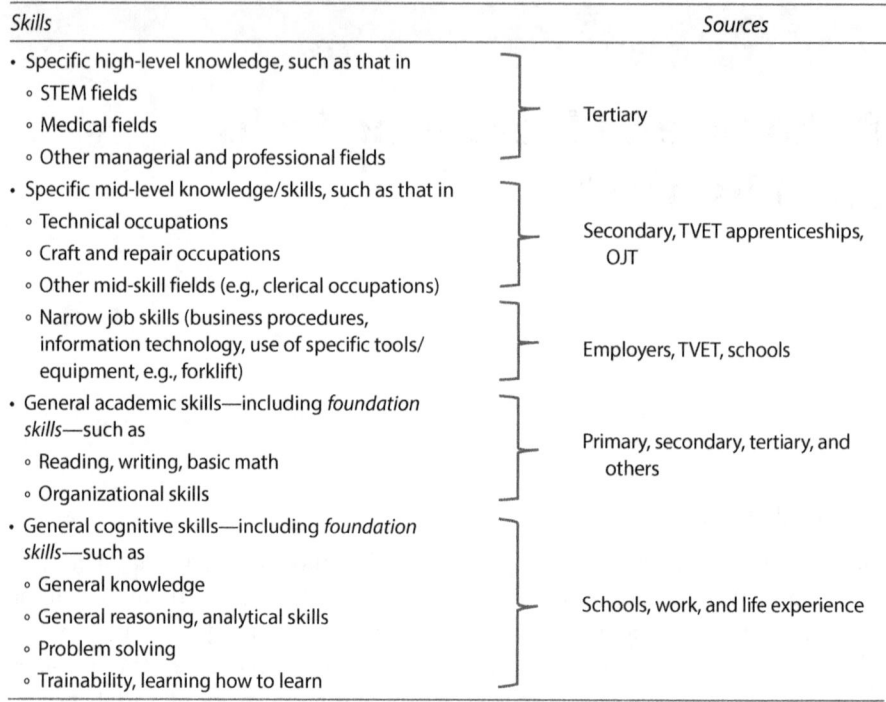

Skills	Sources
• Specific high-level knowledge, such as that in 　◦ STEM fields 　◦ Medical fields 　◦ Other managerial and professional fields	Tertiary
• Specific mid-level knowledge/skills, such as that in 　◦ Technical occupations 　◦ Craft and repair occupations 　◦ Other mid-skill fields (e.g., clerical occupations)	Secondary, TVET apprenticeships, OJT
◦ Narrow job skills (business procedures, information technology, use of specific tools/equipment, e.g., forklift)	Employers, TVET, schools
• General academic skills—including *foundation skills*—such as 　◦ Reading, writing, basic math 　◦ Organizational skills	Primary, secondary, tertiary, and others
• General cognitive skills—including *foundation skills*—such as 　◦ General knowledge 　◦ General reasoning, analytical skills 　◦ Problem solving 　◦ Trainability, learning how to learn	Schools, work, and life experience

Note: STEM = science, technology, engineering, math; TVET = technical and vocational education and training; OJT = on-the-job training; primary, secondary, and tertiary refer to levels of formal education.

found across occupations, industries, firms, and jobs. (Examples are typing, sewing, bookkeeping, and office procedures; competence using specific software or IT hardware; working with specific materials, tools, and mechanical equipment; and procedures such as hazardous materials handling.) Mid-level skills can be acquired in a variety of institutions, such as general and vocational secondary schools and post-secondary/nonuniversity institutions, as well as through some combination of experience, on- or off-job training, and apprenticeships, but narrow job skills are often learned at the workplace.

General academic skills. These are skills used on the job, such as literacy and numeracy, that correspond to curricula at the primary, secondary, and tertiary levels, depending on the skills' complexity level.

General cognitive skills. These include skills such as reasoning and problem solving, which are acquired through life and work experiences as well as schooling at all levels.

The latter two groups are the most transversal. They are often called *foundation skills* because they are necessary for acquiring the occupation-specific skills of varying complexity listed above them. Clearly, a number of the distinctions in table 1.1 are heuristic, and the particular examples may be open to alternative or multiple placement. Nevertheless, this category scheme is a useful framework for understanding the diversity within the cognitive skills domain.

Table 1.1 represents a map of the skills domain that any systematic battery of skill measures must cover and against which the *content validity* of the measures is judged. Most specific examples of what is meant by "skills" can be located in one or more of the categories in this table. A good set of measures should aim for thorough coverage of the categories in this list. It makes no sense to speak about *a* skills mismatch problem without further specifying which skills are the subject of concern, despite the frequency of this approach in public discussion and even in much research. It is clear that even cognitive skills are innumerable, varying both by level or *amount* and by *kind*, and varying as well by the generality of their *applicability* across jobs and by the *sources* from which they are acquired (formal schooling, training, workplaces, general life experience). All of these—amounts, kinds, generality, and sources—affect possible directions for policy.

These four dimensions are highlighted in an alternative representation, shown in table 1.2, which underscores the complexity and diversity of the skills domain and the different perspectives involved in considering skill content, providers, and applicability to varying kinds and numbers of jobs.

General pronouncements that an economy has "a skills mismatch problem" lack policy-actionable content and are essentially empty. Claims that the *level* of education is the source of the mismatch problem are somewhat more specific but still beg the questions of whether the problem lies with foundation skills, vocational or technical middle skills, specific higher-level knowledge (e.g., STEM), or some subset of the innumerable job- and occupation-specific skills. The latter are a constant concern of the particular firms that utilize them and are often channeled into more general calls for improving workforce skill levels. Table 1.2 provides a systematic paradigm for understanding the different meanings of the cognitive skills concept, whose relevance will vary depending on the context.

Table 1.2 Conceptual Map of Cognitive Skills: Three Levels and Four Kinds, Varying Applicability, and Numerous Sources

	3. Applicability to jobs			
	3A. General skills		3B. Specific skills	
1. Skill level	2A. *Kinds* of general skills		2B. *Kinds* of specific skills	
	(a) 3Rs plus	(b) General cognitive	(c) Specific body of knowledge, fields of study	(d) Particular skills (discrete)
1A. High	• math	• general knowledge	*High*: STEM, medical, other managerial & professional, etc.	• use of IT software/ hardware
1B. Medium	• writing	• general reasoning, analytical skills		• business procedures
	• reading			
1C. Low	• general knowledge	• problem solving	*Medium*: technical, craft/ repair, upper clerical, etc.	• working with specific materials, tools, equipment
	• organizational skills	• trainability, learn how to learn		
4. *Source*	Schools (all levels), general life experience	Schools (all levels), life experience, work	*High*: Tertiary education *Medium*: TVET, secondary education, OJT, apprenticeship	Workplace, TVET, schools (tertiary, secondary)

Note: All kinds of skills span all three levels, although (c) *Specific body of knowledge* is rarely found at low skill levels, unlike the more discrete skills and associated knowledge represented in (d), which are specific to particular occupations, industries, firms, or jobs. Sources for each kind of skill are listed in rough order of importance in the bottom row.

From the perspective of research and policy, the easiest skills to measure in greater detail are those acquired in formal education and relatively general (transversal), listed in column (a). However, the skills that matter most to employers are often quite specific, listed in column (d), which creates dilemmas for research and policy.

It is always possible to specify job skill content more finely—indeed in *infinitely* fine detail.[2] The challenge is to reduce the intrinsic complexity of the myriad skills people use at work to a small, usable number of key measures for tracking national progress and identifying the most pressing needs, priorities, and policy gaps. Any tractable number of skill indicators must be selective and necessarily omit detail; there are limits on the granularity with which a general survey can measure specific skills.

The natural starting point in addressing this challenge is to look at the *level* of education required for a given job. Job analysis in industrial/organizational (IO) psychology is the behavioral science field concerned with understanding job requirements (see Harvey 1991). A key principle of job analysis is to *rate the job*, not the person holding it. Just because a job is held by someone with a tertiary degree does not mean the complexity of the tasks requires or uses the skills and abilities conferred by a university education. Reflecting this principle, the gold standard for measuring *job-required education* is on-site observation and interviews by job analysts trained in IO psychology (U.S. Department of Labor 1991). Needless to say, such data are quite scarce and costly to collect. The following are three alternative strategies for determining job-required education.

Statistical methods. Data limitations compel most mismatch researchers to estimate job-required education using the modal or mean personal education of workers within occupations, blurring the distinction between worker traits and job traits. By using realized person-job matches in lieu of direct job measurement, this empirical measurement strategy assumes some level of efficiency and appropriateness of the matching process from the outset, that is, it presumes part of what it seeks to ascertain. This method cannot distinguish education levels that reflect technical job requirements from those reflecting systematic mismatch, such as credential inflation or widespread over-education (such as young university graduates working in coffee shops). It also suffers from some arbitrariness in choosing which measure of central tendency to use (mode vs. mean), whether or not to define a good match using a range of values centered around this value, and, if so, the width of the range (such as mode ± 1 year versus mean ±1 standard deviation). Because there is almost always some variation in education levels within occupations, by construction virtually all occupations will have some workers coded as over- and some coded as under-educated (for example, >±1 standard deviation from mean). The method takes no account of whether or how the task requirements of those workers' jobs may vary from the typical job within the occupation, because job task information is typically not collected.

Researcher judgment. An alternative method used in a few studies involves researchers' assigning educational requirements to jobs based on their judgment of the nature of the work within the occupations. This method usually relies on a high level of occupational aggregation (1-digit occupational categories) because of the difficulty of making judgment-based ratings at finer levels. The approach avoids defining some workers as mismatched based on arbitrary statistical criteria, but the ratings are more subjective and cannot capture variation within highly aggregated occupational groups.

Job-holder surveys. A third method is to ask job-holders to report the education required by their jobs. This is the measure STEP employs. This approach collects data at the *job level* rather than the occupation level. This avoids the problems of defining requirements based on arbitrary ranges and creating groups of over- and under-educated workers within every occupation by construction. It also avoids the opposite limitation of treating all jobs within the same occupation as having identical skill requirements by assigning them a single score.

This last method was used fruitfully in a number of surveys conducted mostly in the 1970s and early 1980s in the United States[3] and has recently been revived by the Survey of Workplace Skills, Technology, and Management Practices (STAMP), with surveys run in 2005 and 2008, and used in both the UK Skills Survey series and the OECD's Programme for the International Assessment of Adult Competencies (PIAAC).[4] Job-required education is a simple, single survey item that is easily implemented and, as this paper hopes to show, is worth adopting as an international standard for use at periodic intervals in national labor force surveys as part of a standard battery of job skill indicators. Although self-report methods raise validity and reliability issues of their own (which will be discussed in an upcoming paper), an extensive review of mismatch research concluded they are the best alternative to job analysis by trained raters (Hartog 2000).

A virtue of job-required education is that it speaks directly to the questions asked by most policy makers and other nonresearchers concerned with skills mismatch. Indeed, it should be underscored that the interpretation of any job skill score is greatly facilitated when it is measured on the *same* scale as the variable with which it will be compared, in this case personal education. When person-measures and job-measures are not expressed in common units—which is often the case for surveys dealing with job-task content (Handel 2003, 2005, 2008)—determining whether there is any mismatch between persons and jobs is much more difficult; mappings between coding systems potentially introduce another source of error variance. Personal education is the most widely used variable in the study of labor markets, but job-required education is found in a much more restricted literature. Although the correspondence between school curricula and job responsibilities is rarely exact, the concept of job-required education is arguably a necessary implication of *human capital theory* (see box 1.1).

After education *level*, the logical extension is to measure the *kind* of skills jobs require. Following are three methods that can help to more accurately determine the quality of matches between persons and jobs. All three methods are represented in the STEP survey, as part 2 will outline in further detail.

Field of study. The STEP survey contains a detailed set of items on field of study at all relevant levels (secondary vocational, postsecondary vocational, apprenticeships, and tertiary). As with job-required education, these items are not

Box 1.1 Human Capital Theory

Human capital theory implies that worker and job characteristics can be measured on the same scale by individuals deciding how much to invest in their own education and skills acquisition. Indeed, quantity of education, along with work experience, is the most common definition of human capital among researchers and is presumed to reflect the education level required by the jobs desired by the future worker.

In practice, most human capital studies simply *assume* perfect labor market matching on principle or for convenience and identify job-required education with the education of job holders themselves. That is, the traits of the job are assumed to be identical to those of the job holder. For anyone concerned about possible mismatch, this more or less settles all issues in advance by assuming them away.

For researchers treating mismatch as an open question, independent measures of job education requirements are necessary in order to avoid such circularity while remaining consistent with the human capital assumption that individuals' conceptions of job requirements and the education and training options available to them are scaled in similar units. If jobs could not be scaled in terms of educational requirements, it is difficult to see how any prospective labor market entrant could make reasoned decisions regarding the educational level necessary for the kind of job she or he desired and how any good labor market matches beyond chance would be possible, much less perfect matching. Economic theory would seem to *require* the concept that jobs can be measured in grade-equivalent units and understood by workers in those terms.

---

unique to STEP, but they are relatively uncommon in surveys focusing on labor market issues. The STEP items and response categories are also considerably more detailed than those used on PIAAC, which only covers field of study at the tertiary level. These data provide much richer detail on national skill stocks than is commonly available (detailed, comparative country profiles will be available in a subsequent report). These person-measures can be compared with jobs to assess (mis-)match using established correspondences between field of study and standard occupation variables, as well as through items specific to STEP, PIAAC, and a few other surveys asking workers how useful their education is for their jobs.

Field of study provides much greater detail for mismatch analyses than level of education alone, and the two together provide reasonable coverage of the first two broad categories in table 1.1, aside from narrow job skills. However, field of study is also likely to be applicable primarily to people with a tertiary education. Most people without a tertiary degree do not complete vocational secondary education or an apprenticeship. They receive a general academic education, whose skills are represented by the third and fourth categories in the skills map given in table 1.1. These general academic and cognitive skills are used also at higher levels of complexity by tertiary- and TVET-educated workers.

Task scales. Directly measuring job skill requirements and the person abilities corresponding to these categories is challenging. STEP follows

STAMP's strategy of *explicit scaling* to measure the reading, writing, math, and problem-solving tasks people perform on the job and in their daily lives. Explicit scaling involves framing items and response categories whenever possible in terms of concrete facts, behaviors, events, and absolute quantities, rather than using relative judgments or rating scales. Following the reasoning behind *criterion-referenced testing*, the task items ask about specific kinds of math performed and the quantity (in page length) and kinds of reading and writing tasks typically performed.

Following the logic of ordinal item response theory, most of these scales were designed as Guttman (or Mokken) scales with a clear difficulty gradient, though not calibrated as finely as parametric scores from models based on Item Response Theory (Handel 2008, 2016).[5] The PIAAC survey used many of these items but STEP goes beyond previous surveys in asking all adults a closely similar battery of task items regarding their daily nonwork lives to understand the skills of the nonemployed, who represent potential labor market participants, and to account for the possibility that employed adults have job-relevant capabilities that are not utilized in their jobs. These measures provide greater substantive detail and finer measurement of the foundational, academic, and transversal specific skills that are required by work and that people are capable of performing. (Note that STEP survey items on *computer* tasks performed on and off the job, as well as other items on technology use also used by STAMP and PIAAC, will be the subject of a separate paper).

It is useful to note in this context that while measures of personal and job education are also straightforward and intuitive and have a natural difficulty gradient, they are also rather coarse and general and do not reference criteria, such as specific literacy or numeracy levels. Therefore, task measures fill in large gaps that mismatch research has identified with established indicators, although these measures present their own challenges in terms of determining grade-equivalence.

Test scores. For a subset of countries, STEP also contains a reading assessment whose content and scoring were designed to be consistent with a similar assessment conducted for PIAAC. Concern with the way skills learned in school are used in the workplace also fed into the design of the PISA assessment conducted by the OECD (Kirsch et al. 2002, p.18). However, it is not clear that any test can avoid the issues associated with establishing grade-equivalence noted earlier.

Both the test scores and task scales permit finer skill distinctions between persons and jobs than is possible based on personal or job education alone, and the task scales use units with absolute rather than relative meanings. But even decades of work in test psychology have not produced a method of equating scores to schooling levels in ironclad fashion. As will be clear from the next section, it is much easier to assess congruence or mismatch when all skill indicators are commensurate, that is, when they have common, preferably objective, metrics.

These complications reflect challenges that are intrinsic in trying to assess mismatch in specific and concrete terms (*What are the skills that people have and jobs require?*). STEP scores measure work-related texts, documents, and math tasks according to frequency and time spent, but the diverse and frequently inconsistent methods for scoring the readability or grade-equivalency of prose, documents, and quantitative tasks attest to the absence of standard or consensus approaches to scoring complexity or grade-equivalency (Klare 1974–1975; Mosenthal and Kirsch 1998; Fernandez 2001). Even when the targets and units of measurement are objective, as they are for task scores, the different behaviors measured are qualitatively diverse and there are no obvious natural or common units to represent different levels of complexity. When constructs are abstractions, such as cognitive abilities, the situation is complicated further. Nevertheless, test scores permit finer discrimination within levels of personal education, and task scores permit finer discrimination within categories of job-required education. Test scores and task scores, especially, permit greater understanding regarding the actual meaning of education categories in concrete terms.

The measures of job-required education, field of study, test scores, and job and daily life tasks involving general academic skills (math, reading, writing) and use of general cognitive skills (problem solving) cover almost all of the skills laid out in the map in table 1.2. The largest remaining gap is in covering the myriad firm-, job- and occupation-specific skills that are acquired mostly *outside* formal schooling, which are often critical for work.

Some of the latter technical, vocational, and career skills are acquired through apprenticeships; through formal training provided by employers, governments, and others; or through on-the-job training, learning-by-doing, or general life experience. Long lists of such skills can be found in sector-based guidelines for skills standards and in some national qualifications frameworks, but the skills listed in those places are both too numerous and apply to groups that are too narrow for their inclusion in a general household survey. Part of the problem with previous work on mismatch is the failure to recognize that skills can be specified at an infinitely fine level of detail but cannot be measured easily at that level of detail. Any practical effort has to decide how to capture narrow skills most effectively.

The STEP survey approached this challenge by collecting information on apprenticeships and formal training and by measuring the amount (but not kind) of job-specific skills in common and objective units by asking about the number of years of prior experience required for the current job and the length of time required for learning the current job. "Time required" is the only obvious basis for consistent cross-job measurement of the effectively infinite number of qualitatively distinct, nontransversal skills used at work. The STEP survey replicated questionnaire items used by job analysts at the U.S. Department of Labor to construct measures of *Specific Vocational Preparation* for the O*NET database, which the agency's public employment service uses to assist the unemployed in searching for new jobs and which is distributed widely to the public as an official source of occupational information for career exploration and guidance (Oswald et al. 1999; Peterson et al. 1999).[6] The measures of required experience and job learning times were also used previously by the STAMP survey (Handel 2008, 2016), and then adopted by the OECD's PIAAC. These measures are not easily equated to levels of schooling, but some of the skills they represent differ in kind from those transmitted through schooling and are too specialized to include as distinct items in a general survey. Nevertheless, the extent to which learning through practice characterizes different jobs or individuals' careers is relevant for the question of mismatch.

Defining Mismatch

The concept of skills mismatch is subject to varying definitions and measurement strategies. Three common conceptions of mismatch are *skills shortage, job shortage,* and *mismatched fields of study.*

Skills shortage. In some contexts, even though some workers want employment or increased work hours and employers have unmet labor needs, the latter will not hire the former at current wages because their skills are inadequate or inappropriate, that is, there is a *skills shortage.* Individuals want more work and employers want more workers, but lack of congruence between persons' skills and job skill requirements produces simultaneous under-employment and vacancies in excess of normal, frictional levels. In many countries there is a concern that insufficient skill formation is a drag on growth and development, although it should be said that simultaneously high levels of idleness and job vacancies would be absent if unskilled jobs were as plentiful as unskilled workers. In such a case, current skills would not be well-matched with a desired *future* state of the job market, which is a reasonable concern for policy and research, but there would be no mismatch relative to *current* job opportunities.

Job shortage. In other contexts there is a concern with over-education, which suggests the possibility that education is valued in the job market for reasons other than its direct, technical relationship to job performance (such as credentialism, screening, signaling), valued by individuals for status reasons, or insufficiently utilized due to weak demand from employers. That is, there is a *job shortage* rather than a skills shortage. When attractive jobs are scarce relative to the skills of the labor force, there are high levels of "wait unemployment" and potential waste of skills due to atrophy and depreciation from underuse. In the case of a jobs shortage, the biggest problems may be inadequate investment, poor investment climate or levels of investment, business inefficiency, inadequate infrastructure, poor macroeconomic conditions, bad policy, weak governance, or other issues relatively unrelated to the performance of the education system. Although there is always the hope that increasing the supply of skills will increase the demand for them, deciding that employment problems dictate producing more graduates when large numbers are not being absorbed currently is unlikely to get at the root of any problem.

Field-of-study mismatch. The possibility that the employment problems of university graduates are due to mismatches between fields of study and the kinds of knowledge valued by the labor market is considered further below. Researchers, practitioners, and governments have spent decades considering a similar issue regarding the value of academic and vocational education for secondary and sub-baccalaureate students.

For the purpose of this research, the term "job shortage" will be used in preference to "education surplus" or "skill surplus," because in most cases the goal is to raise the number of high-skilled jobs rather than to reduce the number of graduates in order to achieve balance between skill supply and demand, and often the main sources of difficulty are on the labor demand side rather than the supply side. This is not meant to rule out the possibility of situations described more aptly as "education surplus," in which universities, in particular, expand enrollments far beyond what the labor market could be expected to absorb under any reasonable scenario. One objection is that the concept of mismatch focuses exclusively on wages rather than tasks, and is described in more detail in box 1.2.

Box 1.2 Mismatch and Wages

One objection to the concept of mismatch focuses exclusively on wages rather than tasks and avoids the issue of directly measuring job skill requirements altogether. In this view, when the number of low-skilled job-seekers exceeds the number of low-skilled jobs, the two sides are brought back into balance simply through wage changes. Declining wages for less-skilled workers induce employers to hire more of them and induce those remaining unemployed to exit the labor force, while wage increases for relatively scarce higher-skilled workers induce some employers to abandon their own searches, shrinking the number of open positions. A similar situation applies in the opposite case of a shortage of high-skilled jobs relative to job-seekers, which also induces declining educational attainment in response to wage signals.

Assuming perfectly flexible prices and agents, there would *never* be mismatch relative to current job opportunities. However, most policy makers, firms, and individuals would probably not consider this kind of equilibrium to be an attractive one, as it leaves wealth generation below potential and leaves some firms and workers idle, underutilized, and discontented. A university graduate in a technical field who works as a salesperson in a small shop selling imported electronics could be considered well-matched simply by virtue of the employment relationship itself, that is, the worker's willingness to trade his or her labor for compensation freely according to the terms offered by the employer. However, most observers would consider it an example of over-education mismatch.

Likewise, unusually large wage differentials by education or large changes in education premiums might be considered the only reliable measures of imbalance or disequilibria. However, there are various institutional forces that affect wages and make them imperfect indicators of the state of the supply of and demand for skills (such as unions, efficiency wages, gender discrimination). Perhaps most importantly, wage series contain little specific information on what people do at work, which means they cannot be used to identify the *nature* of skills that workers possess and that jobs require in any detail, which limits their utility for informing policy and human capital decisions among various actors. Although relative wages are both labor market equilibrators and labor market indicators, *direct* measures of job skill levels as well as worker skills and wages are needed if policy makers, education and training providers, employment counselors, job-seekers, and students are to have a deeper understanding of the state of the labor market.

Table 1.3 Cross-Classification of Workers by Personal and Job-Required Education

	Job-required education			Total
Personal education	Low	Medium	High	
Low	1	2	3	A
Medium	4	5	6	B
High	7	8	9	C
Total	D	E	F	Total

The proposed framework for understanding mismatch is illustrated by the symmetric table below (table 1.3). Individuals are cross-classified by their personal education (rows) and the education required by their jobs (columns), with group totals indicated by letters in the marginal rows and columns and the grand total in the bottom-right cell. This resembles a standard mobility table, except that a person's *origins* are described in terms of educational attainment and *destinations* are represented by job-required education. It is legitimate to treat this square matrix as a kind of mobility table insofar as personal educational attainment precedes the current job held and by all expectations is intended to put the future worker on a certain career trajectory. To the extent that the education required by the current job exceeds or falls below a person's educational level, that person's status may be regarded as representing upward or downward mobility relative to his or her expected trajectory. The table is simplified for purposes of presentation but can be extended easily to finer categories and even to the continuous measurement of persons and jobs in terms of years of education, as was done in early work on occupational mobility (Blau and Duncan 1967, pp. 28ff.), although sophisticated analyses become cumbersome when the number of categories is large.

In table 1.3, any inequality between corresponding row and column totals implies some degree of mismatch. If the total number of highly educated workers (C) is greater than the total number of jobs requiring high education (F), then some workers who might be expected to populate cell 9 will hold jobs requiring less education in cell 8 and possibly cell 7. If cell 6 or even cell 3 is populated, then frequencies for cells 8 and 7 will be even higher than the difference between the aggregate figures in the marginal cells, because some of the relatively scarce high-education jobs will be filled by workers with less than a high education. Whether this mismatch in excess of levels implied by the row and column totals reflects imperfect matching of available workers and positions or proper matching owing to other characteristics besides worker or job education level, such as test scores or specific job tasks, is an empirical question.

Turning to the interior of the table, people who are *well-matched* (that is, whose personal education equals the level required by their job) occupy the blue cells on the diagonal. Workers whose jobs require more education than their own, the *under-educated*, occupy the orange-shaded cells to the right of the diagonal. Workers with more education than their jobs require, the *over-educated*, are in the green cells to the left of the diagonal.

Naturally, a country's leadership wants as many people as possible to become highly skilled and to hold jobs that utilize their skills, the high-skill match situation represented by cell 9. Conversely, the least desirable situation is an economy in which both people and jobs are mostly unskilled, which is the low-skill match situation represented by cell 1. Absence of mismatch, when everyone has minimal skills, is preferable only to mass unemployment; jobs that generally require more education in positions to the right of cell 1 would be an improvement despite ostensible mismatch. Indeed, between the polar cases represented by cells 1 and 9 are various mixed outcomes.

The under-educated appear upwardly mobile in the sense that they hold better jobs than most others with their level of education. Assuming this outcome was unanticipated, it could be a source of increased job satisfaction as well as pecuniary gain. If both personal and job characteristics play a role in wage determination, one would expect the average wages of the under-educated to be *higher than the wages of their classmates*, but *lower than the wages of their coworkers*[7] who are well-matched. For example, workers in cell 2 would be expected to earn more than those in cell 1 because they hold a better job, but less than those in cell 5 due to their lower education, that is, their relative wages would follow the pattern, cell 1 < cell 2 < cell 5.

By contrast, the over-educated appear downwardly mobile insofar as they hold worse jobs than most others with their education, which one would expect produces some level of unhappiness due to frustrated expectations. Their average wages would be expected to be *lower than their classmates' wages* but *higher than their coworkers' wages*. Therefore, average wages for workers in cell 4 would also exceed those of workers in cell 1, in this case due to their greater education, while being lower than those of workers in cell 5 because they hold a worse job, that is, cell 1 < cell 4 < cell 5. More generally, rightward positions within rows are associated with greater advantage due to job-required education level, while lower positions within columns are associated with greater advantage due to personal education level.

Previous research suggests that over-educated persons generally earn more than their most closely related under-educated counterparts, that is, cell 2 < cell 4. In addition, over-education is more common than under-education, which is intuitive given the various ways jobs might fall short of a persons' skills as opposed to the less intuitive scenario that has employers hiring workers with significant deficits. The most straightforward reason would be a shortage of workers with the ideal or preferred level of education, but there are undoubtedly jobs with alternative entry points that would render impressions of "under-qualification" partly an artifact of the method of measuring "required" education, which is considered further below.

Finally, it is worth noting that it is impossible by construction for anyone in the bottom row to be under-educated, because there is no higher job category into which this group can be upwardly mobile, that is, there is a ceiling effect. Likewise, a floor effect precludes those in the top row from being over-educated; there is no lower job category into which the least-educated workers can fall. Models explaining under- and over-education necessarily will omit workers for whom the concepts do not apply. There is also some degree of constraint on rates of mismatch insofar as a country's educational distribution is concentrated in the lowest or highest education categories. In this and other respects, the row and column totals, also known as the unconditional or *marginal distributions*, affect the possible or likely patterns inside the cross-classification region of the table. As will be shown, this is relevant for countries in Europe and Central Asia whose very low rates of under-education reflect their very high shares of workers with tertiary education.

Although the presence of positive returns to both personal and job characteristics means workers who are mismatched have higher average earnings than their reference groups, classmates or coworkers, shifting the comparison to the relative gains of workers and employers suggests that mismatch is suboptimal from a societal perspective. While the under-educated benefit from being hired for jobs that are usually filled by someone from a lower cell in their column, firms that hire them may have lower productivity than they would if more qualified workers were available. Conversely, the over-educated suffer from underemployment, even if firms may benefit from hiring workers who are more productive than the less-educated workers they normally employ, after discounting any effects of lower job satisfaction (such as lower morale/cooperation, higher turnover).

Again, a possible objection to the mismatch framework is that more education is *always* welfare-enhancing for the individual if the wage returns exceed some concept of the cost of acquiring it, as well as producing positive externalities in areas such as health, crime, and social capital (Oreopoulos and Salvanes 2011). Indeed, the social benefits of education are substantial even after accounting for negative social consequences such as widespread frustration among over-educated university graduates.

Nevertheless, restricting attention to the individual level, there is ample evidence that university graduates tend to have certain occupational expectations and experience dissatisfaction when the jobs available do not match them, sometimes motivating migration streams ("brain drains"). Indeed, failure to find a well-matching job domestically represents a pecuniary loss relative to expectations, a perceived "opportunity cost" resulting from an *absence* of opportunities. Few would argue strongly that a university graduate driving a taxi or working in a small retail establishment is well-matched as the concept is understood by policy makers or the public, despite partly offsetting benefits of the extra education for both the individual and society. If education is understood primarily as a means for transmitting objective, technical capacities for accomplishing certain job tasks, rather than as a device for ranking or screening individuals based on trainability or status, it must be acknowledged that it is possible for the skills individuals possess and those required by their jobs to be genuinely mismatched.

Moving from the individual to the systemic level, the institutional differentiation between schools and workplaces makes it likely that all countries have some intrinsic potential for mismatch, though the magnitude of these synchronization issues can be expected to vary by time and place. A country may have more educational achievement than the job market can absorb given current levels of investment and business capacities, or employers may be looking for more skills than the education system can keep up with. In short, there is reason to believe large cell frequencies off the diagonal are a legitimate concern. Both individuals and policy makers in developing countries seek a joint distribution of workers and jobs that clusters toward the lower-right end of the diagonal, and this is a sensible concern.

Finally, the contingency table framework highlights the fact that off-diagonal cell frequencies may be viewed from at least three perspectives:

- Policy makers and others with systemic concerns would want to identify the most prevalent mismatch situations overall, which is indexed by cell frequencies as percentages of all cases, N (table or cell percentages).
- Job-seekers, educators, and education and labor policy makers might focus on job prospects for those acquiring particular levels of qualification, which is best viewed by calculating percentages within education groups using row totals as denominators (row percentages). This is also a natural perspective for researchers insofar as qualifications are temporally prior to job category in most cases.
- Businesses, as well as researchers and policy makers concerned with competitiveness, enterprise, and job quality, might focus more on the shares of jobs that are well-matched or mismatched, which are best measured by calculating percentages using column totals as denominators (column percentages).

Because each cell belongs to a worker education group (row), a job education group (column), and the overall workforce (whole table), each cell frequency can be understood relative to the total sizes of three different groups, depending on whether the purpose is a big-picture view or the situation facing different kinds of workers or job categories.

The choice of perspective can affect conclusions, given unequal and differently distributed row and column totals. A group of workers who share the same level of education may have very high mismatch rates without producing a correspondingly severe mismatch problem for the workforce overall if the row accounts for a small share of the total. For example, the number of cases in cells 4 and 6 in table 1.3 may be very large relative to cell 5, but their sum may be small relative to the total across all cells 1 through 9. In other words, row percentages might suggest a large problem while the cell percentages do not.

Likewise, there may be few problems when job education groups, or column percentages, are considered if cell 5 accounts for nearly all of the jobs in the second column and cells 4 and 6 account for small shares of the first and third columns. In this situation, educators and policy makers might consider how to address mismatch issues for the middle level of education, and students might consider stopping their education at this level since securing matching jobs seems to be a problem for most people at that same level. However, the situation might not pose a large problem for the labor market or for output overall, because no category of employers is adversely affected to any appreciable degree. In this case, the column percentages would not indicate a problem, even though the row percentages exhibit a high rate of mismatch.

In short, this discussion indicates that on a purely descriptive level, each contingency table can be viewed informatively from three different perspectives, which creates challenges common to all high-dimensional data problems when the number of education categories is expanded and tables are compared across countries. Given such complexity, this report will focus on row percentages, that is the incidence of mismatches by worker education group rather than by job education group or relative to the workforce as a whole, which is the typical way mismatch is understood. Nevertheless, it is worth noting that the two alternative perspectives also address other important concerns.

Notes

1. Industrial psychologists and human resource professionals often distinguish between *knowledge*, *skills*, and *abilities* (KSAs), but the term "skills" or "education and skills" will be used for convenience throughout this paper with the understanding that it is intended to cover the entire KSA domain.
2. For example, the International Standard Classification of Occupations (ISCO), maintained by the International Labour Organization, identifies approximately 600 occupations. Industry-based "sector skills councils" in the United Kingdom and elsewhere enumerate skill requirements at an extremely fine level of detail, a refinement that is impractical or impossible for a general labor force survey. The *Journal of Economic Literature* has over 800 key words to describe the subject matter of economics. The issue is not simply academic. In practice, simple generalizations, such as "a shortage of technical skills," frequently break down at finer levels. Some STEM or medical subspecialties face very tight labor markets in developed countries, but the situation for other subspecialties in the same general field can be entirely different (e.g., mechanical engineers vs. petroleum engineers).
3. The Quality of Employment Surveys (1969, 1972–73, 1977) and the Panel Study of Income Dynamics (1976, 1977, 1985).
4. Although they are not as well phrased, similar survey items are also used in the Swedish Level-of-Living surveys (LNU) and in two waves of the European Social Survey (2004, 2010).
5. For more on Mokken scaling, see van Schuur (2011).
6. See also http://www.onetonline.org/help/online/zones and http://www.onetonline.org/help/online/svp (accessed April 27, 2015).
7. For convenience, the terms "classmates" and "coworkers" are used in an extended sense to refer to other individuals with the same educational attainment or holding a job with the same required education, respectively.

References

Blau, Peter M., and Otis Dudley Duncan. 1967. *The American Occupational Structure*. New York: Wiley and Sons.

Carneiro, P., C. Crawford, and A. Goodman. 2007. "The Impact of Early Cognitive and Non-cognitive Skills on Later Outcomes." Discussion Paper 0092, Centre for the Economics of Education, London School of Economics, London.

European Social Survey. 2004. *ESS Round 2 Source Questionnaire*. London: Centre for Comparative Social Surveys, City University London.

European Social Survey. 2010. *ESS Round 5 Source Questionnaire*. London: Centre for Comparative Social Surveys, City University London.

Fernandez, Roberto M. 2001. "Skill-Biased Technological Change and Wage Inequality: Evidence from a Plant Retooling." *American Journal of Sociology* 107: 273–320.

Handel, Michael J. 2003. "Skills Mismatch in the Labor Market." *Annual Review of Sociology*. 29: 135–65.

———. 2005. *Worker Skills and Job Requirements: Is There a Mismatch?* Washington, DC: Economic Policy Institute.

———. 2008. "Measuring Job Content: Skills, Technology, and Management Practices." Discussion Paper 1357-08, University of Wisconsin, Institute for Research on Poverty, Madison, WI.

———. 2015. *Methodological Issues Related to the Occupational Requirements Survey*. Report to the Bureau of Labor Statistics, Department of Labor, Washington, DC. www.bls.gov/ncs/ors/handel_report_feb15.pdf.

———. 2016. "Measuring Job Content: Skills, Technology, and Management Practices." In *Oxford Handbook of Skills and Training*, edited by John Buchanan, David Finegold, Ken Mayhew, and Chris Warhurst. Oxford: Oxford University Press.

Hartog, Joop. 2000. "Over-Education and Earnings: Where Are We, Where Should We Go?" *Economics of Education Review* 19: 131–47.

Harvey, Robert J. 1991. "Job Analysis." In *Handbook of Industrial and Organizational Psychology*, edited by Marvin D. Dunnette and Leaetta M. Hough, 71–163. Palo Alto, CA: Consulting Psychologists Press.

Heckman, J. J., J. Stixrud, and S. Urzua. 2006. "The Effects of Cognitive and Noncognitive Abilities on Labor Market Outcomes and Social Behavior." Paper w12006, Cambridge, MA: National Bureau of Economic Research.

Kirsch, Irwin S., John de Jong, Dominique LaFontaine, Joy McQueen, Juliette Mendelovits, and Christian Monseur. 2002. *Reading for Change: Performance and Engagement across Countries—Results from PISA 2000*. Paris: Organisation for Economic Co-operation and Development.

Klare, George R. 1974–1975. "Assessing Readability." *Reading Research Quarterly* 10: 62–102.

Mosenthal, Peter B. and Irwin S. Kirsch. 1998. "A New Measure for Assessing Document Complexity: The PMOSE/IKIRSCH Document Readability Formula." *Journal of Adolescent and Adult Literacy* 41: 638–57.

Oreopoulos, Philip, and Kjell G. Salvanes. 2011. "Priceless: The Nonpecuniary Benefits of Schooling." *Journal of Economic Perspectives* 25: 159–84.

Oswald, Frederick, John Campbell, Rod McCloy, David Rivkin, and Phil Lewis. 1999. *Stratifying Occupational Units by Specific Vocational Preparation (SVP)*. Raleigh, NC: National Center for O*NET Development, Employment Security Commission.

Peterson, Norman G., Michael D. Mumford, Walter C. Borman, P. Richard Jeanneret, and Edwin A. Fleishman. 1999. *An Occupational Information System for the 21st Century: The Development of O*NET*. Washington, DC: American Psychological Association.

U.S. Department of Labor. 1991. *Dictionary of Occupational Titles*. 4th ed. Revised. Washington, DC: U.S. Government Printing Office.

van Schuur, Wijbrandt H. 2011. *Ordinal Item Response Theory: Mokken Scale Analysis*. Thousand Oaks, CA: SAGE Publications.

CHAPTER 2

Conceptual Framework

Explaining Mismatch: Standard Variables

When numerous workers hold jobs requiring a level of education different from their own, the most straightforward interpretation is that there is an aggregate imbalance between worker skills and skilled jobs at one or more levels (*aggregate mismatch*), suggesting problems with the education system, labor market, or both. The fact that employers hire job-seekers with less education than generally thought needed (under-education) may indicate skill shortage, while the fact that some job-seekers accept positions requiring less education than they have acquired (over-education) may indicate a shortage of better-skilled jobs, or a shortage of employment opportunities more generally. Over-education may also have a cascading effect if there are insufficient jobs at a lower level to accommodate both the downwardly mobile and the well-matched workers at the lower job level, forcing the latter to take yet-lower-skilled jobs themselves and bump well-matched workers at that level downward in turn. Demographic constraints can create their own policy challenges as well, as discussed in box 2.1.

Because over-education tends to be more common than under-education, it would seem that job shortages are more common than workforce skill shortages. Because policy is usually concerned with raising educational attainment, the prevalence of over-education may be perceived as an awkward finding. Nevertheless, over-education need not result solely from aggregate imbalances. Intuition and previous research on mismatch suggest four alternatives to aggregate imbalances that may explain observed patterns: *transitory labor market frictions*, *individual preferences*, *health limitations*, and *the use of experience and education* as equally valid, alternative entry paths for certain occupations (see, e.g., Sloane 2003; Jones et al. 2014). These explanations of off-diagonal cases are treated as potential confounders in this paper because they suggest mismatch is not genuine in important respects or a much less serious problem than it appears, as becomes clear in the brief explanations below.

Transitory labor market frictions. Observed over-education could reflect *search-related frictions* that are common to all job-seekers or are more serious for particular groups, such as those with less experience (young people, recent labor

Box 2.1 Policies to Change Educational Attainment

Although not a focus of this paper, a certain demographic constraint is faced by all countries in adjusting the educational distribution of their populations to the changing composition of employment. Older cohorts are usually less educated and unlikely to return to school or receive effective formal retraining in large numbers, meaning their education and skill levels will remain relatively stable. If the growth of higher-skilled jobs exceeds the growth of well-matched young people, the number of under-educated workers will rise and slow down movement toward a medium- or high-skill match situation (as in table 1.3, cells 5 and 9). Even if the education system is very effective, this issue will be resolved mostly by predictably gradual processes of cohort replacement.

The speed with which educational attainment can be raised in the overall population is constrained by the fact that education levels for young cohorts are the only ones that can be manipulated by policy to any appreciable degree. High growth rates and discontinuous improvements in labor markets are not easy to achieve, but in principle new jobs can be created at a faster rate than new adults. In some contexts, then, mismatch may not signal any underlying problem beyond an unavoidable demographic overhang. Even a relatively rapid flow of educated young people into the workforce will have little effect on a large prior stock of less-educated older workers.

---

market entrants), with poor job search skills, or with poor information networks. For example, recently unemployed workers who accept jobs for which they are over-qualified in order to get back to work may continue to search and eventually find better jobs that more closely match their education. Workers whose jobs are below their potential for these reasons may eventually secure better jobs elsewhere or move up thorough internal promotion, which may or may not have motivated the apparently over-educated worker's initial attraction to the entry-level position.[1] The generally *transitory* nature of these mismatches mitigates their severity, though research in developed countries suggests that some proportion of those affected by transitory shocks may never regain all of their lost ground. Of course, if employment and unemployment rates are persistently weak, there is mismatch as it is conventionally conceived. One analytical problem is that workers "at risk" for upward mobility through internal promotion cannot be as easily associated with specific background characteristics such as age or recent unemployment spells, though employer size might be one possible predictor of promotion probability, following the literature on internal labor markets.

Individual preferences. Observed over-education might partly reflect the decisions of voluntary part-timers, students, and married women, especially those with young children, to take jobs that offer compensating benefits, such as flexible schedules. While over-education due to an insufficiency of jobs that are both flexible *and* higher-skilled is a problem, the severity of mismatch as a social problem is mitigated somewhat when it partly reflects preferences rather than being completely involuntary. Other pecuniary and nonpecuniary *compensating differentials* that may account for apparent mismatches, such as greater employment security, better benefits, and low physical demands, might be captured or proxied by employer size, foreign ownership, public sector, physical task measures, and above-market (that is, efficiency) wages relative to the workers' education level.

Health limitations. Observed over-education may also reflect health-related limitations among some workers, which may be particularly relevant in developing countries. Health status is relatively exogenous to education and labor markets in a narrow sense, that is, aside from the general level of income. Insofar as health issues and disability explain mismatch, one could argue that it is mostly a concern for health policy rather than education or employment policy in a narrow sense. In other words, one could argue that *apparent* mismatch does not reflect genuine mismatch between workers' actual capabilities and job task requirements in this case, even as it points to other significant policy concerns. It is possible that the scale of this problem is significant in some developing countries, though it may affect total work hours more than type of work.

Alternative career paths. Observed under-education may reflect the fact that certain occupations have valid pathways to acquiring necessary skills other than formal educational attainment. While a plurality or slight majority of employers may prefer to hire workers with a given education, it is possible that others rely on demonstrations of occupation-specific competence, which can be acquired and signaled through work experience and other nonformal or informal means (such as webmasters or less technical construction trades like painters). This would be another example of apparent mismatch rather than genuine mismatch because formal education is not a good indicator of skill in such cases. This points to the likelihood that not only the level of required education varies by occupation, but the importance and relevance of formal education for effective job performance varies, as well.

The four scenarios described above are alternatives to pure conventional mismatch explanations insofar as they suggest the problem is not as severe as it might appear or does not reflect poor functioning of the education system or the job market primarily. Demographic and other characteristics widely available in standard surveys will be used to control for these possibilities.

Less recognized in the literature on mismatch is that effects of demographic variables may reflect employer discrimination or societal inequalities based on gender, ethnicity, or socioeconomic origins and that residual mismatch after controlling for covariates may reflect the influence of nepotism and personal networks as much as frictions related to imperfect information. STEP (Skills Toward Employment and Productivity) data can address some of these issues as well, but this paper will focus on other alternatives to conventional mismatch explanations that use information unavailable in most previous data sets, described below.

Using Skill Measures to Investigate Unobserved Heterogeneity

A persistent concern in previous studies is that heterogeneity within worker education groups may explain most of the relatively high rates of observed mismatch. Education level is an informative but a relatively coarse classification scheme.

In every society, there is variation in achievement levels within each education group. If the highest performers within an education level can qualify for jobs usually filled with more educated workers and the lowest performers are forced to accept jobs usually filled by people with less education, then mismatch may be more apparent than genuine (Sloane 2003). In addition, the International Standard Classification of Education (ISCED) guidelines recognize only the highest education level completed, not partial fulfillment of higher levels.[2] Some apparent mismatch may be due to heterogeneity within worker education groups by years of schooling, as well as achievement.

Less commonly recognized is the complementary possibility that task complexity may vary among jobs with the same title or rated as requiring the same level of education, as well. While it is common to focus on normally unobserved differences among seemingly identical *workers*, there are also possibly unobserved differences among the *jobs* they hold. Apparently over-educated workers might perform tasks that are more complex than is typical for their occupation or level of job-required education, while apparently upwardly mobile, under-educated workers may perform less complex tasks than their well-matched coworkers. Thus, apparent mismatch may mask heterogeneity in either *worker skills* or the *complexity of tasks* they perform.

This means apparently over-educated workers could have lower skills and/or more complex jobs than expected on the basis of the education measures, while apparently under-educated workers could have higher skills and/or less complex jobs than expected. Workers and jobs that appear equivalent when classified by broad education categories may be more similar to those in lower or higher education categories when there are finer measures of the skills associated with the education levels persons have attained and jobs require.

If skill distributions for different education groups overlap, apparent mismatch by education may mask effective matching by skill, that is, *education mismatch does not necessarily imply skill mismatch*. Chapter 4 of this report will outline how STEP reading literacy and job task scores are used to measure usually unobserved heterogeneity among workers and jobs, respectively.

This conception of skill distributions nested within education levels for both persons and jobs is represented in stylized fashion in figure 2.1, which assumes for simplicity that worker skills and job skill requirements are unidimensional constructs measured in common units. For convenience, the middle distribution in each panel is centered on 100, the adjacent distributions are centered on 85 and 115, and the standard deviations for all distributions is 15. The top panel shows overlapping skill score distributions for workers in three personal education groups, which is probably similar to many empirical test score distributions. The middle panel assumes job skill requirements can be measured in identical units and shows similar distributions for jobs requiring the same three levels of education. The bottom panel shows how some workers at the middle education level (solid line) might find themselves in jobs with higher or lower educational requirements (dashed lines), assuming matching is sometimes based on skill rather than education. Although the distributions for medium-level-education

Figure 2.1 Distributions of Worker Skills and Job Skill Requirements by Education Group

a. Distribution of worker skills for three education groups

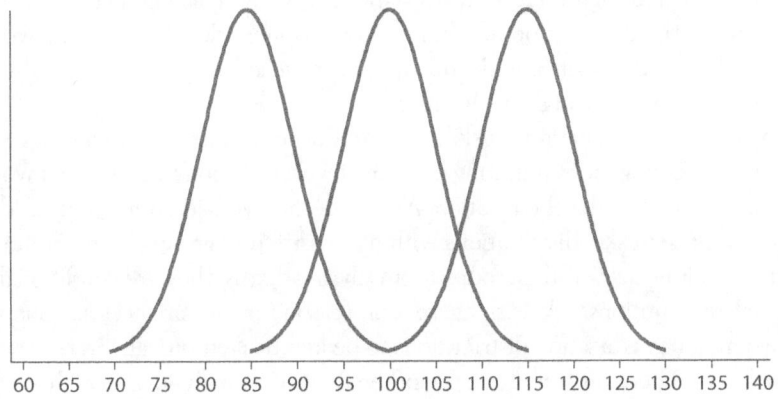

b. Distribution of job skill requirements for three job education groups

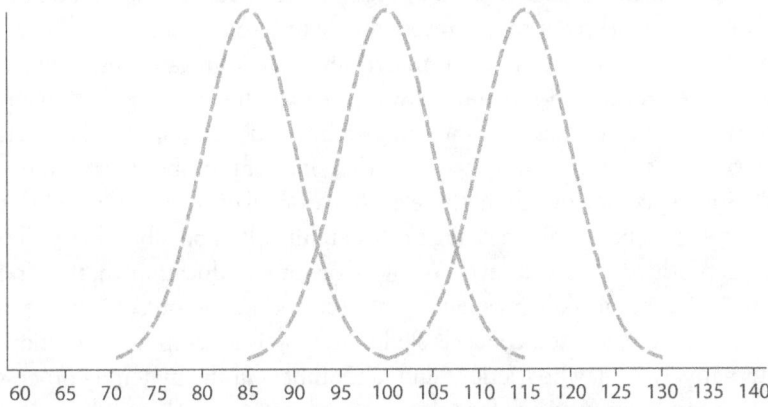

c. Skill distribution for workers with medium education overlapping with skill distributions for three job education groups

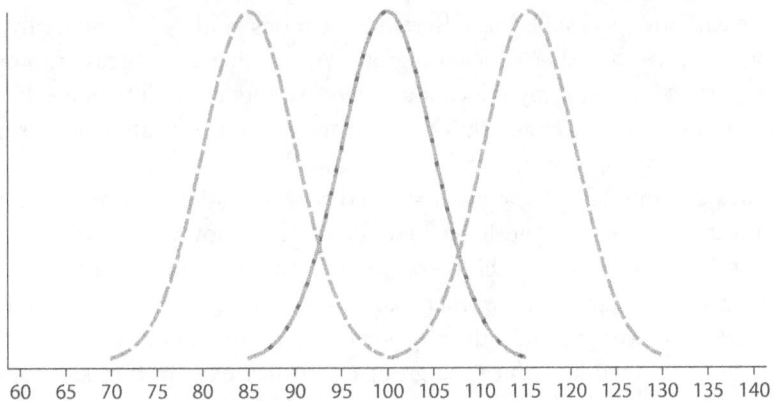

persons and jobs are coterminous when they are overlaid in panel (c), there is no necessity in practice for every realized *skill* match between persons and jobs to be an *education* match as well, given that the skill requirements of jobs rated as requiring low and high education overlap with the actual skill levels of workers in the tails of the distribution of medium-education workers. Thus, some workers with medium education could end up *skill-matched* to jobs that usually hire workers with lower or higher educations.

One possible explanation for skill-match/education-mismatch outcomes is that there are not enough jobs requiring medium-level education to employ all workers who have a medium-level education. Although the overlaid curves appear identical, they represent skill distributions within two different groups, workers and jobs, not the absolute sizes of the groups themselves—that is, they are conditional, not marginal, distributions. Likewise, there is no reason for the variances and shapes of the two medium-education distributions to be identical empirically, as represented in the figure. Therefore, one reason workers with unusually low or high skills for their education group might hold jobs with lower or higher educational requirements is that the numbers of jobs requiring the three education levels do not equal the numbers of workers at the corresponding education levels.

Unbalanced distributions at the macro level, or aggregate mismatch, would compel some workers to move downward or exit the labor market, or provide others with opportunities to move up, or both, depending on the particular pattern. Of course, if the numbers on the two sides of the labor market are unbalanced with respect to education, there is no reason all of the resulting educational mismatch has to be simply masking skill-matching. It is possible that skill or job shortages produce observed levels of over- or under-education that are reliable indicators of genuine skills mismatch, as discussed at the outset. The degree to which aggregate mismatch conceals skill matching is an empirical question.

Alternatively, it may be frictions and randomness in the matching process that produce person-job matches for which the education levels are discrepant but skill levels are congruent. Even if the aggregate distributions permit perfect matching, inefficiencies in the search and hiring processes might result in two workers with identical skills but different educations holding jobs normally filled by workers from the other education group. Again, there is no reason to expect that imperfect matching by education *always* results in good matches by skill, but accounting for worker and skill heterogeneity within education groups might explain some apparent mismatch by education.

Figures 2.2 and 2.3 offer another stylized representation that may be helpful in summarizing the view outlined here. Figure 2.2 shows the distributions of worker skills in three rows, each corresponding to a level of workers' schooling. These curves represent the worker skill distributions shown in panel (a) of figure 2.1. The workers' skill distributions overlap one another as one moves downward across worker education groups, and they overlap the skills found in different job-required education categories as one moves rightward or leftward. However, most of the skill distribution's mass is consistent with jobs that match workers' own levels of education. In addition, the tails of the skill distribution do

Conceptual Framework

Figure 2.2 Distributions of Worker Skills by Worker Education, Overlapping Job-Required Education Levels

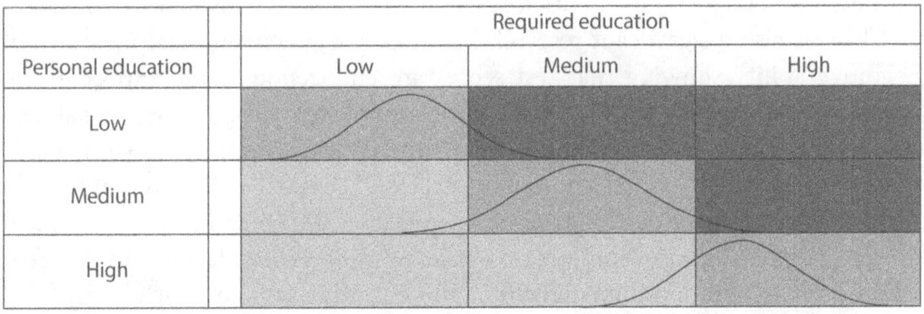

		Required education		
Personal education		Low	Medium	High
Low				
Medium				
High				

Figure 2.3 Distributions of Job Skill Requirements by Job Education, Overlapping Worker Education Levels

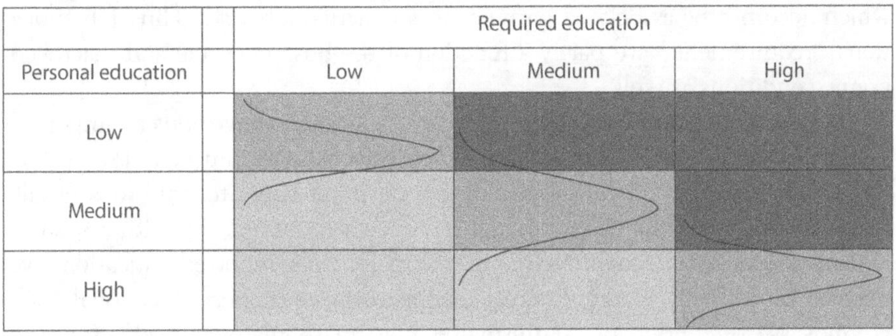

		Required education		
Personal education		Low	Medium	High
Low				
Medium				
High				

not stretch beyond the immediately neighboring level(s) of job education in this representation, that is, there is *no extreme mismatch*. Nevertheless, some workers in the tails of the skill distribution for their education group may be skill-matched to jobs that generally require more or less education than their actual level.

Likewise, the curves in figure 2.3 represent the worker skill distributions shown in panel (b) of figure 2.1. Figure 2.3 shows that the distributions of job task complexity within job education groups represents ranges that overlap with task distributions in other job education groups, and indicate the eligibility of workers in adjacent worker education groups for these jobs. Concretely, the actual task complexity of some jobs requiring high education may be low enough that they could be filled by workers with a medium education if there were an imbalance between supply and demand for education at the aggregate level or if matching processes were imperfect, as is almost certainly the case empirically.

It should be noted at this point that worker skills and job skill requirements have been described in static terms for convenience. It is also the case that workers' skills can *change* in response to the job's requirements. Under-educated workers who are not skill-matched to a job for which they are hired can become so, as shown by studies of workers' *situated learning* and *practical intelligence*

(Scribner 1986; Stasz 2001). The skills workers can develop and for which they are rewarded are partly a function of the jobs employers offer, rather than the intrinsic capacities of individuals acting as a kind of hard constraint.

There is also a significant research literature using conventional measures of cognitive ability showing that test scores are endogenous with respect to job complexity. Using test scores to predict job complexity with cross-sectional data ignores the reciprocal effect of job complexity *on* test scores, as shown by panel models in studies by Kohn and Schooler (1983), Schooler, Mulatu, and Oates (1999), Hauser and Roan (2007), de Grip et al. (2008), and Smart, Gow, and Deary (2014). Likewise, employers can adjust job tasks in response to different labor market conditions, like upgrading the cognitive task content of jobs filled by over-educated workers. Both the skills possessed by individual workers and those required by individual employers are somewhat flexible and endogenous. In addition, it has been shown persuasively that employers raise education requirements in slack labor markets (Modestino, Shoag, and Balance 2015), which need not be associated with changes in actual job tasks. Thus, job educational "requirements" are partly a function of the business cycle and macroeconomic conditions as well.

Despite these complexities, the framework outlined above adds an important dimension to the study of mismatch issues. Persons with unusually low or high test scores for their education group may be more likely to hold jobs usually filled by persons with lower or higher education, while jobs with unusually lenient or demanding cognitive requirements for their reported education level may be more likely to draw persons from lower or higher educational backgrounds as well. Educational mismatch may mask reasonably effective skill matching to some degree.

The preceding discussion treats skills as differing only in magnitude, but the previous section recognized that they differ in kind as well. The demand for skills imparted by different vocational, career, and technical programs at the secondary and post-secondary levels varies, as does the job relevance and marketability of different fields of study at the university level. Some tertiary graduates, as well as those completing occupation-focused secondary education and sub-baccalaureate programs, may be downwardly mobile and compelled to take jobs with lower educational requirements, at least for a certain period, if their field of study is not in high demand. Some apparent mismatch by education level, or *amount-mismatch*, may reflect field of study or *kind-mismatch*.[3]

Possible mismatch by kind of skill fuels continual debates over the relative merits of more academic or career-focused approaches to education at both the secondary/post-secondary and tertiary levels. While large samples would be needed to estimate effects of individual fields of study, smaller samples can be used to investigate whether schooling focused on career preparation is associated with lower levels of education mismatch than general, academic, or liberal arts programs at different levels of attainment.

Finally, while it can be argued that over-education attributable to transitory search frictions and preferences for flexible work means mismatch is not as serious a problem as it might appear, whether to treat low achievement as a confounder in models explaining over-education is more ambiguous. To the degree that the over-educated are not over-skilled because they have low achievement given their education level, the labor market is effectively matching workers to jobs for which they are competent even as the education system is not functioning effectively to impart expected competencies. This would imply that statistics on educational attainment give a misleading picture of human capital stocks, as well. Indeed, demonstrating that apparent over-education is not genuine because workers are not as truly skilled as their education levels imply is an indication of serious problems with worker skills and the education system, rather than weak job creation.

Role of Structural Economic Conditions and Informality

Although aggregate mismatch was discussed earlier, key drivers specific to developing countries require further comment to understand the models estimated in chapter 6. Questions of job quantity and quality are relevant for all economies, but developing countries often experience very low rates of conventional job creation and correspondingly high rates of *informality*. Informality refers to a range of characteristics that are commonly—but by no means invariably—associated with one another, which has produced an array of definitions focusing on different subsets of characteristics. Businesses and jobs considered informal have one or more of the following characteristics:

- *They operate outside of formal legal frameworks* governing business registration, zoning, land titles, permits/licensing, taxation, social insurance contributions, minimum wages, other business and labor regulations, and legally recognized private business contracts;
- *They lack formal organizational frameworks*, such as management structures, specialized job titles, developed accounting practices and detailed written records, and access to bank credit, all of which usually reflects the nature of the operations (such as being small scale, simple in their methods, low in volume, low in profit, or cash-based)[4]; and
- *They lack formal employment frameworks*, such as employment contracts, organizational employment (vs. self-employed and own-account workers), and presumptions of stable tenure and pay (vs. contingent work and pay, such as day laborers and payment by job, commission, or output).

Informal work tends to be labor-intensive and low value-added, with few barriers to entry or shelters from competitive pressures provided by innovative products or methods or scale requirements. In short, these are the very jobs that policies to raise educational attainment aim to supplant. It is reasonable to assume that in many or most cases, informality represents an adaptation to limited opportunities. Formality is more probable when there is an affluent or abundant customer base, modern business practices, access to bank credit, and relatively large, well-capitalized operations. In the absence of abundant formal jobs, individuals must create their own jobs, commonly taking the form of own-account work but sometimes self-employment involving the hiring of others as well.[5]

Even some formal enterprises use informal workers, vendors, and subcontractors to maximize profits or to manage unstable demand while buffering core workers and suppliers from downturns (Portes and Haller 2005). Thus, the extent of informality is an indicator of a country's level of development in various respects, such as the ability to pay on the part of consumers, businesses, and own-account workers; investment levels; labor's bargaining power; and the efficacy and maturity of state/nonstate institutions.

Informal work also tends to be lower-skilled. Although informal work also includes skilled artisanal jobs and those suitable for modern apprenticeships, one would expect that individuals working in the informal sector who pursued nonvocational education make less use of their formal education than their classmates do. In this sense, informality represents a specific mechanism that might account for the aggregate mismatch discussed earlier.

Although some view the informal sector as a source of entrepreneurial energy from which conventional, formal businesses can emerge, a systematic investigation and review concludes that most work and businesses considered informal involve activities that are relatively low value-added, low productivity, small-scale, and labor intensive, rarely evolving into more productive, formal sector jobs or businesses. Informality is widespread and persistent in developing countries because of the large share of consumers whose own low-paid work constrains their demand for goods and services that would be made in formal enterprises using more capital in more developed economies. Country-level cross-sectional and panel models show that the share of the workforce that is self-employed is negatively associated with the level and growth of GDP per capita and positively associated with labor force growth. Informality declines with economic growth, albeit quite slowly overall (La Porta and Shleifer 2014). Not surprisingly, informality and mismatch by education level more generally have been argued to constitute forms of underemployment in countries that lack unemployment insurance and where incomes are too low to give job-seekers the freedom to remain nonworking until employment more congruent with their educational attainment becomes available (Herrera and Merceron 2013).

Thus, high rates of self-employment and other forms of informality would support the argument that a shortage of jobs rather than workforce skills is a key driver of observed mismatch. While it could be argued that high rates of informality or nonemployment among less-educated workers show the need for policies to improve education, the same phenomenon among well-educated workers with high test scores might indicate that more and better jobs are needed if full returns on educational investments are to be realized. *High rates of over-education among tertiary graduates in the informal sector net of controls for preferences, labor market experience, years of education, test scores, and field of study suggest a shortage of skilled jobs, rather than a shortage of skilled workers.* This may reflect some combination of weak investment, unattractive business conditions, low levels of overall economic activity, and/or the quality of institutions and general social conditions.

The key point is that job market woes may reflect job market problems, not necessarily problems with the education system. Indeed, weak job markets are an obstacle to realizing the full potential of educational investments that have been made. More education and training, and even technical assistance and credit for new business development, will not offset insufficient aggregate demand or institutional obstacles to job creation. Because shortages of formal jobs are such a prominent feature of developing economies and can be expected to involve underutilization of formally acquired skills, such structural conditions need to be modeled explicitly in any account of mismatch in developing countries.

Notes

1. This corresponds to a familiar situation in which people accept a job below their qualifications based on a strategic calculation of the advantages of "getting their foot in the door."
2. ISCED levels are defined as follows: < 1 = less than primary education; 1 = primary education; 2 = lower secondary education; 3 = upper secondary education; 4 = post-secondary, nontertiary education; 5 = tertiary education.
3. Although tertiary graduates who hold secondary-level jobs and whose fields of study are irrelevant to their current employment could be considered skill-matched in a narrow sense, there is genuine mismatch between the skills workers acquired and those their jobs demand. The result is a significant underutilization of skills, waste of some or all of the time and resources spent in education, and lower-than-expected earnings and job satisfaction.
4. Many of these correspond to Max Weber's famous definition of what came to be known as formal organizations, which research shows are closely related to organizational size (Handel 2003). For a nice discussion of these and other issues, see Ahmadou Aly Mbaye, Nancy Claire Benjamin, and Stephen Golub, "How the Interplay between Large and Small Informal Firms Affects Jobs in West Africa," published on the World Bank's *Jobs and Development* blog (03/04/2015), http://blogs.worldbank.org/jobs/how-interplay-between-large-and-small-informal-firms-affects-jobs-west-africa.
5. Others treatments of informality emphasize failure to comply with regulations and to pay taxes and social contributions, which may reflect unwillingness to pay, rather than the inability to pay associated with own account and micro/small businesses that operate in survival mode. Operations with more resources may fail to comply either because this is part of a deliberate strategy to maximize profits or because they do not perceive the government to render effective services in return. These aspects of the multifaceted debates on informality are beyond the scope of this report.

References

Davidov, Eldad, Bart Meuleman, Jan Cieciuch, Peter Schmidt, and Jaak Billiet. 2014. "Measurement Equivalence in Cross-National Research." *Annual Review of Sociology* 40: 55–75.

Deaton, Angus. 2005. "Measuring Poverty in a Growing World (or Measuring Growth in a Poor World)." *Review of Economics and Statistics* 87 (1): 1–19.

de Grip, Andries, Hans Bosma, Dick Willems, and Martin van Boxtel. 2008. "Job-Worker Mismatch and Cognitive Decline." *Oxford Economic Papers* 60: 237–53.

Handel, Michael J., ed. 2003. *The Sociology of Organizations*. Thousand Oaks, CA: SAGE Publications.

Handel, Michael J. 2015. *Methodological Issues Related to the Occupational Requirements Survey*. Report to the Bureau of Labor Statistics. Washington, DC: U.S. Department of Labor. www.bls.gov/ncs/ors/handel_report_feb15.pdf.

Hauser, Robert M., and Carol L. Roan. 2007. *Work Complexity and Cognitive Functioning at Midlife: Cross-Validating the Kohn-Schooler Hypothesis in an American Cohort*. Unpublished manuscript. Madison, WI: Center for Demography and Ecology, University of Wisconsin-Madison.

Herrera, Javier, and Sébastien Merceron. 2013. "Underemployment and Job Mismatch in Sub-Saharan Africa." In *Urban Labor Markets in Sub-Saharan Africa*, edited by Philippe De Vreyer and François Roubaud, 83–107. Washington, DC: World Bank.

Jerven, Morten. 2013. *Poor Numbers: How We Are Misled by African Development Statistics and What to Do about It*. Ithaca, NY: Cornell University Press.

Jones, Melanie K., Kostas G. Mavromaras, Peter J. Sloane, and Zhang Wei. 2014. "Disability and Job Mismatches in the Australian Labour Market." *Cambridge Journal of Economics* 38: 1221–46.

Kohn, Melvin L., and Carmi Schooler. 1983. *Work and Personality: An Inquiry into the Impact of Social Stratification*. Norwood, NJ: Ablex Publishing Corporation.

La Porta, Rafael, and Andrei Shleifer. 2014. "Informality and Development." *Journal of Economic Perspectives* 28 (3): 109–26.

Maier, Mark H., and Jennifer Imazeki. 2013. *The Data Game: Controversies in Social Science Statistics*. 4th ed. Armonk, NY: M. E. Sharpe.

Modestino, Alicia Sasser, Daniel Shoag, and Joshua Balance. 2015. "Upskilling: Do Employers Demand Greater Skill When Workers Are Plentiful?" Unpublished manuscript.

Portes, Alejandro, and William Haller. 2005. "The Informal Economy." In *Handbook of Economic Sociology*, edited by Neil J. Smelser and Richard Swedberg, 403–25. Princeton, NJ: Princeton University Press.

Ravallion, Martin. 2010. "Understanding PPPs and PPP-Based National Accounts: Comment." *American Economic Journal: Macroeconomics* 2 (4): 46–52.

Schooler, Carmi, Mesfin Samuel Mulatu, and Gary Oates. 1999. "The Continuing Effects of Substantively Complex Work on the Intellectual Functioning of Older Workers." *Psychology and Aging* 14: 483–506.

Scribner, Sylvia. 1986. "Thinking in Action: Some Characteristics of Practical Thought." In *Practical Intelligence: Nature and Origins of Competence in the Everyday World*, edited by Robert J. Sternberg and Richard K. Wagner, 13–30. London: Cambridge University Press.

Sloane, Peter J. 2003. "Much Ado about Nothing? What Does the Overeducation Literature Really Tell Us?" In *Overeducation in Europe*, edited by Felix Büchel, Andries de Grip, and Antje Merten, 11–48. Northampton, MA: Edward Elgar.

Smart, Emily L., Alan J. Gow, and Ian J. Deary. 2014. "Occupational Complexity and Lifetime Cognitive Abilities." *Neurology* 83: 2285–91.

Stasz, Catherine. 2001. "Assessing Skills for Work: Two Perspectives." *Oxford Economic Papers* 53: 385–405.

CHAPTER 3

About STEP

Introduction

The first part of this report discussed some of the key challenges in measuring education mismatch; those challenges are compounded when investigating mismatch in developing economies. This section provides an overview of the STEP dataset and how the survey is uniquely situated to address such challenges.

STEP (Skills Toward Employment and Productivity) is a household survey of working age adults (ages 15–64) residing in urban areas in most countries that provides new and detailed information on education, employment, and related topics. The sampling strategy was designed to ensure that the target population represents at least 95 percent of the urban working-age population (aged 15–64) in each country.

The 12 countries surveyed represent most of the world's major regions and diverse national incomes, although they mostly span the range within the lower-middle income group.[1] STEP studied urban areas exclusively, except in the Lao People's Democratic Republic and Sri Lanka, whose rural respondents have been excluded from analyses in this report to maintain comparability across countries. Students under age 30 who were currently attending school were excluded, which eliminates one source of artifactual mismatch, as were the very few members of the military, whose circumstances fall outside most discussions of mismatch. In the following regional list of STEP-surveyed countries, the working sample sizes are in parentheses.

- Sub-Saharan Africa
  - Ghana (n = 2,070)
  - Kenya (n = 1,956)
- East, Southeast, and South Asia
  - China—Yunnan Province only (n = 1,268)
  - Lao PDR (n = 1,283)
  - Sri Lanka (n = 579)
  - Vietnam (n = 2,183)

- Europe and Central Asia
  - Armenia (n = 972)
  - Georgia (n = 906)
  - Macedonia, FYR (n = 1,751)
  - Ukraine (n = 941)
- Latin America and the Caribbean
  - Bolivia (n = 1,206)
  - Colombia (n = 1,582)

Respondents in all countries completed a brief battery of reading items, but the full-scale reading assessment was conducted for a subset of participating countries. The STEP survey collects information not typically captured in household surveys, using two distinct instruments, as described next.

Background questionnaire. The background questionnaire consists of household background modules and thematic modules. Modules 2 through 10 are completed by a randomly selected household member (between ages 15 and 64), who completes the remainder of the survey.

- Module 1 conducts a standard background roster of household characteristics.
- Module 2 collects information on education, training, and the respondent's first job.
- Module 3 asks health-related questions.
- Module 4 gathers information on the respondent's current occupation.
- Module 5 includes detailed questions on the respondent's use of reading, writing, and numeracy skills both in daily life and at their job.
- Module 6 collects information on personality traits and behavior.
- Module 7 asks about family background.

Reading literacy assessment. The reading literacy assessment was specifically designed for STEP by Educational Testing Services (ETS) as a direct measure of respondents' reading proficiency. It has three parts:

- Foundational reading skills assessment.
- Core literacy assessment.
- Exercise booklets to evaluate reading proficiency in more depth (only administered to respondents who passed the core literacy assessment).

Dependent variable. In separate and widely spaced sections, the household survey asks respondents for their level of education and how much education was required for their job (if they hold one), using identical response categories. Respondents are coded as over-educated, well-matched, or under-educated based on the difference between their responses to these questions.[2]

Analyses do not control for the possibility that some mismatches reflect incomplete schooling, which is a potentially important issues for multiple reasons.

If those who break off schooling still qualify for jobs at the higher level of job education, that would help explain some apparent under-education—that is, employers would not be reaching as far down the education queue as they seem to be, perhaps reaching down only half a level instead of a full level. Insofar as noncompleters fail to qualify for such jobs, this is an indication of the limited gains from partially completing degree requirements.

In the absence of strong evidence to the contrary, all analyses for this report presume acceptable levels of reliability, validity, and accuracy for key variables such as self-reported education, job-required education, cognitive tasks performed at work and outside work, and reading test scores. Although the test scores may appear more objective than the others, it is not always possible to exclude threats to the validity of this low-stakes assessment, such as domestic distractions, fatigue, lack of interest or comfort, or informal assistance from others. For these and other reasons common to educational testing everywhere, actual reading ability may be higher or lower than measured on the assessment.

Issues regarding data quality are a common concern in social science and currently a lively subject of discussion in research on developing countries.[3] Cross-national surveys raise well-known issues of measurement equivalence across contexts (Davidov et al. 2014). STEP has the advantage of conducting employer surveys in a number of countries that ask identical or closely similar questions regarding job skill demands as are asked in the household surveys. Comparing patterns of task requirements by occupation across employers and households will provide cross-validation in future work.

Notes

1. For details, see http://data.worldbank.org/about/country-and-lending-groups (accessed April 26, 2015). China is classified as an upper-middle-income country, but STEP covered only Yunnan Province, where GDP per capita is below the national average.
2. The question on job education is, "What minimum level of formal education do you think would be required before someone would be able to carry out this work?" Although exact wording varies among surveys asking about job-required education it is not clear that they affect results (Hartog 2000, pp.132f.). Responses to both questions on personal educational attainment and job requirements in terms of national educational systems are recoded into consistent ISCED levels for the analyses in this report.
3. See Jerven (2013) and the related special issue of the *Journal of Development Studies* (vol. 51, 2015). See also studies by Angus Deaton (2005, 2008) as well as Martin Ravallion's (2010) comment in the *American Economic Journal: Macroeconomics*. For examples from a recent controversy on the subject in South Asia, see Manoj Kumar, "Economic Growth Revised Up by Almost 50 Percent" (Reuters, India, Jan. 30, 2015, at http://in.reuters.com/article/2015/01/30/india-gdp-idINKBN0L319Z20150130); Ruchir Sharma, "6.9% Growth? World Laughing at This Bad Joke." (*The Times of India*, blog, Feb. 22, 2015, at http://blogs.timesofindia.indiatimes.com/toi-edit-page/6-9-growth-world-laughing-at-this-bad-joke/); and Sandrine Rastello, "India's New GDP Data Join Global Revisions: India's Not the First to Get a Boost from Changing the Way

It Measures GDP" (*BloombergBusiness*, Feb. 10, 2015, at http://www.bloomberg.com/news/articles/2015-02-10/no-1-for-now-india-s-new-gdp-data-join-global-revisions). For a useful survey of similar issues with respect to official statistics and notable private surveys in the United States, see Maier and Imazeki (2013). For a recent report on measurement issues related to skills and occupational requirements, see Handel (2015).

References

Davidov, Eldad, Bart Meuleman, Jan Cieciuch, Peter Schmidt, and Jaak Billiet. 2014. "Measurement Equivalence in Cross-National Research." *Annual Review of Sociology* 40: 55–75.

Deaton, Angus. 2005. "Measuring Poverty in a Growing World (or Measuring Growth in a Poor World)." *Review of Economics and Statistics* 87 (1): 1–19.

Deaton, Angus, and Alan Heston. 2008. "Understanding PPPs and PPP-Based National Accounts." Paper w14499, Cambridge, MA: National Bureau of Economic Research.

Handel, Michael J. 2015. *Methodological Issues Related to the Occupational Requirements Survey*. Report to the Bureau of Labor Statistics. Washington, DC: U.S. Department of Labor. www.bls.gov/ncs/ors/handel_report_feb15.pdf.

Hartog, Joop. 2000. "Over-Education and Earnings: Where Are We, Where Should We Go?" *Economics of Education Review* 19: 131–47.

Jerven, Morten. 2013. *Poor Numbers: How We Are Misled by African Development Statistics and What to Do about It*. Ithaca, NY: Cornell University Press.

Maier, Mark H., and Jennifer Imazeki. 2013. *The Data Game: Controversies in Social Science Statistics*. 4th ed. Armonk, NY: M. E. Sharpe.

Ravallion, Martin. 2010. "Understanding PPPs and PPP-Based National Accounts: Comment." *American Economic Journal: Macroeconomics* 2 (4): 46–52.

CHAPTER 4

Findings: Country Context

National Income and Employment Rates

The STEP (Skills Toward Employment and Productivity) countries differ significantly in their levels of development and their labor markets. Figure 4.1 shows that GDP per capita varies significantly across the STEP countries, both at the time of the survey in 2013 (shaded blue) and 10 years earlier, in 2003 (shaded orange).

There is very strong persistence in country rankings over the 10-year period ($r = 0.89$), suggesting powerful country fixed effects reflecting a range of country characteristics, including the persistence of demographic forces described earlier. China's growth exceeds levels predicted by this association, but the other countries seem to be facing enduring forces that must be overcome for the economy, and therefore employment, to grow faster than average.

Employment-to-population ratios vary widely across countries in ways that are unlikely to reflect differences in the size of the working-age population alone (figure 4.2). The employment-to-population ratio in the former Yugoslav Republic of Macedonia is strikingly low, for example. It is reasonable to expect that the relative importance of problems relating labor supply, demand, and mismatch for different education levels and selection effects will vary significantly across countries due to differences in income levels and employment rates. If joblessness is high among university graduates, using workers to calculate mismatch rates will underestimate mismatch prevalence, since joblessness itself is arguably a serious form of mismatch.

The patterns in figure 4.2 are also found in roughly similar form among STEP survey samples, as can be seen in table 4.1.[1] Employment rates in the Lao People's Democratic Republic and Bolivia are centered on 85 percent, while those for Armenia and Georgia are closer to 35 percent. Clearly, there is reason to suspect that countries with such low employment rates have general problems with job generation. These issues will be understated in the main findings on mismatch rates, which are restricted to current workers.

Because employment rates differ across countries, sample selection effects will limit the comparability of results across countries to some extent. For example,

Figure 4.1 GDP per Capita, by Country, 2003 and 2013

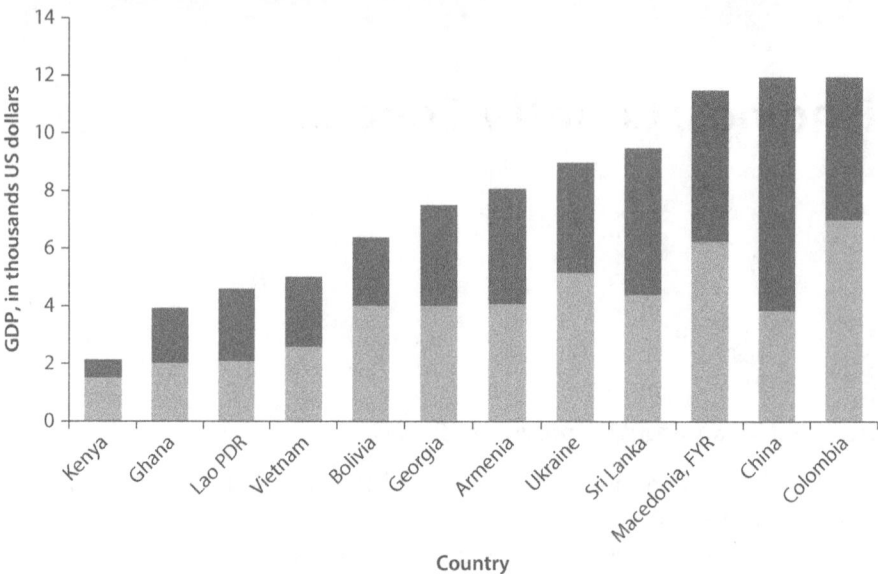

Source: World Development Indicators.
Note: Blue indicates 2013; orange indicates 2003.

results will suggest that the employment situation in the Europe and Central Asia region compares favorably with the situation in other STEP countries, but this must be balanced against the fact that much larger proportions of the potential workforce in Europe and Central Asia (ECA) countries are omitted from the analyses because they are jobless. Observed mismatch is only the tip of the iceberg, since there are unusually large numbers of unemployed and inactive persons in those countries, many of whom would likely be mismatched if they were employed currently. The very high unemployment rates in Armenia and Georgia (table 4.1), which mirror national figures, speak for themselves.

STEP also includes information on reasons for inactivity, which help explain the varying employment rates (table 4.1). Across all countries, about 45 percent of the inactive are keeping house, although the figures are much higher for Bolivia (65 percent of inactive keep house) and Sri Lanka (67 percent), while the figures for FYR Macedonia (27 percent) and Ukraine (7 percent) are much lower (not shown). Most of those keeping house are female. In contrast, retired and discouraged workers account for large shares of the inactive in FYR Macedonia (46 percent) and Ukraine (56 percent), which, along with their elevated unemployment rates, reinforce the impression that jobs are relatively scarce in those countries, raising rates of labor force exit. In short, the smaller share of employed persons among the working-age population in ECA countries needs to be kept in mind when analyses shift to the employed because it is a smaller group overall compared to other countries and likely a more selective group as a consequence.

Findings: Country Context

Figure 4.2 Employment to Population Ratios, by Country, 2012

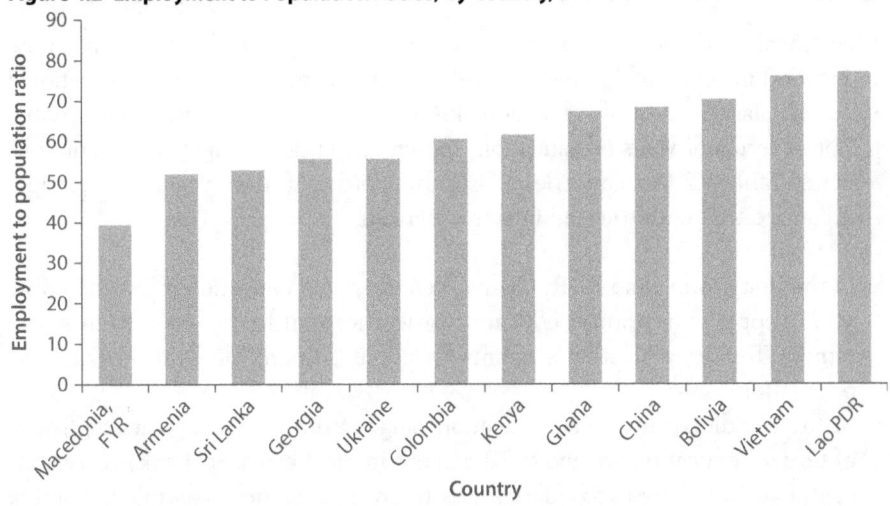

Source: World Development Indicators.

Table 4.1 Labor Force Status of STEP Respondents and Selected Reasons for Inactivity

	1. Employed, percent of total	2. Unemployed, percent of total	3. Inactive, percent of total	4. Inactive and housekeeping, percent of total	5. Inactive and retired, percent of total	6. Inactive and discouraged, percent of total
Lao PDR	88.4	0.8	10.8	5.7	2.4	0.4
Bolivia	83.5	4.8	11.7	7.6	0.9	0.1
Ghana	80.8	6.1	13.1	3.2	1.0	1.3
Vietnam	74.8	2.1	23.1	9.5	8.2	0.2
Colombia	71.8	9.6	18.6	9.2	2.6	0.7
Kenya	66.8	16.2	17.0	8.5	1.0	2.1
Yunnan Province	66.2	3.2	30.7	10.0	13.0	1.4
Ukraine	61.1	10.3	28.7	2.4	12.6	6.9
Macedonia, FYR	57.2	15.0	27.9	7.4	9.2	3.6
Sri Lanka	55.0	2.9	42.1	28.3	3.3	0.7
Armenia	36.6	20.1	43.3	20.3	2.1	7.6
Georgia	33.0	23.8	43.2	20.7	3.7	9.8
Mean	64.6	9.6	25.9	11.1	5.0	2.9

Source: World Bank STEP Skills Measurement Program.
Note: Columns 4–6 show a partial breakdown of the Inactive persons (column 3). Unweighted means of country values in bottom row. Figures in **blue** exceed cross-country means by a substantively significant amount and figures in **orange** are lower than means by similar magnitudes, which vary by column. All figures calculated after excluding rural residents, members of the military, and students under age 30.

Educational Attainment, Achievement Levels, and Fields of Study

Educational attainment varies greatly across countries, as well. Education can be understood in terms of completed level using the categories of the International Standard Classification of Education (ISCED), shown in the left panel of table 4.2, or in terms of years of education, shown in the table's right panel. For convenience, table 4.2 lists countries in ascending order of mean years of education. One can see that countries fall into three groups:

- In the first group (Lao PDR, Ghana, Kenya), mean education is less than nine years. People with primary education or less account for 35–44 percent of the sample. Tertiary education accounts for about 10 percent of the working-age population.
- In the middle group, mean education ranges from 10 to 12 years, and rates of tertiary education are above 20 percent in most cases. Sri Lankans are concentrated in the two secondary levels to an unusual degree, while Colombia has a large share with only a primary education compared to other countries in this group.
- In the third group are the Europe and Central Asia countries, whose mean years of education range from 12.5 to over 14. Rates of tertiary education are generally very high, which will limit potential rates of under-education for these countries. Very few people have only a primary education or less, even in FYR Macedonia, whose rate of tertiary education is more similar to the middle group. Nevertheless, only 21 percent of Macedonians have less than upper secondary, while the average for the middle group is 41 percent.

Table 4.2 ISCED Levels and Mean Years of Education, by Country

	ISCED level (percent)							Years	
	<1	1	2	3	4	5	Total	Mean	SD
Lao PDR	20	24	23	15	7	11	100	8.3	4.9
Ghana	21	14	36	20		10	100	8.4	5.3
Kenya	14	23	17	31	8	8	100	8.9	4.8
Sri Lanka	4	9	25	55		8	100	9.9	3.1
Colombia	8	24	8	38		22	100	10.0	3.8
Vietnam	4	13	25	34	1	22	100	10.8	3.9
Bolivia	11	5	21	30	11	23	100	10.9	4.2
Yunnan Province	2	11	35	29		23	100	11.8	3.6
Macedonia, FYR	1	2	19	54		25	100	12.5	3.6
Ukraine			6	36	13	45	100	12.9	2.3
Armenia		1	10	39		50	100	12.8	3.1
Georgia		2	8	32		58	100	14.3	3.2
Mean	7	11	19	34	3	25		10.9	3.8

Note: Blank cells indicate either no cases or too few cases for reliable estimates. Last row shows unweighted means across countries. Figures in **blue** exceed cross-country means by more than five percentage points and figures in orange are more than five percentage points below cross-country means. Figures cover the working age population excluding rural residents, members of the military, and students under 30 years old.

Looking across the 12 countries, rates of post-secondary, nontertiary education (ISCED level 4)[2] are meaningful for only four countries and show no particular pattern by region, level of development, or country mean education level. This is not an entirely reliable guide to rates of job- and career-focused education because some proportion of both secondary and tertiary graduates have been coded separately as having completed such a program as part of their studies based on country-specific information regarding their degree type.

A natural question is the degree to which the ISCED codes are comparable across countries in terms of years of schooling, achievement, or fields of study, which are also important in their own right in the study of mismatch as controls for usually unobserved heterogeneity. Comparability in terms of expected years of education is relatively high. In a pooled regression, ISCED category accounts for a very large share of the variance of years of education across countries ($\bar{R}^2$ = 0.92). The incremental explained variance after adding country dummies is modest ($\Delta\bar{R}^2 = 0.01$).

Nevertheless, breakdowns show variation in years of education by ISCED level even when current students under 30 years old are excluded, as in all analyses in this report. Notable variations include these:

- In some countries persons with *less than primary* have no education (Ghana, Kenya, FYR Macedonia), while in others they have close to two years (Lao PDR) or three years (Bolivia, Colombia, Sri Lanka, Vietnam).
- *Primary schooling* corresponds to four years of education in FYR Macedonia and five years in Lao PDR, Sri Lanka, and Vietnam, compared to six years in others (Bolivia, Colombia, Georgia, Ghana, Kenya, Yunnan Province).
- *Lower secondary* implies eight to nine years of education in all countries except Colombia and Yunnan Province, where it is 10 years.
- Somewhat more significantly, *upper secondary education* implies 12 years of education for half the countries (Bolivia, Georgia, Kenya, Lao PDR, FYR Macedonia, Vietnam), but
    - 40–60 percent of upper secondary graduates have just 10 years in Armenia and Sri Lanka;
    - 75 percent of students have 11 years in Colombia and Ukraine; and
    - 90–100 percent have 13 years in Ghana and Yunnan Province.

The distribution of years of education for tertiary graduates is particularly complex (table 4.3). The diversity is driven partly by the inclusion of sub-baccalaureate and post-baccalaureate degrees, as well as bachelor's degrees, in a single ISCED category, but it is important to understand the different meanings of this ISCED category in interpreting results both within and across countries.

Given that significant numbers of tertiary graduates hold less than a bachelor's degree, the probability of over-education may be greater even as the extent

Table 4.3 Distribution of Years of Education among Tertiary Graduates, by Country
percent

	Detailed breakdown						Summary breakdown		
	<13	13	14	15	16	>16	<16	16	>16
Armenia		36			40	24	36	40	24
Bolivia				40	3	58	40	3	58
Colombia	5	39	18	3	23	12	65	23	12
Georgia			28		20	52	28	20	52
Ghana					50	50	–	50	50
Kenya				23	65	13	23	65	13
Lao PDR				39		61	39	–	61
Macedonia, FYR			15			85	15	–	85
Sri Lanka				34	49	18	34	49	18
Ukraine		25	7	8	59	1	40	59	1
Vietnam				24	65	11	24	65	11
Yunnan Province					57	43	–	57	43
Mean							29	36	36

Source: World Bank STEP Skills Measurement Program.
Note: Blank cells indicate either no cases or too few cases for reliable estimates. Rows sum to 100 percent aside from rounding. Figures cover the working-age population with ISCED = 5, excluding rural residents, members of the military, and students under 30 years old. Unusually large values in left panel in **blue** and unusually small values in orange. Seventh column sums percentages in first four columns.

of downward mobility is less than might be assumed otherwise. A similar breakdown for the employed differs by only a few percentage points, except in the case of Armenia, where only a quarter of employed tertiary graduates have 13 years of education and the share with bachelor's degrees absorbs almost all the difference (not shown).

Test scores vary greatly both between and within countries (figure 4.3). These gaps shrink substantially once education is controlled for, as shown in the box plots for secondary and tertiary graduates in figure 4.4 and the means in table 4.4. Nevertheless, substantial test score variation remains within ISCED groups for each country, and the distributions for ISCED-3 and ISCED-5 overlap within all countries. Some people with a given education level function at a different level from others in their countries, providing ample reason to investigate the contribution of achievement differences to education mismatch. Likewise, while the range of scores across countries is much narrower after controlling for ISCED level, it is clear that educational attainment levels are not directly comparable across countries. Mean scores for tertiary graduates in Bolivia, Kenya, and Ghana are lower than means for upper secondary graduates in Ukraine and Armenia (table 4.4, columns 2 and 3), some of which may reflect differences in linguistic homogeneity across countries. The gap in mean literacy scores between secondary and tertiary graduates averages 25 points but can be one-half or twice that amount for different countries (table 4.4, column 4). Because the meaning

Figure 4.3 Reading Score Distributions, by Country

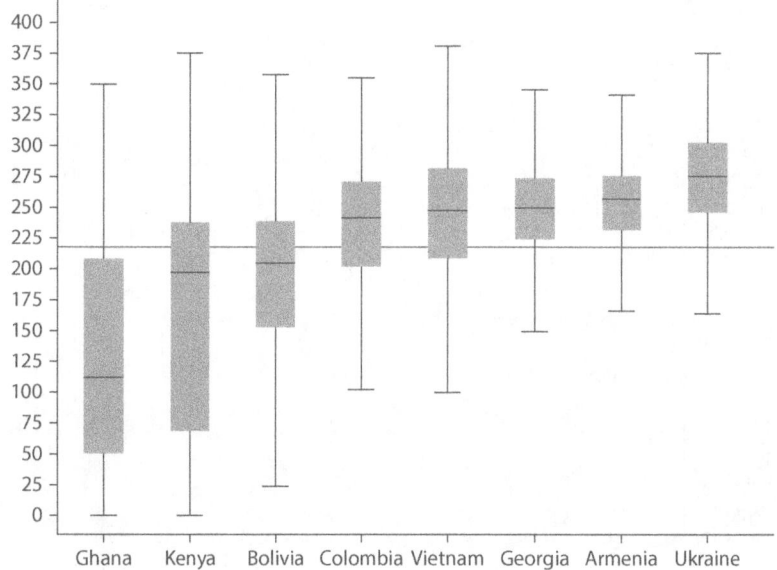

Source: World Bank STEP Skills Measurement Program.

of education level can differ greatly across countries, all models will be estimated separately by country.

Nearly everyone with post-secondary education reports having a specialized field of study, but the number of secondary graduates reporting specialized study varies greatly. This raises the question of the *kind or content* of schooling, addressed in table 4.5. Most of the country variation in the percentage reporting no specialization (column 1) reflects different rates of post-secondary attainment and the relative degree of subject specialization at the secondary level. The degree to which selection into employment alters this picture is shown in column 1a, which shows the change in column 1 values when the sample is restricted to employed persons. (Figures sum to 100 percent across rows excluding column 1a and allowing for the omission of low-skill service and unspecified "other" fields that account for an additional 2–5 percent of persons in most countries.)

None of the broad groupings of fields of study accounts for as much as 10 percent of the workforce on average (bottom row), and the relatively few exceptions within countries are highlighted in blue. Even the shares of graduates for such job-relevant fields as business (column 4) and technical subjects at the tertiary level (column 5) do not particularly stand out. Although patterns vary by country, there is no obvious overemphasis on fields of study assumed to face low demand or low rewards in the labor market. Business management and general office subjects are the most popular, followed by technical subjects

Figure 4.4 Reading Score Distributions for Upper Secondary and Tertiary Levels, by Country

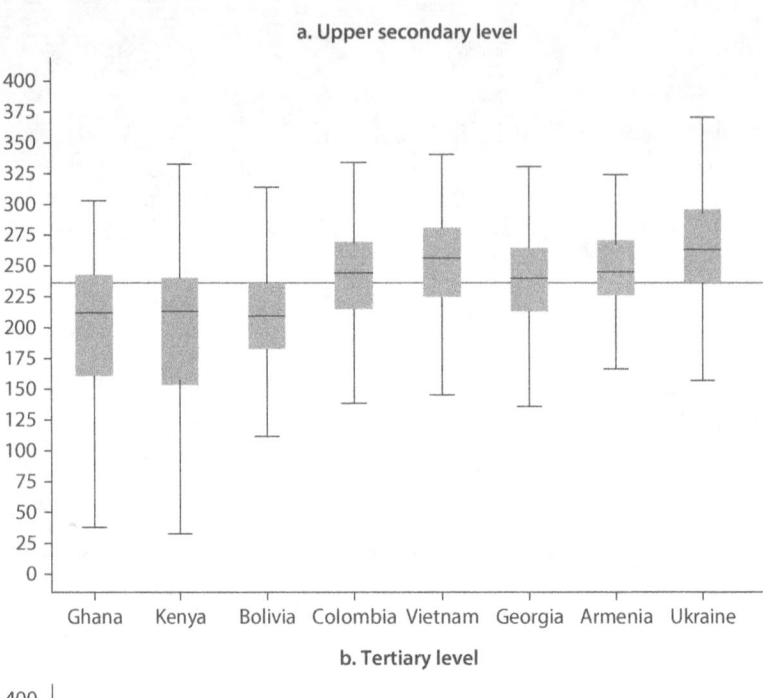

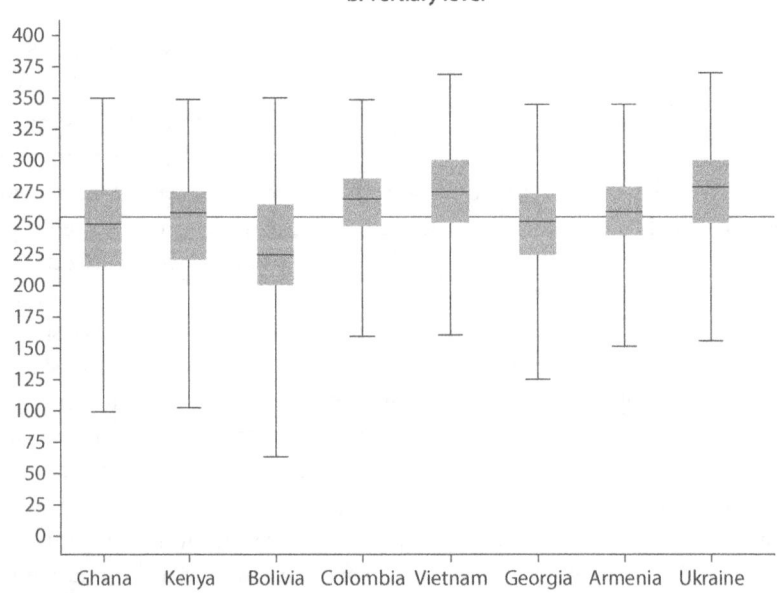

Source: World Bank STEP Skills Measurement Program.

Table 4.4 Mean Literacy Score by ISCED Level and Secondary-Tertiary Gap, by Country

	All	ISCED level 3	ISCED level 5	Difference
Ukraine	268	264	274	10
Armenia	253	247	260	13
Georgia	242	234	247	13
Vietnam	235	251	274	23
Colombia	228	241	265	25
Bolivia	183	206	229	23
Kenya	163	189	238	49
Ghana	125	191	238	47
Mean	**212**	**228**	**253**	**25**

Source: World Bank STEP Skills Measurement Program.
Note: Means for tertiary graduates in **orange** (column 3) are less than means for secondary graduates in **blue** (column 2). Fourth column values are tertiary means minus secondary means. Sample is working age population excluding rural residents, members of the military, and students under 30 years old.

Table 4.5 Broad Fields of Study, by Country
percent

	1. None full sample	1a. None employed only (Δ percent)	2 Education and social services	3 Humanities and social sciences	4 Business and office	5 STEM, trades tertiary	6 STEM, trades secondary	7 Law and health
Armenia	38	−16	10	15	5	13	4	11
Bolivia	56	−6	5	2	13	9	4	7
Colombia	79	−3	2	1	7	8	0	4
Georgia	31	−14	6	17	7	14	2	14
Ghana	77	−2	2	5	6	2	4	1
Kenya	71	−6	4	3	6	4	4	2
Lao PDR	77	−3	6	1	5	4	1	3
Macedonia, FYR	31	−13	5	11	8	7	23	8
Sri Lanka	63	−10	2	7	10	2	13	1
Vietnam	74	−4	3	2	9	6	2	2
Yunnan Province	57	−10	8	2	13	5	6	4
Mean	**54**	**−8**	**5**	**6**	**8**	**7**	**6**	**5**

Source: World Bank STEP Skills Measurement Program.
Note: "None" indicates no field of study. Except for column 1a figures cover the working-age population excluding rural residents, members of the military, and students under 30 years old. Column 1a shows the difference between column 1 and percentage values recalculated restricting samples to employed respondents. Unusually large values in **blue** and unusually small values in **orange**.

at the tertiary level. Whether particular fields of study or specialized study itself accounts for mismatch to an appreciable extent will be investigated further below, though assessing individuals' level of learning or knowledge achieved within these diverse fields is clearly beyond the scope of a general household survey.

Selection into Employment by Education and Achievement Level

Figure 4.2 and table 4.1 showed significant variation in employment rates by country, raising possible issues of sample selectivity and introducing an element of noncomparability across countries. They also complicate conclusions within countries with low employment rates, because outcomes are unobserved for a large proportion of cases, and the extent to which this represents weak labor markets or personal preferences is difficult to determine for many female and older persons, in particular. Table 4.6 shows employment rates by ISCED level, giving some sense of selection into employment. Employment rates below 55 percent are shown in orange; almost all of these countries are in the Europe and Central Asia region, with rates for Armenia and Georgia much lower than the other countries.

Within every country, tertiary graduates have the highest rates of employment, averaging 75 percent. However, the countries with the highest rates of tertiary education have the lowest employment rates overall (final column), and the lowest rates for tertiary graduates themselves (column 5). Thus, the different employment-to-population ratios shown earlier cannot be ascribed simply to compositional differences with respect to education level across countries. Indeed, the most educated countries have the *lowest* employment rates overall and within each ISCED group. In Georgia, the employment rate for tertiary graduates is *one-half* the average across countries (38 percent vs. 75 percent). Although education is positively associated with employment in Georgia and Armenia, employment rates for tertiary graduates are below those of secondary school graduates in every other country, and almost every other ISCED level

Table 4.6 Employment Rates by ISCED Level, by Country
percent

	<1	1	2	3	4	5	All
Lao PDR	86	87	86	88	94	96	88
Ghana	86	75	80	75		87	81
Kenya	64	62	70	65	70	82	67
Sri Lanka	48	58	50	54		69	55
Colombia	64	67	70	73		78	72
Vietnam	77	73	76	68		83	75
Bolivia	73	91	81	83	79	91	83
Yunnan Province		45	57	69		89	67
Macedonia, FYR		14	32	59		71	57
Ukraine			49	56	56	68	61
Armenia			29	25		45	37
Georgia			19	23		38	33
Mean	**71**	**64**	**58**	**62**	**75**	**75**	**65**

Source: World Bank STEP Skills Measurement Program.
Note: Blank cells indicate either no cases or too few cases for reliable estimates. Last row shows unweighted means across countries. Figures below 55 percent in **orange**. Figures exclude rural residents, members of the military, and students under age 30.

Table 4.7 Mean Literacy Score by Employment Status, by Country

	All	Employed	Unemployed	Inactive
Ukraine	268	270	271	262
Armenia	253	256	251	252
Georgia	242	248	240	239
Vietnam	235	238	244	223
Colombia	228	230	229	216
Bolivia	183	185	183	168
Kenya	163	169	163	139
Ghana	125	122	154	131
Mean	212	215	217	204

Source: World Bank STEP Skills Measurement Program.
Note: Values in orange are unusually small and the value in blue are unusually large. Sample is working-age population excluding rural residents, members of the military, and students under 30 years old.

outside the Europe and Central Asia group. It is likely that many tertiary graduates in Georgia and Armenia are unable to find suitable work and would be counted as mismatched if the definition of mismatch were broadened to include nonemployed persons.

Given the observed selection into employment based on education level, it is surprising to find relatively modest selection into employment based on test score means for the employed, unemployed, and inactive (table 4.7) and various score percentiles (not shown). Note that only eight of the 12 countries completed the full literacy assessment, hence the absence of Lao PDR, FYR Macedonia, Sri Lanka, and Yunnan Province. While the main analyses will examine the extent to which test scores affect the probability of education mismatch among the employed, it does not appear that test scores strongly affect the probability of employment itself in many cases.

Quality of Employment

Some indication of the kinds of jobs workers hold, which relates to structural conditions in the labor market, can be gained by examining the distribution of jobs according to (1) whether they are in the public or private sectors, (2) whether they are formal or informal (as defined by the presence/absence of pension benefits), and (3) the nature of the employment relationship (employee, self-employed, unpaid family worker).

These three category schemes may cross-cut one another, though in practice the vast majority of public sector jobs are formal and almost all self-employed workers are informal, as are all unpaid family workers. However, employees show significant variation across the public/private and formal/informal categories. The major exception to the preceding is Georgia, where nearly 45 percent of public sector workers are informal by the preceding definition. If informality were defined more narrowly, the fact that the vast majority of public sector workers in Georgia have written employment contracts and permanent positions would reduce the informal share in that country significantly.

These distinctions reflect some of the structural issues discussed previously. While some state-owned enterprises may be solid, there is concern that some countries have used public sector employment to substitute for a weak private sector as an incentive for people to pursue higher education, and there is also some concern that the pursuit of public sector employment spontaneously motivates students to enter higher education and queue for public sector jobs after graduation.

Likewise, high rates of informality are seen widely as an indicator of poor job market conditions. It is also widely recognized that much self-employment in developing countries is a response to a shortage of more productive, formal jobs, though there is some question as to whether some of the self-employed may be considered entrepreneurs with significant potential for income generation.

Table 4.8 sheds light on job conditions across countries. Figures in blue exceed the cross-country (unweighted) means in the final row by at least ten percentage points, while figures in orange fall below those means by an equal amount. The following patterns are evident.

Public employment is very high in Armenia, Georgia, and Ukraine, and, to a lesser extent, in Yunnan Province and FYR Macedonia. All of these countries have low rates of self-employment (about 13 percent), as well. For this reason and because of low rates of informal private sector employment, rates of informality are very low in Armenia, Ukraine, and FYR Macedonia (about 16 percent).

Table 4.8 Employment by Public/Private and Formal/Informal Sectors

| | 1. Public sector | 2. Informal sector | 3a. Employees | | | | 3b. Self-employed | 3c. Unpaid family workers |
			All	Public, formal	Private, formal	Private, informal		
Lao PDR	18	87	30	11	2	11	59	10
Ghana	10	84	34	8	7	17	62	4
Kenya	7	76	55	6	17	31	41	4
Sri Lanka	21	64	57	17	16	20	40	3
Colombia	4	62	53	4	31	17	46	1
Vietnam	25	60	54	22	13	16	39	7
Bolivia	12	77	47	10	12	23	50	3
Yunnan Province	34	47	83	28	23	27	13	4
Macedonia, FYR	31	15	83	30	48	4	16	1
Ukraine	36	13	87	36	51	0	12	0
Armenia	57	19	88	56	23	7	11	1
Georgia	45	62	84	25	13	26	14	1
Mean	25	56	63	21	21	17	34	3

Source: World Bank STEP Skills Measurement Program.
Note: Last row shows unweighted means across countries. Figures in **blue** exceed cross-country means by at least 10 percentage points and figures in **orange** are at least 10 percentage points below cross-country means. Figures cover the working-age population excluding rural residents, members of the military, and students under 30 years old.

Informality is more common in Georgia (62 percent) both for the reasons already noted and also because of relatively high levels of informality among private sector employees, a pattern also found in Yunnan Province. It should be noted that rates of public sector employment are much higher for tertiary graduates than less educated workers in many countries, which may explain their lower probability of mismatch to some extent.

Lao PDR and Ghana have the highest rates of informality (about 85 percent) and the highest rates of self-employment (about 60 percent). Formal employment in the private sector is extremely low (about 5 percent), and formal employment in the public sector is among the lowest as well (about 10 percent).

Patterns are more diverse among the other countries. Informality ranges from 60 to 77 percent and self-employment is in the range of 40–50 percent. Private, formal employment is quite low (about 15 percent), except for Colombia (31 percent), as is public sector formal employment (about 7 percent in Kenya, Colombia, and Bolivia).

Formal private sector jobs are most common in Ukraine and FYR Macedonia, accounting for about 50 percent of all employment. However, 22 percent of private employment in Ukraine is in privatized state enterprises. Given the relatively high rates of formal public sector employment in both countries, it is no coincidence that they have the lowest rates of mismatch (about 28 percent), followed by Armenia and Georgia (about 34 percent), as shown in the next chapter. Jobs tend to be scarce in these countries, but employment is similar to that in developed countries, where it exists.

The Task Content of Jobs

The previous sections provide information on personal and job characteristics and broader labor market conditions that are expected to help account for observed mismatch by education level. Just as literacy scores and field of study provide finer detail than education level regarding worker skills, STEP's measures of cognitive job tasks provide finer detail than required education level does regarding job skill demands. And just as apparent mismatch based on education level raises questions regarding the equivalence of workers with the same level of education, it also raises the question of the equivalence of jobs within job-required education categories. Finally, just as apparently over-educated workers may have lower achievement and less marketable specialized knowledge than their classmates, they may also have more cognitively complex jobs than their well-matched, less educated coworkers.

This report uses STEP's measures of the complexity of reading, writing, math, and problem solving performed on the job to measure job skill requirements more finely and specifically. Other measures, such as computer and noncomputer technology used at work, as well as a parallel set of items on tasks performed outside work, which provide comparable information on capacities, will be used in further studies. The measures aim to cover, as much as possible, the content of the cognitive skills domain specified previously, as can be seen in the shaded entries in table 4.9, which reproduces key content of table 1.2 from chapter 1 for convenience. Table 4.9 shows that the comprehensive cognitive skills map developed in chapter 1 is covered reasonably well by measures in the STEP survey.

STEP task items aim to be as concrete and objective as possible, and most incorporate a clear difficulty gradient. The goal is to move beyond ordinal-level measures using vague quantifiers and Likert-style response options toward measures that give some indication of the *absolute* levels of cognitive complexity involved in work and personal life. Rather than items that simply rank respondents, STEP measures provide information on what people actually do at their jobs.

Ideally, a correspondence could be established between values on these task scales and education level such that one could determine not only the percentage of *jobs* requiring reading, writing, math, and problem solving at different ISCED levels, but also the percentage of *people* with those skills and how many people work in jobs that involve using them. This would not only locate people and jobs on a common education scale, but also cross-reference those values to the presumed content of education at different levels to the extent possible.

Needless to say, continued ambiguity within the education field as to what constitutes grade-level reading, writing, and problem solving, as well as the constraints of large-sample surveys, place limits on how effectively this can be achieved. The number of survey questions and level of detail in the instructions to respondents are limited and the data are self-reports. There is not even a consensus within IO psychology on rating methods using external observation by trained job analysts that can equate job task complexity to education levels. Nevertheless, few previous surveys have approached the issue of job skill requirements as systematically as STEP, and insofar as self-reports are biased upward then rates of self-reported task performance represent an upper bound, which in this case remains informative because they are well below the scales' ceilings.

Table 4.9 Cognitive Skills Domain

Skill level	General skills		Specific skills	
	3Rs plus	General cognitive skills	Knowledge, field of study	Particular skills
High	• Math	• General knowledge	*High level*, such as STEM, medical, other managerial & professional	• IT software, hardware skills
	• Writing	• General reasoning, analytical skills		• Business procedures
Medium	• Reading	• Problem solving	*Medium level*, such as technical, craft/repair, upper clerical	• Handling of specific materials, tools, equipment
	• General knowledge	• Trainability, learning how to learn		
Low	• Organizational skills			

Findings: Country Context

Some indication of the quality of the measures as well as the level of job skill requirements by country is shown by rates of task performance by ISCED level. For presentation purposes, tables 4.10, 4.11, and 4.12 recode task variables into three levels and show rates of simple and complex task performance by ISCED category. Rates of performing moderately complex tasks can be recovered by subtracting the sum of rates of simple and complex task performance from 100 percent. All tables refer only to employed persons, excluding those whose personal education or job-required education is post-secondary nontertiary (ISCED = 4), who are excluded from the main analyses due to the small and specialized nature of these groups. Rates that are at least 10 percentage points above (below) cross-country averages are shaded blue (orange). Thus, countries with unusually skilled jobs have values in the first row shaded orange and/or values in the second row shaded blue (orange-blue), while the

Table 4.10 Level of Reading Complexity at Work, by Worker ISCED Level, by Country
percent

	Document length by ISCED level						Kinds of reading by ISCED level					
	<1	1	2	3	5	All	<1	1	2	3	5	All
Lao PDR												
Low	100	98	97	92	64	93	89	84	71	46	10	67
High	0	0	0	2	14	2	1	3	4	12	59	11
Ghana												
Low	100	99	98	75	47	88	100	93	88	57	16	77
High	0	0	1	17	43	9	0	1	3	14	55	10
Kenya												
Low	99	92	75	75	29	79	96	83	58	56	8	66
High	0	4	15	19	63	15	2	4	19	20	61	16
Sri Lanka												
Low		99	96	62	37	71		99	86	39	8	53
High		0	0	26	45	20		1	5	40	67	31
Colombia												
Low	95	93	97	81	50	78	80	76	72	49	24	54
High	5	5	3	11	37	15	4	7	8	22	43	21
Vietnam												
Low	100	93	91	79	35	74	89	85	71	52	18	55
High	0	4	4	11	50	18	1	1	7	18	46	19
Bolivia												
Low	96	100	95	80	39	72	88	91	82	66	24	59
High	2	0	2	15	51	22	3	4	4	13	44	20
Yunnan Province												
Low		87	79	62	33	60		68	50	21	8	30
High		6	10	23	48	25		8	17	40	59	36

table continues next page

Table 4.10 Level of Reading Complexity at Work, by Worker ISCED Level, by Country (continued)

	Document length by ISCED level						Kinds of reading by ISCED level					
	< 1	1	2	3	5	All	< 1	1	2	3	5	All
Macedonia, FYR												
Low			94	70	27	57			82	47	11	**38**
High			3	20	61	33			8	31	66	**41**
Ukraine												
Low				79	55	64				50	20	**32**
High				11	32	24				33	62	**50**
Armenia												
Low			94	85	47	60			88	70	32	**45**
High			2	9	34	26			7	9	33	**26**
Georgia												
Low				80	53	59				75	40	**47**
High				13	34	30				13	26	**23**
Mean												
Low	98	95	91	77	43	71	90	85	75	52	18	**52**
High	1	2	4	15	43	20	2	4	8	22	52	**25**

Source: World Bank STEP Skills Measurement Program.
Note: Blank cells indicate either no cases or too few cases for reliable estimates. *Document length* refers to the longest document read normally at work, where *low* = 0–5 pages, *medium* = 6–10 pages (not shown), *high* = over 10 pages. *Kinds of reading* refers to the number of different types of materials read regularly at work (forms, bills, manuals, reports, newspapers/magazines/books), where *low* = 0–1, *medium* = 2–3 (not shown), *high* = 4–5. Because Ukraine survey includes only four types of reading, *low* = 0–1, *medium* = 2 (not shown), *high* = 3–4.

Table 4.11 Level of Writing at Work, by Worker ISCED Level, by Country
percent

	< 1	1	2	3	5	All
Lao PDR						
Low	96	89	81	63	27	77
High	0	2	1	2	25	4
Ghana						
Low	99	91	87	62	21	78
High	0	0	3	12	40	8
Kenya						
Low	95	84	66	65	17	71
High	0	1	7	11	52	9
Sri Lanka						
Low		98	88	55	37	65
High		0	3	20	32	16
Colombia						
Low	91	89	84	72	47	72
High	1	1	6	5	24	8

table continues next page

Findings: Country Context

Table 4.11 Level of Writing at Work by Worker ISCED Level, by Country *(continued)*

	< 1	1	2	3	5	All
Vietnam						
Low	95	94	88	73	29	69
High	0	2	1	6	35	11
Bolivia						
Low	94	94	85	74	27	64
High	1	1	2	5	42	17
Yunnan Province						
Low		78	62	31	12	38
High		6	8	21	48	24
Macedonia, FYR						
Low			89	64	20	51
High			2	13	48	24
Ukraine						
Low				73	33	49
High				8	29	21
Armenia						
Low			79	70	30	43
High			0	8	36	27
Georgia						
Low				83	55	61
High				1	22	18
Mean						
Low	95	89	81	65	30	61
High	0	2	3	9	36	16

Source: World Bank STEP Skills Measurement Program.
Note: Writing refers to the length of the longest document written normally at work, where *low* = 1 page or less, *medium* = 2–5 pages (not shown), *high* = over 5 pages.

pattern is reversed (blue-orange) for countries whose rates of job task complexity are unusually low.

Table 4.10 presents results for complexity of reading at work as measured by (1) length of the longest document normally read on the job and (2) the number of different kinds of reading materials normally used at work. Reading complexity is *low* if the longest document is five pages or less or if respondents indicated they read no more than one out of the four or five kinds of reading materials about which they were queried. Reading complexity is considered *high* if they normally read documents over 10 pages long and use all or nearly all of the different kinds of reading materials asked about in the survey.

There is a clear gradient by worker education for both measures of reading complexity. Aside from Kenya and Yunnan Province, almost no one with less than upper secondary education reads documents longer than five pages as a

Table 4.12 Levels of Math Use and Problem Solving at Work, by Worker ISCED Level, by Country
percent

	Math by ISCED level						Problem solving by ISCED level					
	<1	1	2	3	5	All	<1	1	2	3	5	All
Lao PDR												
Low	16	7	6	3	4	8	92	91	84	75	67	84
High	2	4	3	9	16	5	4	2	11	9	11	7
Ghana												
Low	9	9	10	9	12	10	78	70	67	58	27	64
High	0	0	0	2	22	3	19	25	26	34	62	30
Kenya												
Low	19	19	14	11	5	15	67	67	64	49	21	57
High	0	0	5	5	31	5	25	26	24	41	69	34
Sri Lanka												
Low		20	18	12	14	14		68	61	45	29	49
High		4	2	12	25	10		22	28	42	62	39
Colombia												
Low	23	22	9	15	13	17	59	53	43	57	34	50
High	1	2	5	9	16	8	20	41	49	33	51	39
Vietnam												
Low	19	14	16	12	15	14	94	91	81	73	48	72
High	0	2	2	5	19	7	2	7	12	20	40	20
Bolivia												
Low	11	4	10	9	10	9	70	64	56	48	26	47
High	2	7	3	5	28	12	21	29	36	33	63	42
Yunnan Province												
Low		36	27	17	15	21		83	84	67	56	70
High		0	2	7	13	7		7	9	21	28	18
Macedonia, FYR												
Low			35	26	22	25			77	52	28	46
High			2	6	22	11			21	42	64	48
Ukraine												
Low			22	15	18					63	36	46
High				7	22	16				24	50	40
Armenia												
Low			26	32	22	25			81	64	49	55
High			3	7	17	13			10	26	41	35

table continues next page

Findings: Country Context

Table 4.12 Levels of Math Use and Problem solving at Work by Worker ISCED Level, by Country *(continued)*

	Math by ISCED level						Problem solving by ISCED level					
	< 1	1	2	3	5	All	< 1	1	2	3	5	All
Georgia												
Low				43	32	35				84	64	68
High				6	10	9				12	27	24
Mean												
Low	16	16	17	17	15	18	77	74	70	61	40	59
High	1	2	3	7	20	9	15	20	22	28	47	31

Source: World Bank STEP Skills Measurement Program.
Note: Blank cells indicate either no cases or too few cases for reliable estimates. *Math* refers to the kinds of math used normally at work, where *low* = no math at all, *medium* = arithmetic, including calculations with fractions, decimals, and percents (not shown), *high* = any math above arithmetic (e.g., algebra, geometry, trigonometry). *Problem solving* refers to the frequency of performing tasks that require at least 30 minutes of thinking to figure out how they should be done, where *low* = less than once a month, *medium* = less than once a week but at least once a month (not shown), *high* = at least once a week.

normal part of their job. Required reading levels are somewhat higher when measured by the percentages using a moderate number of different kinds of reading materials at work, but the generally low literacy demands of jobs held by workers without upper secondary education is notable.

Analyses of STEP's information on test scores and literacy practices can shed light on the extent to which the low workplace demands are a response to low worker abilities or are determined exogenously and indicative of skill underutilization. However, even the vast majority of upper secondary graduates read documents no longer than five pages at work (mean = 77 percent), though, again, reading complexity is higher when measured by the variety of reading materials used at work. Likewise, the share of tertiary graduates reading documents over 10 pages exceeds 50 percent in only three countries (Bolivia, Kenya, FYR Macedonia), though the vast majority in most countries read more than one kind of reading material.

Table 4.11 shows that about 90 to 95 percent of workers with primary education or less do not write text longer than a page as a normal part of their job. About 15–25 percent of workers with lower and upper secondary education write moderately long text (two to five pages) as part of their job, but even tertiary graduates do not write text longer than five pages at rates exceeding 45 percent outside of Kenya, Yunnan Province, and FYR Macedonia.

In short, although there is much imprecision in equating document length and document variety to education levels, it does not seem that literacy practices at work are typically high relative to the curriculum content one assumes for tertiary, upper secondary, and the other education levels.

Information on math used at work (table 4.12) generally reinforces impressions from the evidence on literacy practices. There is much less variation in math use at work by education level, and only 15–25 percent of any ISCED group reports using no math at all in most countries. Moderate math complexity involves using arithmetic at work, even though it is typically learned by the end of primary school; this level of math is commonly used on the job. However, higher levels of math, defined as anything above arithmetic, are rarely used on the job by any education group. Aside from Sri Lanka, less than 10 percent of upper secondary graduates in any country use secondary school math at work, and only about 15–25 percent of tertiary graduates in most countries use any math beyond arithmetic as a regular part of their jobs.

Of course, it is possible that the critical skills for most jobs are general reasoning and problem solving, skills that are part of the general cognitive development fostered by schooling, rather than math, writing, or reading extended text specifically. STEP defines complex problem solving as tasks requiring at least 30 minutes of thinking to figure out how they should be accomplished. This item uses time as an objective basis to define complexity for a concept ("problem solving") that has no other obvious basis for a natural unit, unlike reading, writing, and math.

When respondents are asked how often they have to solve problems at work requiring at least 30 minutes of thinking, the average percentage across countries saying they do so with high frequency (at least once a week) seems larger than the corresponding percentages for other tasks. For example, 28 percent of upper secondary graduates say they are faced with such tasks at least once a week, but only 15 percent say they regularly read documents at least 10 pages long, which might be expected to take the average reader about 30 minutes as well. Comparing the frequency of complex problem solving to the other tasks is not so straightforward and may produce other rankings. Likewise, the time required to solve a problem is partly dependent on the ability of the problem solver as well as the intrinsic difficulty of the problem, so the standard unit is less fixed than page length. Nevertheless, it seems likely that problem solving contributes unique information on general skills developed significantly through education that is distinct from literacy and numeracy practices.

A useful point to note is that the education gradients for all tasks, apart from simple math use, are nonlinear. The difference in rates between tertiary and upper secondary is typically much greater than the difference for any other pair of adjacent groups, and the contrast between upper and lower secondary ranks second. Contrasts between rates for lower secondary and primary and for primary versus less than primary tend to be smaller. This is suggestive of the differential substitutability of workers with different levels of education. It is also possible that job-required education is a softer constraint on hiring when the level required is lower secondary and below.

In addition to providing baseline information on the levels of job task complexity, Tables 4.10 through 4.12 provide evidence of the strong discriminating power of most of the job skill measures and their construct validity. The different ISCED groups would be expected to differ in their rates of task performance, and the evidence of such differences offers support for their construct validity according to the *principle of known groups*. Evidence of convergent construct validity that is especially relevant to the study of mismatch is provided by the correlations between the task items and job-required education, and the intercorrelations among tasks themselves, shown as a heat map in table 4.13.

Findings: Country Context

The sample in table 4.13 is identical to that used in tables 4.10–4.12, but responses to the task items are not collapsed. Overall, it depicts the types of patterns we would expect in terms of job-required education and job tasks. Job-required education (shortened to "job education" in the table) is strongly related to the three reading and writing variables; nearly all 36 correlations are between

Table 4.13 Correlations of Job Tasks and Job-Required Education, by STEP Country

	Job education	Reading length	Reading type	Writing	Math 1	Math 2	Math 3
Armenia							
Job education	1.00						
Reading, length	0.56	1.00					
Reading type	0.53	0.75	1.00				
Writing	0.49	0.68	0.60	1.00			
Math, all	0.20	0.21	0.33	0.20	1.00		
Math, arithmetic	0.18	0.19	0.32	0.19	0.98	1.00	
Math, advanced	0.19	0.20	0.21	0.16	0.55	0.39	1.00
Problem solving	0.33	0.33	0.25	0.32	0.21	0.19	0.19
Bolivia							
Job education	1.00						
Reading, length	0.65	1.00					
Reading type	0.63	0.82	1.00				
Writing	0.62	0.71	0.63	1.00			
Math, all	0.21	0.25	0.31	0.24	1.00		
Math, arithmetic.	0.15	0.16	0.24	0.17	0.98	1.00	
Math, advanced	0.32	0.43	0.39	0.37	0.51	0.31	1.00
Problem solving	0.34	0.40	0.38	0.42	0.20	0.16	0.23
Colombia							
Job education	1.00						
Reading, length	0.51	1.00					
Reading type	0.47	0.74	1.00				
Writing	0.42	0.56	0.49	1.00			
Math, all	0.20	0.26	0.32	0.27	1.00		
Math, arithmetic	0.18	0.24	0.30	0.25	0.99	1.00	
Math, advanced	0.19	0.20	0.23	0.18	0.44	0.28	1.00
Problem solving	0.24	0.26	0.24	0.31	0.29	0.28	0.16
Georgia							
Job education	1.00						
Reading, length	0.56	1.00					
Reading type	0.49	0.69	1.00				
Writing	0.44	0.57	0.49	1.00			
Math, all	0.14	0.23	0.37	0.23	1.00		
Math, arithmetic	0.13	0.21	0.36	0.19	0.99	1.00	
Math, advanced	0.13	0.23	0.23	0.30	0.52	0.39	1.00
Problem solving	0.31	0.29	0.30	0.29	0.21	0.21	0.14

table continues next page

Table 4.13 Correlations of Job Tasks and Job-Required Education, by STEP Country *(continued)*

	Job education	Reading length	Reading type	Writing	Math 1	Math 2	Math 3
Ghana							
Job education	1.00						
Reading, length	0.63	1.00					
Reading type	0.66	0.82	1.00				
Writing	0.61	0.69	0.64	1.00			
Math, all	0.19	0.18	0.25	0.22	1.00		
Math, arithmetic	0.15	0.15	0.21	0.19	0.99	1.00	
Math, advanced	0.31	0.28	0.32	0.23	0.37	0.24	1.00
Problem solving	0.34	0.36	0.34	0.32	0.12	0.10	0.17
Kenya							
Job education	1.00						
Reading, length	0.55	1.00					
Reading type	0.57	0.78	1.00				
Writing	0.56	0.71	0.66	1.00			
Math, all	0.36	0.39	0.42	0.42	1.00		
Math, arithmetic	0.31	0.34	0.39	0.36	0.99	1.00	
Math, advanced	0.40	0.42	0.35	0.47	0.44	0.29	1.00
Problem solving	0.33	0.35	0.33	0.36	0.34	0.33	0.22
Lao PDR							
Job education	1.00						
Reading, length	0.67	1.00					
Reading type	0.69	0.79	1.00				
Writing	0.64	0.76	0.68	1.00			
Math, all	0.36	0.44	0.43	0.39	1.00		
Math, arithmetic	0.35	0.42	0.41	0.38	0.98	1.00	
Math, advanced	0.22	0.24	0.25	0.23	0.45	0.29	1.00
Problem solving	0.25	0.27	0.29	0.25	0.26	0.24	0.19
Macedonia, FYR							
Job education	1.00						
Reading, length	0.58	1.00					
Reading type	0.53	0.79	1.00				
Writing	0.56	0.71	0.65	1.00			
Math, all	0.24	0.40	0.51	0.37	1.00		
Math, arithmetic	0.21	0.38	0.50	0.35	0.99	1.00	
Math, advanced	0.26	0.28	0.27	0.29	0.55	0.40	1.00
Problem solving	0.40	0.43	0.43	0.41	0.33	0.31	0.24
Sri Lanka							
Job education	1.00						
Reading, length	0.54	1.00					
Reading type	0.55	0.80	1.00				
Writing	0.50	0.71	0.61	1.00			
Math, all	0.21	0.31	0.36	0.25	1.00		

table continues next page

Findings: Country Context

Table 4.13 Correlations of Job Tasks and Job-Required Education, by STEP Country *(continued)*

	Job education	Reading length	Reading type	Writing	Math 1	Math 2	Math 3
Math, arithmetic	0.18	0.29	0.34	0.23	0.98	1.00	
Math, advanced	0.24	0.22	0.24	0.22	0.46	0.29	1.00
Problem solving	0.27	0.31	0.27	0.25	0.23	0.23	0.12
Ukraine							
Job education	1.00						
Reading, length	0.45	1.00					
Reading type	0.50	0.64	1.00				
Writing	0.46	0.73	0.61	1.00			
Math, all	0.32	0.35	0.51	0.44	1.00		
Math, arithmetic	0.30	0.33	0.51	0.41	0.98	1.00	
Math, advanced	0.25	0.28	0.25	0.34	0.58	0.41	1.00
Problem solving	0.41	0.45	0.37	0.47	0.36	0.34	0.27
Vietnam							
Job education	1.00						
Reading, length	0.63	1.00					
Reading type	0.62	0.73	1.00				
Writing	0.59	0.68	0.61	1.00			
Math, all	0.23	0.23	0.33	0.31	1.00		
Math, arithmetic	0.19	0.19	0.30	0.27	0.99	1.00	
Math, advanced	0.33	0.29	0.29	0.32	0.46	0.30	1.00
Problem solving	0.49	0.43	0.42	0.40	0.29	0.27	0.24
Yunnan Province							
Job education	1.00						
Reading, length	0.50	1.00					
Reading type	0.47	0.70	1.00				
Writing	0.53	0.70	0.61	1.00			
Math, all	0.26	0.38	0.50	0.40	1.00		
Math, arithmetic	0.24	0.37	0.50	0.39	0.99	1.00	
Math, advanced	0.19	0.21	0.17	0.26	0.42	0.28	1.00
Problem solving	0.36	0.32	0.35	0.37	0.29	0.28	0.18

| 0.60–0.89 | 0.40–0.59 | 0.30–0.39 | 0.20–0.29 | 0.10–0.19 |

Source: World Bank STEP Skills Measurement Program.

0.45 and 0.69. Job education is also associated with problem solving (mean correlation = 0.34), while correlations with math tasks average 0.25, using either a scale with all math items or a single dichotomous indicator of advanced math tasks. Turning to the intercorrelations among the task variables, the three reading and writing variables are quite strongly associated among themselves, while problem solving and math show associations with reading and writing that are similar to their correlations with required education. The weakness of the math task variables undoubtedly reflects their relatively low variation despite their concreteness.

Correlations with wages (not shown) reinforce the conceptual arguments and the table's empirical evidence that the job task variables pick up meaningful variation in job cognitive skill demands that make them promising candidates for testing whether or to what extent apparent mismatch by education level masks heterogeneity of the skills actually used at work.

Of course, the additional information that the task items contribute must be balanced against the likelihood that ratings of job-required education reflect in part some weighted sum or average of these tasks made by the respondents in answering the question on job-required education. Insofar as these tasks partly define the meaning of job-required education in the minds of respondents, there is a limit on how similarly one might expect workers would rate the task requirements of their jobs if they report having the same education but working in jobs that do and do not match that education level. The fact that workers report different job-required education likely implies they will *not* report similar levels of reading, writing, math, and problem solving on the job, but the extent to which their tasks are more similar to the tasks of their coworkers or to their classmates is an empirical question, addressed in chapter 6.

Implications for Analyses

The STEP countries vary significantly in terms of national income, which, together with country-specific factors, affects education levels, employment rates, and selection into formal and public sector employment. All of these differences could be expected to be associated with differences in observed rates of mismatch.

In addition, there is variation within education levels in terms of years of education, test scores, fields of study, and job tasks. This raises the possibility that observed mismatch by education level masks important complicating and/or mitigating circumstances that are usually unobserved, such as low achievement, specialization or skill kind mismatch, and job skill upgrading. At the same time, very high rates of informality, self-employment, and nonemployment raise the possibility that structural labor market conditions are significant drivers of mismatch net of education level, indicating a genuine under-supply of good jobs relative to skill stocks. Even the highly educated may be forced into work that does not utilize their skills if formal jobs are scarce, or they may remain nonemployed as in the Europe and Central Asia countries. *A key policy implication is that if results show the biggest problem is a shortage of good jobs, education policy is unlikely to be able to reverse the situation on its own.*

Notes

1. Unless noted, all data from this point onwards are from World Bank analyses of the STEP database.
2. The ISCED (International Standard Classification of Education) levels were developed by UNESCO to facilitate comparisons of education statistics and indicators across countries on the basis of uniform and internationally agreed definitions.

CHAPTER 5

Patterns of Educational Mismatch: Findings

Introduction

Applying the conceptual framework discussed earlier, this chapter describes patterns of mismatch in the 12 participating countries using the contingency table framework developed in chapter 1.

The marginal distributions of personal education and job-required education for employed persons are compared in the section titled "Aggregate Distributions: Workers' Education and Job Education Requirements." The differences between the two aggregate distributions provide lower-bound estimates of mismatch at the individual level and give some indication of the role of absolute job availability in producing mismatch for different education groups. The section titled "Aggregate Imbalances and Individual-Level Mismatch" presents these figures and their contrast with actual mismatch rates, which exceed the lower bounds set by aggregate mismatch rates.

The section titled "Joint Distributions of Personal and Job-Required Education" presents the joint distributions of personal and job-required education by country in contingency table charts to show the full profile of match/mismatch by education levels and to permit easy comparison across countries. From these figures it is easy to calculate conditional distributions showing how well different education groups fare in the labor market (row percentages) and how effectively jobs at different skill levels can be filled with well-matched workers (column percentages). Comparisons of marginal, joint, and conditional distributions across countries show their relative performance with respect to workers, firms, and the economy overall. Finally, the section titled "Summary of Descriptive Mismatch Results" summarizes the pattern of descriptive results.

Aggregate Distributions: Workers' Education and Job Education Requirements

Figure 5.1 shows the distribution of employed adults by International Standard Classification of Education (ISCED) education level, with countries ordered by the proportion of tertiary graduates. Treating education as a scalar can be convenient, though it masks diversity in distributions across educational categories. Figure 5.2 converts ISCED codes to equivalent years of education and orders countries by mean, which alters some rankings; a horizontal reference line shows the unweighted mean across countries.

Both the levels and the distributions of educational attainment vary widely across countries. About 45 percent of employed, urban adult residents in the Lao People's Democratic Republic have primary education or less, followed by Ghana and Kenya, where one-third of urban adult residents have this level of education. By contrast, urban workers in Ukraine, Armenia, and Georgia report extraordinarily high levels of tertiary education, though generally low

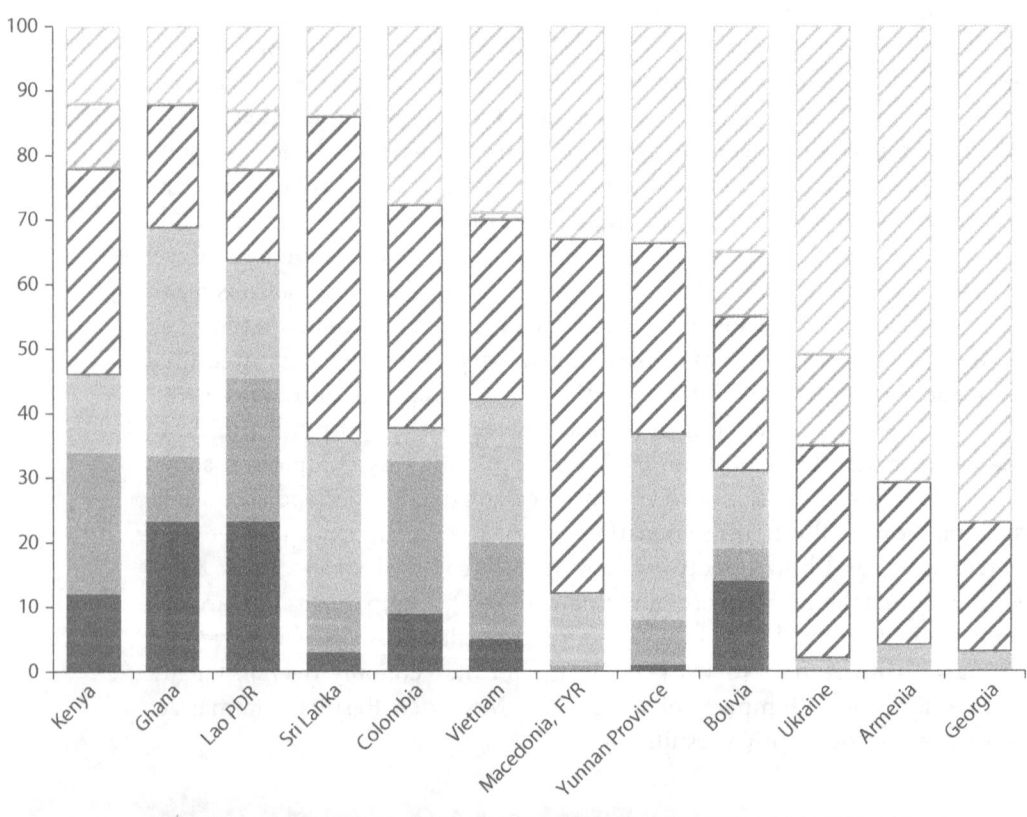

Figure 5.1 Educational Distribution of Employed Persons, by STEP Country
percent

■ < ISCED 1   ■ ISCED 1   ■ ISCED 2   ▨ ISCED 3 and 4A   ▨ ISCED 4B   ▨ ISCED 5 and 6

Source: World Bank STEP Skills Measurement Program.
Note: "Employed persons" is here defined as employed urban adults.

Figure 5.2 Employed Mean Years of Education, by STEP Country

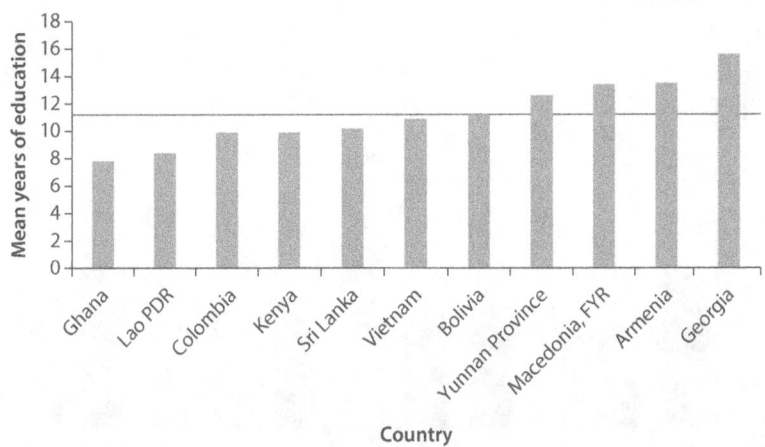

Source: World Bank STEP Skills Measurement Program.
Note: Horizontal reference line shows the unweighted mean across countries. "Employed persons" is here defined as employed urban adults.

employment-population rates argue for caution in interpreting these figures. Medium levels of schooling (lower and upper secondary) tend to predominate in Sri Lanka, the former Yugoslav Republic of Macedonia, and Yunnan Province (China). The prevalence of vocational or career education (ISCED level 4B) is surprisingly similar in Kenya, Lao PDR, Bolivia, and Ukraine (9–14 percent), while this kind of education is virtually absent elsewhere.

Clearly, the potential for under- and over-education may be affected by the different educational distributions for purely mechanical reasons. For example, only 23 percent of urban workers in Georgia can be under-educated using this set of categories, but because more than 85 percent of urban workers in Kenya, Ghana, Lao PDR, and Sri Lanka are below the top category, far more of them are at risk for under-education in those countries, in principle.

Figure 5.3 shows the distribution of jobs according to their required education level, ordered in terms of the proportion requiring tertiary education, which differs slightly from figure 5.1.[1] Key patterns evident in the distribution include these:

- Large differences between worker education and job-required education are immediately evident for Ghana, Lao PDR, and Vietnam, where the proportions of jobs requiring less than primary education are very large and exceed the shares of workers with less than primary education by wide margins.
- The shares of jobs requiring tertiary education in Ukraine, Armenia, and Georgia clearly fall short of the shares of workers with tertiary education in those countries.
- There are interesting shortfalls in the total number of jobs requiring vocational education in the four countries with significant numbers of workers with vocational education.

Figure 5.3 Distribution of Jobs by Job-Required Education Levels, by STEP Country
percent

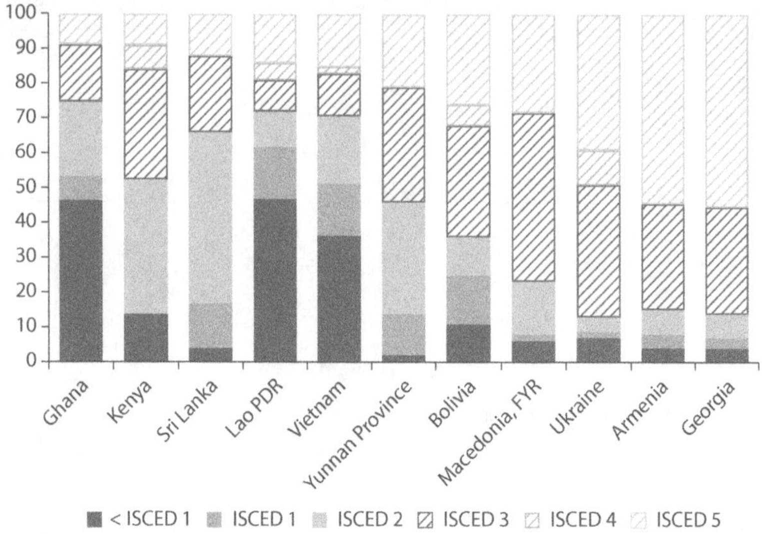

[Bar chart showing distribution of jobs by job-required education level for countries: Ghana, Kenya, Sri Lanka, Lao PDR, Vietnam, Yunnan Province, Bolivia, Macedonia FYR, Ukraine, Armenia, Georgia. Legend categories: < ISCED 1, ISCED 1, ISCED 2, ISCED 3, ISCED 4, ISCED 5.]

Source: World Bank STEP Skills Measurement Program.

Given the relatively small numbers of both workers and jobs at the ISCED level 4B, they are excluded from further analyses in this paper for the sake of simplicity (but will receive detailed treatment in separate work). The provisional conclusion is that job-oriented education below the tertiary level is relatively underdeveloped in most countries relative to general secondary and tertiary education, and there are relatively few jobs for which this is a well-identified pathway for qualification.

Aggregate Imbalances and Individual-Level Mismatch

Table 5.1 shows the distribution of worker education and job-required education, as well as the difference between them at each level (worker education *minus* job education). Countries are listed in descending order according to the share of workers that has not completed primary education. Large negative values, indicating more jobs than workers at that education level, are shown in orange. Large positive values, indicating more workers than jobs at that level, are shown in green.

Overall, it appears that the skills required by jobs lag behind the skills of workers. Three countries have far more jobs requiring less than a primary education than workers with that level of education: Vietnam (gap = 32.5 percent), Lao PDR (26.6 percent), and Ghana (22.3 percent); no other country comes close to these mismatch rates for these education levels based on differences in the aggregate distributions. Kenya and Sri Lanka have far more jobs requiring lower secondary education than workers with that education level. Although workers in Lao PDR, Ghana, and Kenya have much less education than workers in the other countries,

Table 5.1 Aggregate Match Rates between Worker Education and Job-Required Education, by Country
percent

	ISCED Level				
	<1	1	2	3	5
Lao PDR					
Worker	25.4	26.8	20.1	14.6	13.1
Job	52.0	16.1	9.7	8.8	13.4
Difference	−26.6	10.8	10.4	5.8	−0.4
D index					27.0
Ghana					
Worker	25.0	10.4	33.4	19.3	11.9
Job	47.3	6.2	21.1	17.0	8.5
Difference	−22.3	4.2	12.4	2.4	3.4
D index					22.3
Kenya					
Worker	17.1	25.8	14.9	32.8	9.5
Job	16.3	0.0	44.8	29.7	9.2
Difference	0.8	25.8	−29.9	3.1	0.2
D index					29.9
Bolivia					
Worker	16.5	6.4	15.9	25.8	35.4
Job	12.2	15.9	11.9	36.1	23.9
Difference	4.3	−9.5	4.0	−10.3	11.4
D index					19.8
Vietnam					
Worker	5.4	15.5	23.2	29.6	26.4
Job	37.9	16.7	19.5	12.1	13.9
Difference	−32.5	−1.2	3.7	17.5	12.5
D index					33.7
Sri Lanka					
Worker	2.9	10.2	20.9	53.5	12.5
Job	5.2	12.1	50.5	21.2	11.0
Difference	−2.3	−1.9	−29.6	32.3	1.5
D index					33.8
Yunnan Province					
Worker	0.7	7.5	30.9	29.8	31.1
Job	1.7	12.3	33.4	33.4	19.2
Difference	−1.0	−4.9	−2.5	−3.5	11.9
D index					11.9
Macedonia, FYR					
Worker	0.2	0.4	8.6	56.8	34.0
Job	5.5	1.2	13.6	50.4	29.2
Difference	−5.3	−0.8	−5.1	6.4	4.8
D index					11.2

table continues next page

Table 5.1 Aggregate Match Rates between Worker Education and Job-Required Education, by Country *(continued)*

	ISCED Level				
	<1	1	2	3	5
Armenia					
Worker	0.2	0.5	5.2	26.1	68.1
Job	4.0	4.3	8.1	31.4	52.1
Difference	−3.9	−3.9	−3.0	−5.3	16.0
D index					16.0
Georgia					
Worker	0.1	0.6	2.6	19.5	77.2
Job	3.5	2.4	5.8	32.2	56.1
Difference	−3.4	−1.8	−3.2	−12.8	21.2
D index					21.2
Ukraine					
Worker	0.0	0.2	1.8	35.8	62.2
Job	6.3	1.4	3.5	39.8	49.1
Difference	−6.2	−1.3	−1.7	−4.0	13.1
D index					13.1
Mean					
Difference	−9.0	1.4	−4.1	2.9	8.7
D index					20.6

Source: World Bank STEP Skills Measurement Program.
Note: Column numbers represent ISCED levels (< primary, primary, lower secondary, upper secondary, tertiary). *Difference* = Worker education share minus job-required education share. Categories for which the share of workers (jobs) exceed jobs (workers) by at least 10 percentage points are indicated in **Green (Orange)**. *D index* (index of dissimilarity) = The total mismatch at the aggregate level, shown in light **blue**.

it appears that the skill levels of their jobs lag even further. By contrast, Georgia, Armenia, Ukraine, Vietnam, China-Yunnan Province, and Bolivia, where the difference is shaded green, have significantly more workers than jobs at the tertiary level.

Aggregate mismatch rates range from about 11 percent to nearly 34 percent. The total imbalance at the aggregate level, equal to the index of dissimilarity between the marginal distributions, is shown below each country panel in blue. This indicates the percentages of workers who would need to shift job or education categories to bring the two aggregate distributions into balance and is one indicator of structural conditions affecting the probability of mismatch in different countries. If there is imperfect matching, the actual rates of mismatch will be greater, that is, these are lower-bound figures based on the differences between the marginal distributions of the two variables.

The individual-level match rate varies from 26 percent in Vietnam to nearly 73 percent in FYR Macedonia (table 5.2). The values in columns 1–3 are also shown graphically in figures 5.4, 5.5, and 5.6. Subtracting the matched share from 100 percent or, equivalently, adding rates of over-education and under-education yields the actual mismatch rate shown in column 4. These figures are at least double

Patterns of Educational Mismatch: Findings

Table 5.2 Individual-Level (Actual) Match Rates, by STEP Country

	1	2	3	4	5	6
	Well-matched	Over-educated	Under-educated	Actual mismatch	Aggregate mismatch	Difference (column 4 minus column 5)
Lao PDR	45.1	41.1	13.7	54.9	27.0	27.9
Ghana	47.7	39.5	12.8	52.3	22.3	30.0
Kenya	34.5	24.9	40.4	65.5	29.9	35.6
Bolivia	40.1	34.6	25.2	59.9	19.8	40.1
Vietnam	26.0	70.0	4.0	74.0	33.7	40.3
Sri Lanka	43.5	46.1	10.4	56.5	33.8	22.7
Yunnan Province	56.6	32.6	10.7	43.4	11.9	31.5
Macedonia, FYR	72.6	22.3	5.1	27.4	11.2	16.2
Armenia	66.2	28.0	5.8	33.8	16.0	17.8
Georgia	66.4	29.4	4.0	33.4	21.2	12.2
Ukraine	72.1	24.0	3.8	27.9	13.1	14.8
Mean	51.9	34.2	12.4	48.1	21.8	26.3

Source: World Bank STEP Skills Measurement Program.

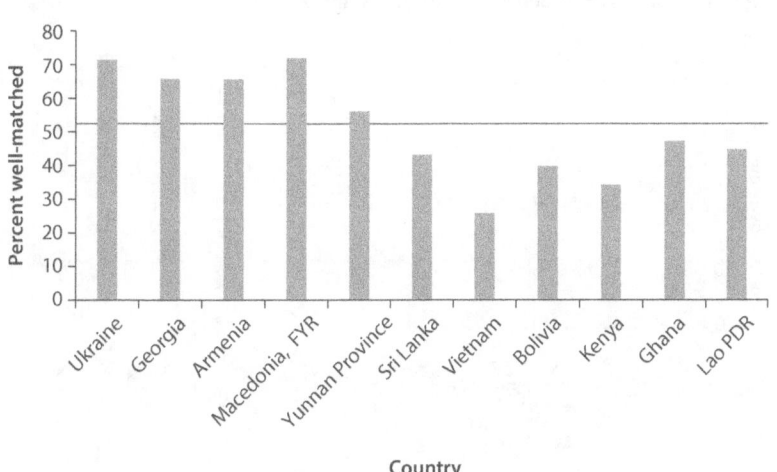

Figure 5.4 Education Match Rates, by Country
percent

Source: World Bank STEP Skills Measurement Program.
Note: Horizontal reference line shows the unweighted mean across countries.

the lower-bound values based on the marginal distributions for every country other than Sri Lanka and Georgia (columns 5 and 6). Conceptually speaking, some portion of the differences may reflect "exchange" or "swapping" of positions of differently educated workers across job education categories beyond the theoretical minimum set by the marginals. In other words, *there are some jobs requiring completed secondary education that are filled by those with lower secondary educations and*, for example, that are in excess of the mismatch rates that are implied directly by the marginal distributions of worker education and job education.

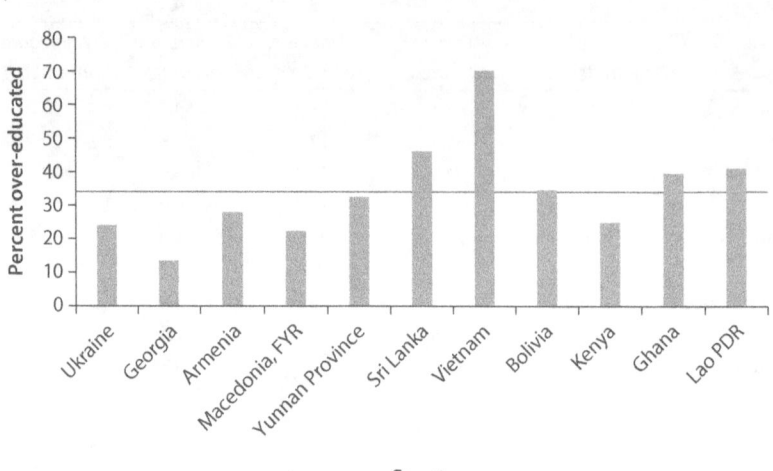

Figure 5.5 Rates of Over-Education, by Country
percent

Source: World Bank STEP Skills Measurement Program.
Note: Horizontal reference line shows the unweighted mean across countries.

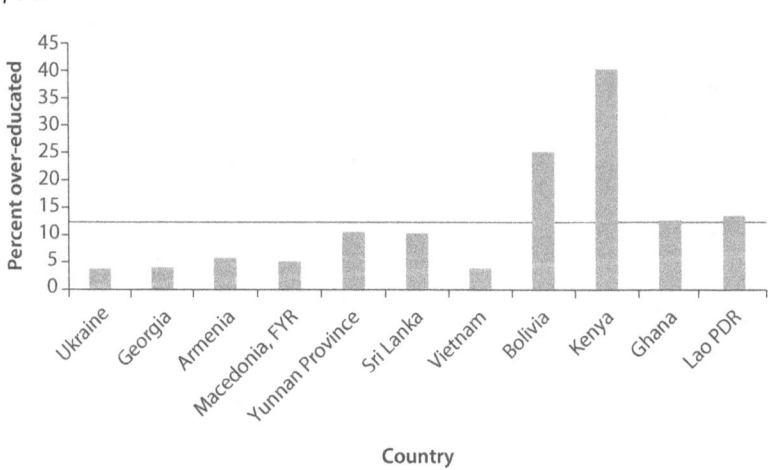

Figure 5.6 Rates of Under-Education, by Country
percent

Source: World Bank STEP Skills Measurement Program.
Note: Horizontal reference line shows the unweighted mean across countries.

If the marginals were identical, the rates of over-education and under-education would be identical because one worker's mismatch would have to be offset exactly by someone else "exchanging places" with them. However, the two marginal distributions are not identical in any country, so there is no arithmetic or mechanical necessity for the rates of over- and under-education to be equal.

Over-education rates exceed under-education rates by a substantial margin in all countries studied, except Kenya, where under-education is unusually common. Apart from outliers, over-education affects between 15 and 45 percent of workers, while under-education affects about 4–14 percent. As one might expect, under-education is somewhat more common among countries in the upper rows with lower levels of educational attainment, but over-education tends to be more common in those countries, as well, despite the smaller shares of the workforce "at risk" for over-education. These latter countries appear to have a generally more severe problem with the synchronization of their education and employment systems.

Not only are rates of over-education much higher than rates of under-education, the range of over-education rates is much wider. The scatterplot in figure 5.7 gives an overview of over- and under-education rates for all countries on identically scaled axes. Not surprisingly, under-education rates tend to be quite low among countries in Europe and Central Asia, reflecting the ceiling effect of the concentration of workers at the maximum level of personal education. There also seems to be a positive relationship ($r = 0.58$) between the two mismatch rates after excluding the two most extreme values, Vietnam and Kenya, which is even stronger after excluding Bolivia ($r = 0.83$), suggesting the possibility that some labor markets are more efficient generally or have fewer

Figure 5.7 Rates of Over- and Under-Education, by Country

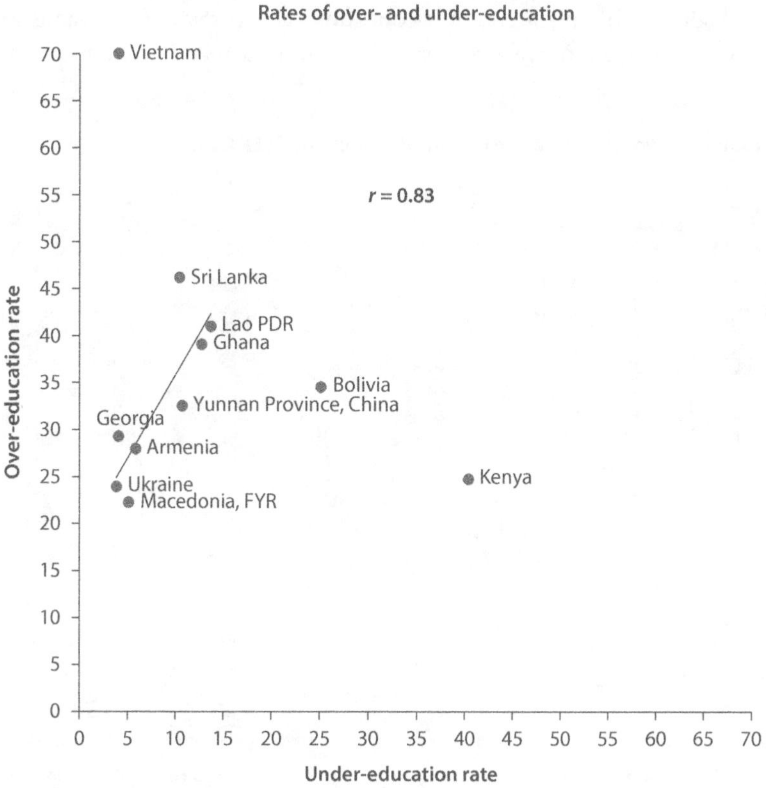

Source: World Bank STEP Skills Measurement Program.

distortions (such as due to discrimination) than others. The plot underscores the unusually high rates of over-education in Vietnam and under-education in Kenya and, to a lesser extent, Bolivia. From this evidence, it appears that there is a great deal of underutilization of education in Vietnam (or a skilled job shortage) and a severe under-provision of education in Kenya relative to the job requirements there.

Joint Distributions of Personal and Job-Required Education

The country panels in figure 5.8 show the distributions of worker education (on the y-axis) by job-required education (on the x-axis), as in the mobility table shown in table 1.3. All values on the diagonal show percentages of the workforce that are matched at various levels. Values to the left and below the diagonal show the percentages of the workforce who are over-educated (for example, 15 percent of employed Laotians have a primary education but work in jobs requiring less than primary). Values to the right and above the diagonal show percentages of workers who are under-educated (for example, 2 percent of Laotian workers have a secondary education but work in jobs requiring tertiary education). Cells accounting for less than one percent of the workforce are unmarked; otherwise, cell values sum to 100 percent. Key features of each country's distribution are discussed in box 5.1.

Both high rates of under- and over-education can exist within the same country. These figures highlight the puzzle of simultaneous under- and over-education in the

Figure 5.8 Joint Distribution of Worker Education by Job Education, by STEP Country
Cell percentages sum to ~100

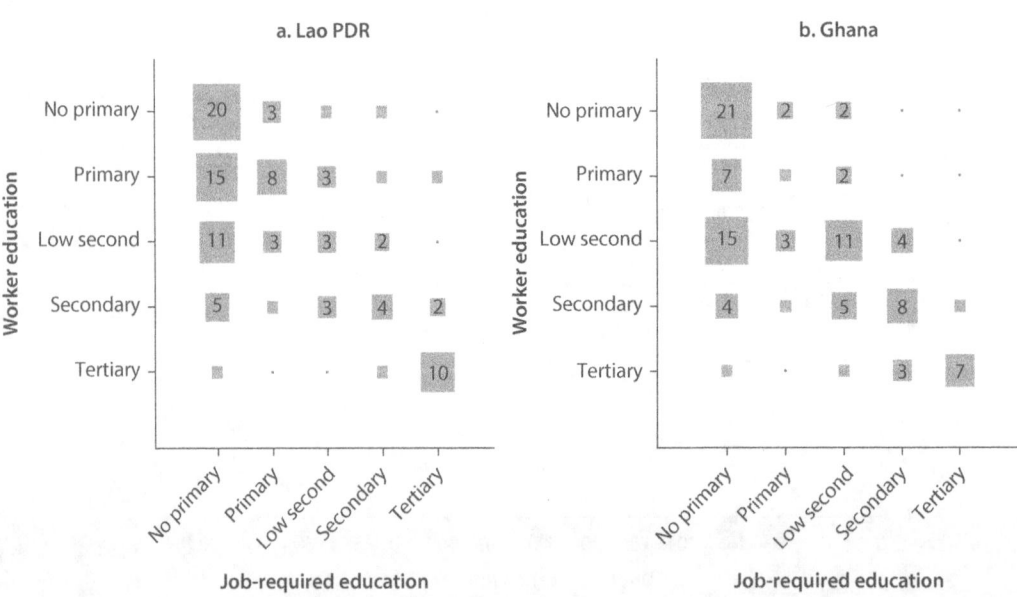

figure continues next page

Patterns of Educational Mismatch: Findings 71

Figure 5.8 Joint Distribution of Worker Education by Job Education, by STEP Country *(continued)*

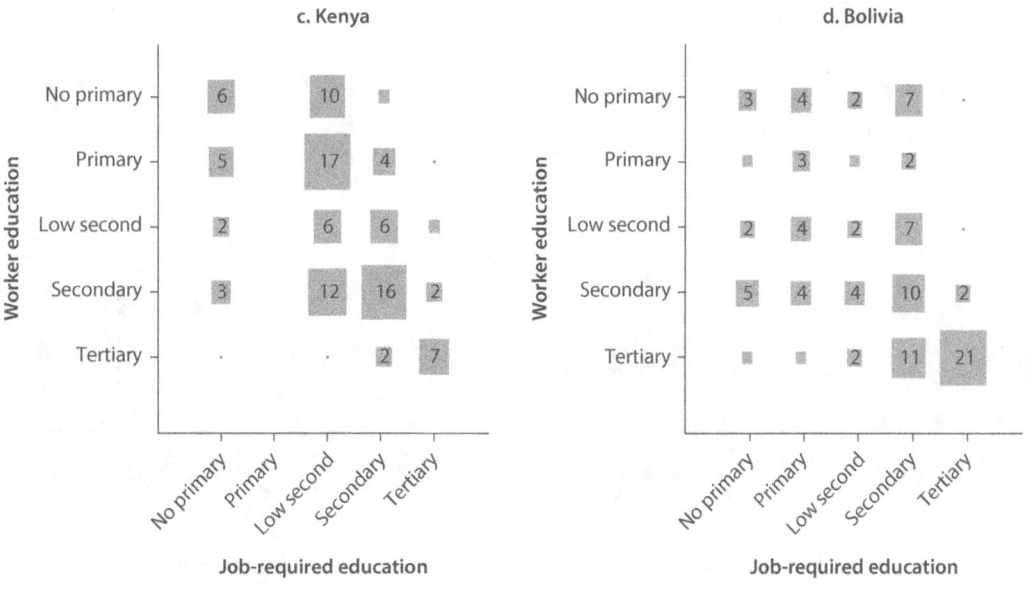

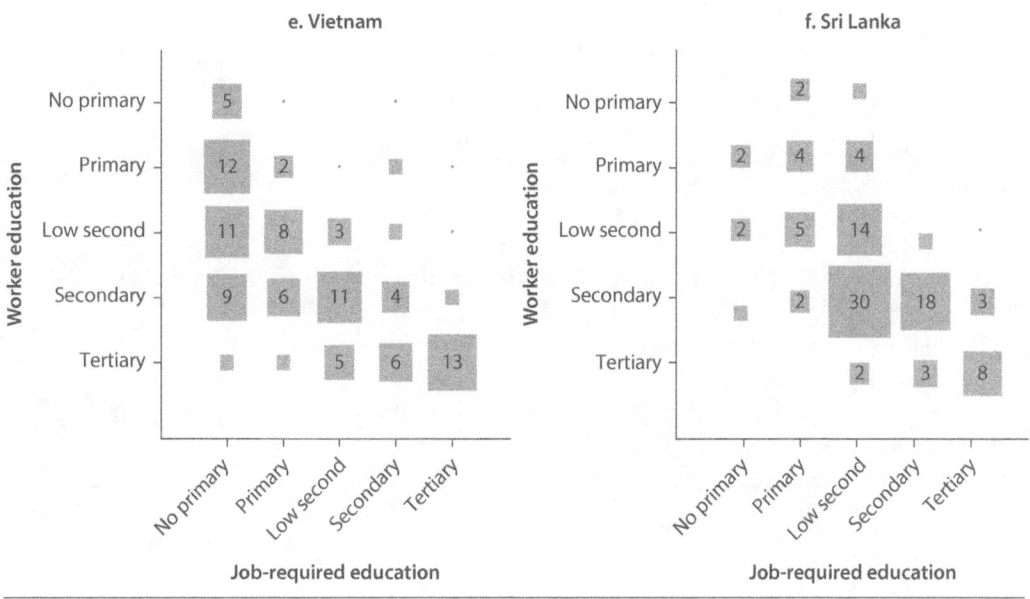

figure continues next page

Figure 5.8 Joint Distribution of Worker Education by Job Education, by STEP Country *(continued)*

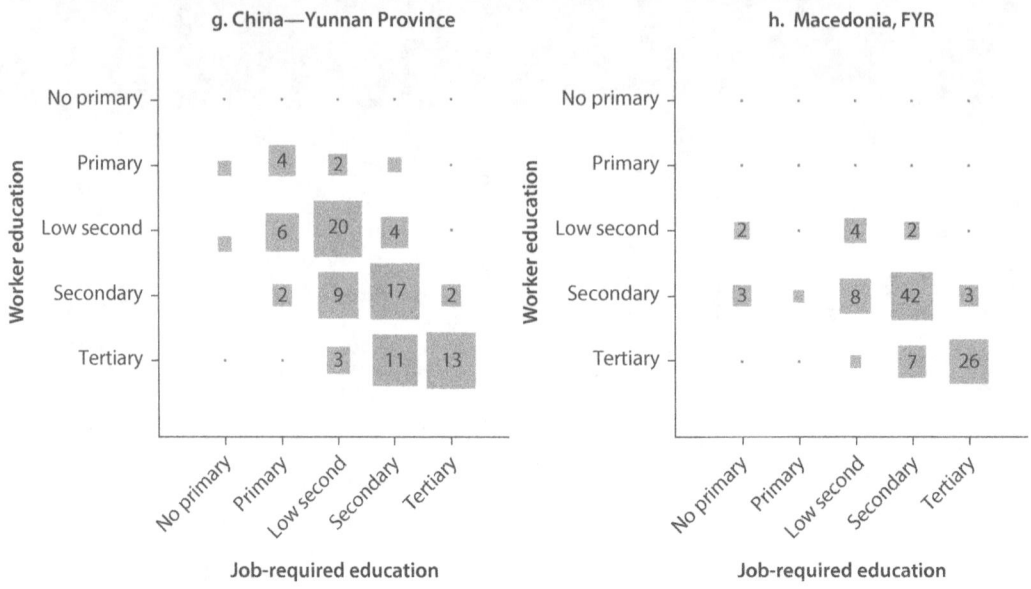

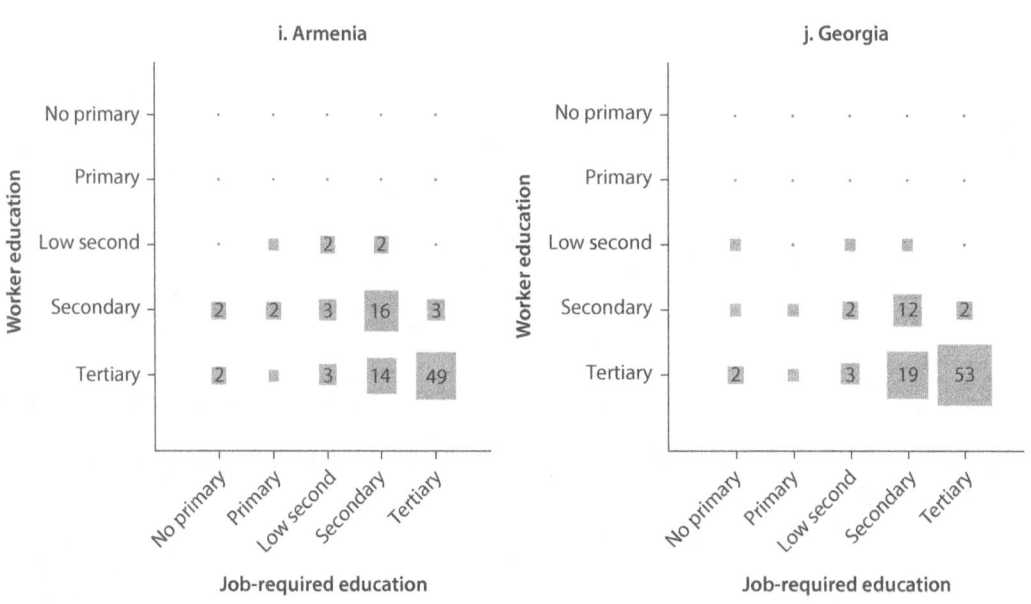

figure continues next page

Figure 5.8 Joint Distribution of Worker Education by Job Education, by STEP Country *(continued)*

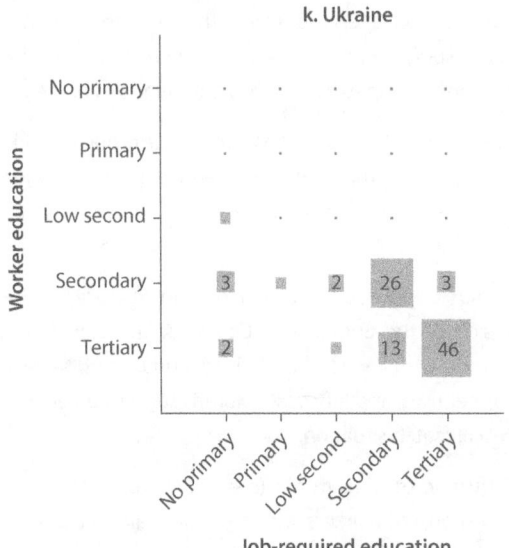

k. Ukraine

Source: World Bank STEP Skills Measurement Program.
Note: Unlabeled squares represent 1 percent of workers. Dark gray dots indicate figures that fall below 1 percent after rounding.

Box 5.1 Discussion: Joint Distributions of Worker Education by Job Education

Lao People's Democratic Republic (Lao PDR) (see figure 5.8, panel a). Lao PDR has a large share of well-matched workers with less than a primary education, occupying the low-skill match cell. However, large groups of workers with primary and secondary education also work in jobs requiring less than a primary education, and these workers who are over-educated relative to complexity of their jobs account for nearly one-third of total employment.

Ghana (see figure 5.8, panel b). The pattern for Ghana is similar to that of Lao PDR but somewhat less pronounced. There appears to be significant underutilization of the education of the current workforce before controlling for covariates.

Kenya (see figure 5.8, panel c). Kenya has large groups with primary education or less working in jobs requiring lower secondary education (under-educated), and a significant group of workers with complete secondary education working in such jobs, as well (over-educated). None reports that their job requires a primary education. Kenya's largest problem appears to be under-education relative to job requirements.

Bolivia (see figure 5.8, panel d). Bolivia has a large share of workers with less than a primary education working in jobs requiring various levels of more education (under-educated). More than half of all workers with secondary education in Bolivia are evenly distributed across jobs requiring less education (over-educated), and a large group of tertiary graduates work in jobs requiring no more than a secondary education (over-educated).

box continues next page

Box 5.1 Discussion: Joint Distributions of Worker Education by Job Education *(continued)*

Vietnam (see figure 5.8, panel e). Vietnam has surprisingly few workers on the diagonal, and large numbers of workers at all levels report that their jobs require less education than their actual level of schooling, suggesting a very large problem with over-education or the generation of sufficient jobs whose complexity matches the capacities of the workforce.

Sri Lanka (see figure 5.8, panel f). Sri Lanka has a very large group of workers with a completed secondary education reporting that their jobs require lower secondary education (over-educated), but otherwise jobs are reasonably well-matched with most workers clustering at mid-skill levels.

Yunnan Province, China (see figure 5.8, panel g). Yunnan Province has the strongest clustering on the diagonal outside of the Europe and Central Asia region. There is significant over-education among workers with lower secondary, secondary, and tertiary educations, but the sparsely populated upper rows and leftmost columns suggest an economy that is transitioning to a mid- to high-skill match situation.

Former Yugoslav Republic of Macedonia (see figure 5.8, panel h). FYR Macedonia has a moderately significant group of workers with secondary and tertiary educations working in jobs requiring less education (under-educated), but the workforce is otherwise well-matched at a relatively high skill level.

Armenia (see figure 5.8, panel i). Armenia shows a similar pattern except that the greater mass of workers at the tertiary level is accompanied by a larger group of workers with tertiary education who are over-educated.

Georgia (see figure 5.8, panel j). The profile for Georgia is very similar to that seen for Armenia (see above).

Ukraine (see figure 5.8, panel k). The profile for Ukraine is very similar to that seen for Armenia (see above).

---

absence of absolute shortfalls in workers at given education levels. For example, in Kenya 6 percent of the workforce has a lower secondary education but works in jobs requiring a completed secondary education, while 12 percent are secondary school completers who work in jobs requiring only lower secondary education. That means that one-half of the latter, over-educated group could be well-matched, in principle, if none of the under-educated group were in those positions. This kind of pattern reflects either (1) worker and/or job heterogeneity, (2) some kind of measurement error, or (3) imperfect matching, insofar as this mismatch exceeds levels implied by the marginal distributions. In other words, an absolute shortage of workers with secondary schooling does not explain this kind of pattern, because there are enough over-educated secondary school graduates to satisfy employer needs without resorting to hiring those with less education. It is also possible that controlling for other variables might explain some portion of the apparent anomaly.

The joint distributions in figure 5.8 permit identification of the largest and most seriously mismatched subgroups in each country. In addition, it is easy to use these

Patterns of Educational Mismatch: Findings

figures to calculate conditional distributions showing how well different education groups fare in the labor market (row percentages) and how well jobs at different skill levels can find well-matched workers (column percentages). Appendix A shows these conditional distributions in pairs of charts for each country.

Figure 5.9 shows row percentages for workers with upper secondary and tertiary education, permitting easy comparisons across countries. (Panels for the

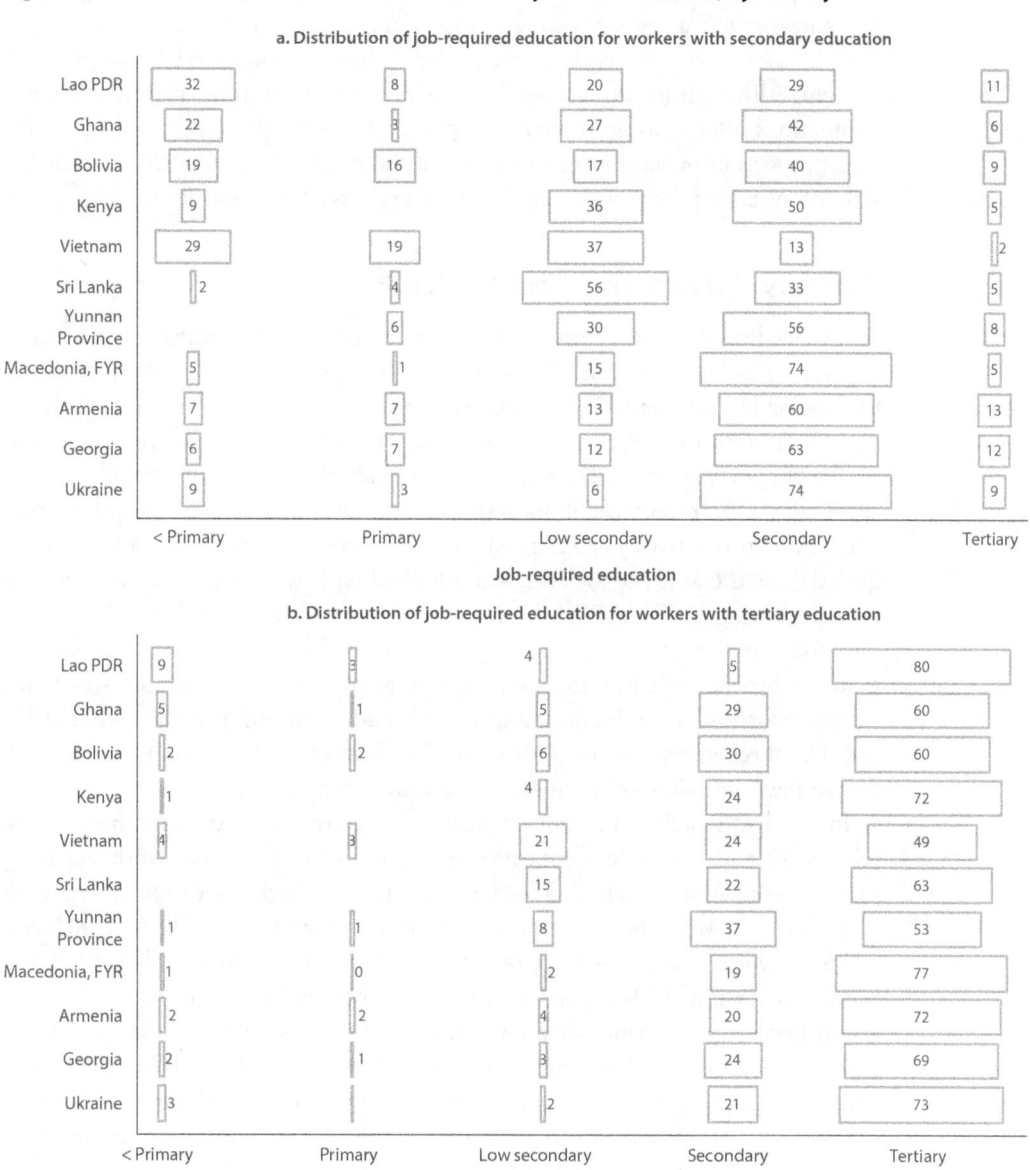

Figure 5.9 Conditional Distributions of Job Education by Worker Education, by Country

Source: World Bank STEP Skills Measurement Program.
Note: Row percentages sum to 100 percent aside from rounding.

three other levels of education may be found in appendix B, where figures omit countries whose sample sizes are too small for the conditional distributions to be reliable.) The bars show the percentage of workers at a given education level who work in jobs requiring different levels of education; figures sum to 100 percent across rows. Insofar as the longest bars fall short of 100 percent, or are not located in the appropriate column, as with Sri Lanka's secondary graduates, there is mismatch. Levels of mismatch can be compared easily across countries for each level of education.

The panels in appendix B indicate that outcomes seem most heterogeneous for workers with a primary or lower secondary education; match rates are much higher among workers with a tertiary education, though rarely exceeding 75 percent. Although improving worker skills is one of the most common recommendations offered to promote development, these results suggest that a significant proportion of skills remains underutilized at the highest levels and that the skill intensity of jobs tends to lag behind the skills of the workforce.

Summary of Descriptive Mismatch Results

The preceding suggests that countries can be classified according to patterns of (1) worker skills, (2) job skill requirements, and (3) their intersection in its manifold possible representations, with each pattern useful in revealing different aspects of labor market conditions. That is, worker skill patterns are consequential for the society overall (aggregate and individual mismatch rates, cell percentages), job skill requirement patterns are consequential for different worker education groups (row percentages), and the patterns of intersections are consequential for the kinds of jobs that can be filled with well-matched workers (column percentages). Table 5.3 summarizes country results along these dimensions. Divisions into low, medium, and high categories should be considered approximate, and there are a few cases on the border of or in a wide gap between two categories whose assignment to a given or an adjacent group is somewhat artificial. The three groups are meant to describe country clusters *within* columns and do not have similar absolute meanings across columns.

In the left panel of the table ("Education marginals"), the countries divide relatively clearly into a low-education group with large shares of workers having primary education or less (~33–45 percent) and a high-education group with large shares of workers having post-secondary education (~65–77 percent), and a more diverse medium-education group. An exception to this division is the borderline case of FYR Macedonia, which was included in the high-education group because of its singularly low shares of workers with less than complete secondary education. The unusually low employment rate in FYR Macedonia argues for caution, however, and the assignment of Yunnan Province, China, to the medium-education group may give a misleading impression of the two regions' relative ranks given Yunnan's much higher employment rate. The medium-education country group is more variegated, with lower and upper secondary accounting for 50–75 percent, except for Bolivia, whose medium

Table 5.3 Summary of Country Results

	Education marginals[a]		Mismatch rates[b]				Over-education rates (row percent)		
	Workers	Jobs	Aggregate	Individual	Over-education	Under-education	Secondary	Tertiary	Most
	1	2	3	4	5	6	7	8	9
Lao PDR	Low	Low	High	Medium	High	Medium	60	20	Primary, lower secondary
Ghana	Low	Low	Medium	Medium	High	Medium	52	40	Lower secondary
Kenya	Low	Medium	High	High	Low	Very high	45	28	Secondary
Bolivia	Medium	Medium	Medium	Medium	Medium	High	51	40	Secondary
Vietnam	Medium	Low	High	High	Very high	Low	85	51	All
Sri Lanka	Medium	Medium	High	Medium	High	Medium	62	37	Secondary
Yunnan Province	Medium	Medium	Low	Medium	Medium	Medium	36	47	Tertiary
Macedonia, FYR	High	Medium	Low	Low	Low	Low	21	23	—
Armenia	High	High	Low	Low	Low	Low	27	28	Tertiary
Georgia	High	High	Medium	Low	Medium	Low	25	31	Tertiary
Ukraine	High	High	Low	Low	Low	Low	18	27	Tertiary

Source: World Bank STEP Skills Measurement Program.
Note: All level categories (*low, medium, high*) are relative to the distribution of values within columns and comparable across columns only in terms of ranks, not absolute magnitudes (see Key, below, for values that define the categories within columns). Cells shaded blue are in the highest-ranked groups, which includes *low* mismatch rates, while cells shaded orange are in middle-ranked and those shaded green are in low-ranked (high mismatch) categories. Cells shaded gray are very-low-ranked outliers. The cell for secondary over-education in Yunnan Province is unshaded because it does not fit the categories of the classification system shown in the key below. The final column shows the personal education groups that account for the greatest number of over-educated workers in each country.
a. Columns 1 and 2 are based on a three-category classification of education (see key below).
b. Columns 3 and 4 are based on a five-category educational classification.

Key to Table 5.3 (ranges are trimmed to exclude any outliers)

	Worker education			Job education			Mismatch rates			
	Primary or below	Lower secondary/ secondary	Post-secondary	Primary or below	Lower secondary/ secondary	Post-secondary	Aggregate	Individual	Over-educated	Under-educated
Low	33–45%			51–62%			11–16%	27–34%	22–28%	4–6%
Medium		50–75%			63–71%		20–22%	43–60%	33–35%	10–13%
High			65–77%			49–56%	27–34%	66–75%	40–46%	25%

share is lower (36 percent) but whose shares for tertiary graduates *and* workers with primary or less are both a bit higher than for other countries in this group.

The composition of jobs in most countries clusters in groups that are ranked in relatively similar fashion to their workforces, but this does not imply the jobs match worker education levels, because the ranking in column 2 is simply a categorization scheme for the job-education marginals taken in isolation. Countries with large shares of jobs requiring primary education or below

(51–62 percent) or post-secondary education (~49–56 percent) are somewhat more homogeneous than those requiring lower and upper secondary education (63–71 percent) when Bolivia is included in the latter, because Bolivia's medium-education share is low (43 percent). However, Bolivia's shares of jobs requiring lower education (25 percent) or higher education (32 percent) are even lower, ruling out inclusion in those groups. The unusual patterns of worker versus job-required education for Kenya and Vietnam, noted previously, are circled. For example, Vietnam ranks in the middle of the pack with respect to worker education but ranks much lower in terms of the education required by jobs.

In the middle panel ("Mismatch rates"), aggregate mismatch rates implied by differences in the marginals are coded as high (~27–34 percent), medium (20–22 percent), and low (11–16 percent). These are lower-bound estimates, and the individual-level mismatch rates are higher for all categories used in the next column: high (66–75 percent), medium (43–60 percent), and low (27–34 percent). Mismatch at the individual level is clearly the more important indicator for both individual well-being and economic development, but the difference between the two gives some indication of the underlying processes at work insofar as it represents mismatch in excess of what seems to be implied by imbalances between the aggregate distributions representing structural conditions.

Over-education is more common than under-education, so the rates associated with categories for the former (High, 40–46 percent; Medium, 33–35 percent; Low, 22–28 percent) are consistently higher than for the latter (High, 25 percent; Medium, 10–13 percent; Low, 4–6 percent). These ranges exclude Vietnam's over-education rate (70 percent) and Kenya's under-education rate (40 percent), which are both positive outliers.

Because most concerns relate to the fate of secondary and tertiary graduates, and over-education is more serious as a manifest mismatch problem than under-education, the right panel of table 5.3 shows the over-education rates for secondary and tertiary graduates. Countries with the lowest levels of worker education also tend to have the highest rates of underutilization as well. The educational system may not be producing enough graduates, but the economy is producing too few jobs to utilize the current graduates who are working, leaving aside the issue of cross-national variation in employment rates. This inference takes measures of worker and job-required education at face value, something that the next section investigates in detail by considering variation in academic achievement and task complexity within worker and job-education levels, respectively. Finally, the last column in table 5.3 shows the personal education groups that account for the most over-educated workers in each country—that is, the largest cell percentages. (Note that for presentational convenience, a summary of results for the column percentages does not appear in table 5.3.)

Note

1. Note that Colombia is excluded due to data limitations at the time of publication.

CHAPTER 6

Explaining Education Mismatch

Introduction

The magnitude of worker-job mismatch by education suggests a serious issue and raises questions as to the validity of measured mismatch and the nature of its underlying drivers. These are assessed in this chapter using multinomial and binary logit models, but the interpretive challenges of the log odds metric and the particular interest in tertiary education also argue for a closer look at the relationship between key variables and over-education among tertiary graduates in a more intuitive fashion before proceeding to multivariate results.

Predictors of Mismatch among Tertiary Graduates

Given the high rates of over-education observed among tertiary graduates, along with the perceived scarcity of human capital in developing countries, it is natural to ask whether apparent mismatch masks low levels of achievement among a large segment of tertiary graduates. This possibility, as depicted in figure 2.2, embodies the natural assumption that tertiary graduates working in jobs requiring no more than secondary education would be drawn exclusively from the bottom of the test score distribution, that is, if 30 percent of tertiary graduates were over-educated they would be expected to be drawn overwhelmingly from the bottom 30 percent of test scorers.

Table 6.1 shows the rates of over-education among tertiary graduates by test score decile for each country under this assumption. For example, because 28 percent of tertiary graduates in Ukraine are over-educated, over-education rates are expected to be 100 percent for the bottom two test score deciles and 80 percent for the third decile. While no one expects test scores to explain over-education entirely, the extent to which actual rates in table 6.2 depart from this expectation may be surprising. Although there is a clear tendency for the lower (upper) deciles to contribute more (less) to the ranks of the over-educated, over-education is spread remarkably broadly throughout the test score distribution in most countries.

It is certainly not the case that the over-educated are drawn exclusively or overwhelmingly from the lowest achievers among tertiary graduates, as measured

Table 6.1 Hypothetical Rates of Tertiary Over-Education by Test Score Decile
percent

	Overall percent	Hypothetical rates by test score decile (percent)									
		1	2	3	4	5	6	7	8	9	10
Armenia	29	100	100	90							
Bolivia	40	100	100	100	100						
Colombia	42	100	100	100	100	20					
Georgia	31	100	100	100	10						
Ghana	40	100	100	100	100						
Kenya	26	100	100	60							
Ukraine	28	100	100	80							
Vietnam	51	100	100	100	100	100	10				

Note: Table depicts the actual rates of tertiary over-education in the first column and conditional rates by test score decile, assuming the over-educated are drawn exclusively from the bottom of the test score distribution. Hypothesis predicts no cases of over-education for empty cells.

Table 6.2 Actual Rates of Over-Education among Tertiary Graduates by Test Score Decile
percent

	Overall (percent)	Tertiary over-education rates by test score decile (percent)									
		1	2	3	4	5	6	7	8	9	10
Armenia	29	26	34	37	27	33	26	30	21	29	24
Bolivia	40	60	52	55	41	50	38	15	42	30	15
Colombia	42	63	39	43	43	25	36	54	29	44	46
Georgia	31	34	45	32	42	30	28	28	22	22	25
Ghana	40	52	76	65	14	16	36	59	19	26	39
Kenya	26	29	42	39	31	33	17	33	16	8	7
Ukraine	28	26	58	30	27	33	23	31	24	9	16
Vietnam	51	55	65	46	55	52	43	49	60	58	29

Source: World Bank STEP Skills Measurement Program.
Note: Values in **orange** are unusually small and values in **blue** are unusually large relative to overall rates.

by test scores. Because each decile represents 10 percent of the workforce, it is easy to calculate each decile's contribution to the overall over-education rate in the first column. For example, rather than contributing nothing to the ranks of over-educated tertiary graduates, workers above the 40th test score percentile in Bolivia account for 19 percent (= 5 + 3.8 + 1.5 + 4.2 + 3 + 1.5) of the 40 percent of Bolivian tertiary graduates who are over-educated, nearly half of the total (47.5 percent). Using the values in the first column as country-specific test score cut-points, one finds that the percentiles above those levels account for 46–68 percent of the over-educated across countries, or 56 percent on average. Likewise, deciles above country medians account for 32–50 percent of the over-educated, or 41 percent on average. Relatively high test scores clearly do inoculate tertiary graduates from over-education.

The pattern of over-education is much clearer when tertiary graduates are divided by years of education and grouped into three categories. In every country, the worker group with the fewest years of tertiary education faces much greater risk of working in a nontertiary job than the adjacent group with more years of tertiary education. The differences are about 20 percentage points for three countries (the Lao People's Democratic Republic, Ghana, and Ukraine), 27–36 points for five countries (Colombia, Kenya, Yunnan Province, the former Yugoslav Republic of Macedonia, and Armenia), and 40–46 points for the other four countries (Sri Lanka, Bolivia, Vietnam, Georgia), while the mean across countries is 32.8 percentage points. In most countries with three categories of tertiary education, there is a large difference between the middle and top group, as well, though the average difference is exactly half as large, 16.9 percentage points. Clearly, heterogeneous levels of educational attainment among the tertiary educated are an important predictor of over-education.

By contrast, the picture is quite murky with respect to the *content* of tertiary education. Rates of over-education for tertiary fields of study that are technical are close to average within countries, while over-education among for graduates in the humanities and social sciences and graduates in law and health tends to be below country averages. Rates for business graduates tend to be above average. In short, mismatch by *kind* of skill, rather than level, is not highly pronounced in the STEP (Skills Toward Employment and Productivity) data, and the level that seems to matter most is formal educational attainment rather than reading test scores.

Finally, the patterns by job type are clear and sharp (table 6.4).

- Rates of over-education for tertiary graduates in the *private sector* are nearly 30 percentage points higher than in the public sector on average.
- Over-education in the *formal sector* is comparable or somewhat higher than rates for the public sector, probably reflecting their significant overlap in many countries.
- Rates of over-education among *self-employed workers in the informal sector* average 65 percent and exceed 50 percent in all countries except FYR Macedonia, where the category represents a relatively small share of employment (16 percent) in any case.
- Over-education rates for *wage and salary workers in the informal sector* are intermediate, averaging about 20 percentage points lower than for self-employed informal workers and about 20 percentage points higher than for formal and public sector workers.
- Rates for *unpaid family workers* are the highest overall, but this group is surprisingly small in most countries (see table 4.8).

As these observations indicate, the total contribution of the different education groups and job types to tertiary over-education rates depends not only on the conditional rates shown in tables 6.3 and 6.4, but also on the relative sizes of the different categories. The sizes of the test score groups (deciles) in tables 6.1 and 6.2 are equal and convenient for calculating group contributions to overall rates. Because this does not hold for the sizes of the education and job categories, it is possible for conditional rates to give a misleading impression of overall importance if some categories are relatively small. This is most clearly the case for unpaid family

Table 6.3 Rates of Over-Education among Tertiary Graduates by Employer Type and Sector, by Country
percent

	Overall	Employer		Formal sector	Informal sector		
		Public	Private		Wage	Self-employed	Unpaid
Armenia	28	21	43	24	65	64	51
Bolivia	40	10	51	15	46	66	85
Colombia	42	19	45	29	42	63	68
Georgia	31	20	41	20	31	64	57
Ghana	40	24	53	27	45	78	100
Kenya	26	10	31	18	33	53	
Lao PDR	20	3	62	4	6	66	94
Macedonia, FYR	23	7	36	20	44	40	95
Sri Lanka	37	22	63	33	9	78	N/A
Ukraine	27	15	38	24	N/A	53	N/A
Vietnam	51	40	61	45	63	75	86
Yunnan Province	47	40	57	43	61	81	67
Mean	34	19	48	25	41	65	78

Source: World Bank STEP Skills Measurement Program, wb/box/overed.log.
Note: Values in orange are unusually small and the value in blue are unusually large.

Table 6.4 Over-Education Rates among Tertiary Graduates by Years of Education and Field of Study, by Country
percent

	Years of education				Field of study				
	Overall	<16	16	>16	Education and social services	Humanities and social sciences	Business	STEM, ICT, manufacturing, architecture	Law and health
Armenia	28	55	19	21	24	19	30	40	27
Bolivia	40	69		24	40	17	50	44	33
Colombia	42	54	27	9	40	55	45	45	20
Georgia	31	66	20	22	17	21	57	33	28
Ghana	40		51	31	41	32	41	45	40
Kenya	26	47	19	14	30	34	21	26	0
Lao PDR	20	33		14	24	0	30	20	13
Macedonia, FYR	23	53		18	20	23	32	23	16
Sri Lanka	37	72	32	2	19	26	49	35	11
Ukraine	27	42	21		N/A	N/A	N/A	N/A	N/A
Vietnam	51	90	45	11	61	34	55	42	41
Yunnan Province	47		61	29	29	24	57	47	46
Mean	34	58	33	18	31	26	42	36	25

Source: World Bank STEP Skills Measurement Program.
Note: Values in orange are unusually small and values in blue are unusually large. Fields of study unavailable for Ukraine.

workers, whose high rates of over-education must be balanced against the small size of the category, but similar issues apply to other groups in less extreme form.

For example, although there is a strong gradient in over-education rates by years of tertiary education in Vietnam, the three groups differ in size, accounting for one-quarter, two-thirds, and one-tenth of tertiary graduates, respectively (see table 4.3). Therefore, the two groups with more education account for nearly 60 percent of the over-educated despite their significantly lower rates of over-education relative to the group with the fewest years of education. Belonging to the two most educated groups is protective, but they still account for a clear majority of over-educated tertiary graduates.

The next section models these relationships net of the others and additional explanatory variables using logistic regression. Although the main results of regression models are in terms of conditional rates and do not capture the influence of varying group sizes, regressions have the advantage of permitting inclusion of multiple predictors simultaneously and sequentially, isolating partial effects, and testing hypotheses.

Models of Mismatch among All Workers

Given the heterogeneity of country conditions described in chapter 4, as well as differences in the administration of the literacy assessment, country-specific models are estimated on varying subsets of countries. Table 6.5 presents the pattern of country coverage of the country-specific logistic regression models predicting mismatch for all workers (net of certain sample exclusions) based on educational attainment, test scores, and predictors testing the different explanations for

Table 6.5 Coverage of Regression Models, by Country

	Under-education models		Over-education models	
	Test scores in model		Test scores in model	
	No	Yes	No	Yes
Armenia	—	—	X	X
Bolivia	X	X	X	X
Colombia	X	X	X	X
Georgia	—	—	X	X
Ghana	X	X	X	X
Kenya	X	X	X	X
Lao PDR	X	—	X	—
Macedonia, FYR	—	—	X	—
Sri Lanka	X	—	X	—
Ukraine	—	—	X	X
Vietnam	X	X	X	X
Yunnan Province	X	—	X	—
N	8	5	12	8

Note: An X indicates the model could be estimated for the country, while dashes indicate the model could not be estimated.

mismatch described previously. Only eight countries have sufficient numbers of under-educated workers to predict both under- and over-education relative to being well-matched (reference category) using multinomial logit models. Binary logit models predicting the odds of being over-educated relative to well-matched are used for the four Europe and Central Asia countries. To maintain consistency, estimation samples for these countries are restricted to all workers with tertiary education and workers with secondary education who are not under-educated. Models with test scores cannot be estimated for a different set of four countries that did not include the reading assessment in their survey. Only FYR Macedonia is doubly limited by the absence of both test scores and sufficient numbers of under-educated workers. Only models predicting over-education that omit test scores can be estimated for all 12 STEP countries (column 3).

The analyses first predict mismatch using baseline models that include only dummies for ISCED education levels. The reference category for personal education is upper secondary (ISCED 3) for all models. A second model adds the literacy test scores if available. The next model omits test scores if present previously and adds all other predictors, as well as replacing the single dummy for ISCED = 5 with dummies for different years of education among tertiary graduates in the models predicting over-education. A final model adds test scores to this model, if available. Note that because tertiary graduates cannot be under-educated and workers with less than primary education cannot be over-educated, there are no coefficients for these combinations of groups and outcomes. Well-matched workers are the reference outcome in both the multinomial and the binary logit models.

Because of the sheer quantity of results produced by estimating even these few models over so many countries, table 6.6 (under-education) and table 6.7 (over-education) summarize results, which are presented in detail in tables 6.8 through 6.15. All figures in tables 6.8 through 6.15 show the multiplicative change in the odds of mismatch for unit changes in the predictors, that is, the coefficients are in exponentiated form. Tables 6.6 and 6.7 show the number of coefficients significant

Table 6.6 Summary of Significant Logistic Regression Results, Under-Education

		1	2	3	4
		Baseline	Literacy	No literacy	All
Experience	10–29 years			2/8	2/5
<10 years = 0	30+ years			2/8	2/5
Male = 0	Female, no young kids			−1/8	−1/5
	Female, young kids			−1/8	−1/5
Yes = 1	Voluntary part-time			−2/8	−2/5
Yes = 1	Health problem			(1/8)	0/5

table continues next page

Table 6.6 Summary of Significant Logistic Regression Results, Under-Education *(continued)*

		1	2	3	4
		Baseline	Literacy	No literacy	All
Private = 0	Public sector			(1/8)	(1/5)
Formal = 0	Informal employee			−5/8	−4/5
	Informal self-employed			−3/8	−2/5
	Informal family			−1/8	−1/5
ISCED	< Primary	5/8	3/5	4/8	4/5
ISCED 1	Primary	7/8	5/5	6/8	5/5
ISCED 2	Low secondary	6/8	5/5	6/8	5/5
	Literacy score		0/5		0/5

Source: World Bank STEP Skills Measurement Program.
Note: Figures are number of coefficients significant at 0.05 level or better out of total number possible. Negative signs indicate direction of relationships. Values without parentheses refer to number of significant coefficients with expected signs, while values inside parentheses indicate number with unexpected signs. Total possible number of significant coefficients for all predictors within models are given in denominators. Gray cells indicate values are not applicable.

Table 6.7 Summary of Logistic Regression Results, Over-Education

		1	2	3	4
Predictors		Baseline	Literacy	No literacy	All
Experience	10–29 years			0/12	0/8
	30+ years			(4/12)	(1/8)
	Female, no young kids			2/12 (−1/12)	3/8 (−1/8)
	Female, young kids			5/12	3/8
Yes = 1	Voluntary part-time			1/12	1/8
Yes = 1	Health problem			0/12	0/8
Private = 0	Public sector			−11/12	−7/8
Formal = 0	Informal employee			11/11	7/7
	Informal self-employed			11/12	7/8
	Informal, family			6/12	3/8
ISCED 1	Primary	2/8, −3/8	2/7, −2/7	2/8, −4/8	2/7, −2/7
ISCED 2	Low secondary	3/8, −3/8	1/7, −1/7	1/8, −3/8	1/7, −1/7
ISCED 5	Tertiary <16 years			6/10	5/7
ISCED 5	Tertiary 16 years			−4/9	−4/7
ISCED 5	Tertiary >16 years			−5/11	−3/7
ISCED 5	Tertiary, all	−7/12	−5/8		
	Literacy		−6/8		−3/8

Source: World Bank STEP Skills Measurement Program.
Note: Figures are number of coefficients significant at 0.05 level or better out of total number possible. Negative signs indicate direction of relationships. Values without parentheses refer to number of significant coefficients with expected signs, while values inside parentheses indicate number with unexpected signs. Total possible number of significant coefficients for all predictors within models are given in denominators. Gray cells indicate values are not applicable.

Table 6.8 Logistic Regressions Predicting Mismatch, by Country—Bolivia
t-statistics in parentheses

		Baseline	Literacy	No literacy	All
Under-education					
Experience	10–29 years			2.093**	2.081**
<10 years = 0				(2.446)	(2.422)
	30+ years			2.713***	2.712***
				(2.786)	(2.782)
Male = 0	Female, no young kids			0.723	0.721
				(−1.281)	(−1.290)
	Female, young kids			0.815	0.811
				(−0.752)	(−0.767)
	Voluntary part-time			1.274	1.266
				(0.702)	(0.683)
	Health problem			1.340	1.339
				(1.243)	(1.237)
Private = 0	Public sector			0.751	0.733
				(−0.379)	(−0.409)
Formal = 0	Informal employee			0.462**	0.460**
				(−2.055)	(−2.059)
	Informal self-employed			0.418**	0.411**
				(−2.424)	(−2.464)
	Informal family			0.304	0.303
				(−1.497)	(−1.497)
ISCED	< Primary (ISCED = 0)	12.78***	11.36***	15.38***	14.24***
Upper secondary = 0		(9.798)	(8.616)	(8.074)	(7.353)
	Primary (ISCED = 1)	6.210***	5.610***	6.629***	6.191***
		(5.504)	(4.986)	(5.052)	(4.676)
	Low secondary (2)	9.714***	9.133***	10.80***	10.41***
		(7.808)	(7.446)	(7.297)	(7.040)
	Literacy (1 = 25 pts.)		0.970		0.979
			(−1.033)		(−0.654)
Over-education					
Experience	10–29 years			1.003	1.000
				(0.0188)	(0.000241)
	30+ years			1.862**	1.712*
				(2.267)	(1.944)
	Female, no young kids			1.371	1.325
				(1.637)	(1.452)
	Female, young kids			1.911***	1.848***
				(3.241)	(3.047)
	Voluntary part-time			1.385	1.464
				(1.378)	(1.607)
	Health problem			0.875	0.896
				(−0.658)	(−0.541)
	Public sector			0.582	0.527*
				(−1.594)	(−1.865)

table continues next page

Table 6.8 Logistic Regressions Predicting Mismatch, by Country—Bolivia *(continued)*

	Baseline	Literacy	No literacy	All
Informal employee			3.520***	3.470***
			(4.871)	(4.785)
Informal self-employed			3.434***	3.302***
			(5.045)	(4.844)
Informal family			5.747***	5.646***
			(2.896)	(2.833)
Primary (ISCED = 1)	0.507*	0.293***	0.385**	0.258***
	(−1.906)	(−3.219)	(−2.530)	(−3.386)
Low secondary (2)	1.737**	1.232	1.451	1.133
	(2.235)	(0.802)	(1.435)	(0.461)
Tertiary <16 years (5)			1.722**	1.843**
			(2.157)	(2.400)
Tertiary 16 years (5)			1.260	1.313
			(0.353)	(0.415)
Tertiary >16 years (5)			0.426***	0.530***
			(−4.116)	(−2.923)
Tertiary, all (5)	0.387***	0.476***		
	(−6.068)	(−4.562)		
Literacy (1 = 25 pts.)		0.862***		0.889***
		(−4.897)		(−3.475)
N	1,206	1,206	1,113	1,113
Pseudo R²	0.265	0.275	0.334	0.340
Log likelihood	−940.0	−927.4	−792.3	−786.0

Note: Empty cells indicate values are not applicable.
*** p<0.01, ** p<0.05, * p<0.1.

Table 6.9 Logistic Regressions Predicting Mismatch, by Country—Colombia
t-statistics in parentheses

		Baseline	Literacy scores	No literacy	All
Under-education					
Experience	10–29 years			1.249	1.257
				(0.941)	(0.969)
	30+ years			1.586*	1.648*
				(1.716)	(1.850)
	Female, no young kids			1.045	1.054
				(0.238)	(0.284)
	Female, young kids			0.740	0.745
				(−1.204)	(−1.175)
	Voluntary part-time			0.425**	0.426**
				(−2.230)	(−2.229)
	Health problem			0.938	0.948
				(−0.303)	(−0.250)

table continues next page

Table 6.9 Logistic Regressions Predicting Mismatch, by Country—Colombia *(continued)*

		Baseline	Literacy scores	No literacy	All
	Public sector			1.893	1.850
				(1.132)	(1.089)
	Informal employee			0.589**	0.585**
				(−2.131)	(−2.159)
	Informal self-employed			0.834	0.823
				(−0.925)	(−0.992)
	Informal family			1.577	1.715
				(0.529)	(0.632)
	< Primary (ISCED = 0)	12.57***	14.92***	16.22***	19.97***
		(10.76)	(9.745)	(9.663)	(9.289)
	Primary (ISCED = 1)	3.927***	4.255***	4.572***	5.053***
		(7.373)	(7.338)	(6.943)	(7.080)
	Low secondary (2)	10.84***	11.23***	12.29***	12.92***
		(6.779)	(6.852)	(6.853)	(6.949)
	Literacy (1 = 25 pts.)		1.043		1.058
Over-education			(1.204)		(1.520)
Experience	10–29 years			1.126	1.124
				(0.824)	(0.808)
	30+ years			1.141	1.119
				(0.611)	(0.512)
	Female, no young kids			1.068	1.065
				(0.456)	(0.437)
	Female, young kids			1.129	1.128
				(0.669)	(0.662)
	Voluntary part-time			0.717	0.723
				(−1.203)	(−1.172)
	Health problem			1.180	1.181
				(0.926)	(0.934)
	Public sector			0.280***	0.280***
				(−2.778)	(−2.776)
	Informal employee			2.717***	2.721***
				(5.414)	(5.419)
	Informal self-employed			2.645***	2.629***
				(6.353)	(6.309)
	Informal family			2.710	2.626
				(1.535)	(1.483)
	Primary (ISCED = 1)	0.578***	0.507***	0.449***	0.431***
		(−3.298)	(−3.774)	(−4.346)	(−4.357)
	Low secondary (2)	2.601***	2.457***	2.125**	2.085**
		(2.830)	(2.649)	(2.180)	(2.119)
	Tertiary <16 years (5)			1.483**	1.507**
				(2.384)	(2.459)

table continues next page

Table 6.9 Logistic Regressions Predicting Mismatch, by Country—Colombia *(continued)*

	Baseline	Literacy scores	No literacy	All
Tertiary 16 years (5)			0.423***	0.436***
			(−3.075)	(−2.933)
Tertiary >16 years (5)			0.294**	0.303**
			(−2.396)	(−2.327)
Tertiary, all (5)	0.707***	0.750**		
	(−2.577)	(−2.086)		
Literacy (1 = 25 pts.)		0.938**		0.975
		(−1.978)		(−0.731)
N	1,582	1,582	1,509	1,509
Pseudo R^2	0.169	0.171	0.219	0.221
Log likelihood	−1,366	−1,363	−1,228	−1,227

Note: Empty cells indicate values are not applicable.
*** $p<0.01$, ** $p<0.05$, * $p<0.1$.

Table 6.10 Logistic Regressions Predicting Mismatch, by Country—Ghana
t-statistics in parentheses

		Baseline	Literacy scores	No literacy	All
Under-education					
Experience	10–29 years			1.706**	1.735**
				(2.288)	(2.349)
	30+ years			2.408***	2.329***
				(3.110)	(2.985)
	Female, no young kids			0.532***	0.542***
				(−2.991)	(−2.898)
	Female, young kids			0.575**	0.585**
				(−2.448)	(−2.355)
	Voluntary part-time			0.484**	0.475**
				(−2.040)	(−2.090)
	Health problem			1.493	1.520
				(1.505)	(1.572)
	Public sector			1.490	1.522
				(1.183)	(1.245)
	Informal employee			0.416***	0.435***
				(−2.793)	(−2.643)
	Informal self-employed			0.571*	0.595*
				(−1.856)	(−1.709)
	Informal family			0.567	0.620
				(−0.957)	(−0.804)
	< Primary (ISCED = 0)	1.481	1.728*	3.561***	4.373***
		(1.430)	(1.807)	(3.655)	(3.968)

table continues next page

Table 6.10 Logistic Regressions Predicting Mismatch, by Country—Ghana *(continued)*

		Baseline	Literacy scores	No literacy	All
	Primary (ISCED = 1)	28.62***	33.92***	45.24***	55.66***
		(9.403)	(9.190)	(9.607)	(9.547)
	Low secondary (2)	3.403***	3.876***	4.513***	5.328***
		(4.520)	(4.656)	(4.876)	(5.123)
	Literacy (1 = 25 pts.)		1.036		1.049
			(1.229)		(1.576)
Over-education					
Experience	10–29 years			1.244	1.202
				(1.547)	(1.293)
	30+ years			1.916***	1.936***
				(3.152)	(3.182)
	Female, no young kids			1.340**	1.331**
				(2.089)	(2.033)
	Female, young kids			1.460**	1.401**
				(2.498)	(2.212)
	Voluntary part-time			1.072	1.085
				(0.331)	(0.384)
	Health problem			1.291	1.308
				(1.202)	(1.259)
	Public sector			0.638**	0.616**
				(−2.014)	(−2.166)
	Informal employee			1.991***	1.982***
				(3.328)	(3.294)
	Informal self-employed			3.044***	2.902***
				(5.439)	(5.177)
	Informal family			6.027***	5.820***
				(4.587)	(4.479)
	Primary (ISCED = 1)	5.244***	3.405***	3.378***	2.598***
		(6.215)	(4.358)	(4.424)	(3.288)
	Low secondary (2)	1.237	0.870	0.837	0.679**
		(1.608)	(−0.921)	(−1.214)	(−2.358)
	Tertiary 16 years (5)			1.581*	1.675**
				(1.903)	(2.128)
	Tertiary >16 years (5)			0.682	0.803
				(−1.431)	(−0.801)
	Tertiary, all (5)	0.526***	0.642***		
		(−3.923)	(−2.610)		
	Literacy (1 = 25 pts.)		0.910***		0.943***
			(−4.911)		(−2.875)
	N	2,070	2,070	1,789	1,789
	Pseudo R^2	0.208	0.217	0.215	0.220
	Log likelihood	−1,595	−1,577	−1,379	−1,371

Note: Empty cells indicate values are not applicable.
*** $p<0.01$, ** $p<0.05$, * $p<0.1$.

Table 6.11 Logistic Regressions Predicting Mismatch, by Country—Kenya
t-statistics in parentheses

		Baseline	Literacy scores	No literacy	All
Under-education					
Experience	10–29 years			1.003	0.997
				(0.0179)	(−0.0203)
	30+ years			0.673	0.666
				(−1.518)	(−1.558)
	Female, no young kids			0.740	0.734
				(−1.588)	(−1.627)
	Female, young kids			0.774	0.774
				(−1.360)	(−1.357)
	Voluntary part-time			1.580	1.573
				(1.586)	(1.573)
	Health problem			1.317	1.325
				(0.826)	(0.844)
	Public sector			6.287***	6.288***
				(4.314)	(4.309)
	Informal employee			0.416***	0.416***
				(−3.369)	(−3.355)
	Informal self-employed			0.568**	0.572**
				(−2.167)	(−2.143)
	Informal family			0.274**	0.272**
				(−2.353)	(−2.367)
	< Primary (ISCED = 0)	19.81***	21.59***	39.28***	39.60***
		(12.91)	(11.34)	(11.64)	(10.81)
	Primary (ISCED = 1)	77.24***	79.99***	151.8***	152.5***
		(17.61)	(17.27)	(16.38)	(16.16)
	Low secondary (2)	11.76***	11.81***	19.21***	19.23***
		(10.16)	(10.17)	(10.16)	(10.16)
	Literacy (1 = 25 pts.)		1.016		1.001
			(0.614)		(0.0414)
Over-education					
Experience	10–29 years			1.142	1.133
				(0.970)	(0.912)
	30+ years			0.941	0.911
				(−0.224)	(−0.345)
	Female, no young kids			1.101	1.104
				(0.616)	(0.633)
	Female, young kids			1.380**	1.365*
				(2.010)	(1.935)
	Voluntary part-time			1.944***	1.923***
				(2.695)	(2.647)
	Health problem			1.108	1.110
				(0.320)	(0.328)
	Public sector			0.373***	0.376***
				(−2.629)	(−2.604)

table continues next page

Table 6.11 Logistic Regressions Predicting Mismatch, by Country—Kenya *(continued)*

	Baseline	Literacy scores	No literacy	All
Informal employee			2.578***	2.548***
			(4.838)	(4.771)
Informal self-employed			2.609***	2.617***
			(4.935)	(4.947)
Informal family			1.720	1.724
			(1.213)	(1.217)
Primary (ISCED = 1)	2.045***	1.916***	1.628**	1.531**
	(3.755)	(3.316)	(2.413)	(2.062)
Low secondary (2)	0.556***	0.552***	0.471***	0.468***
	(−3.079)	(−3.110)	(−3.778)	(−3.801)
Tertiary <16 years (5)			1.059	1.123
			(0.166)	(0.332)
Tertiary 16 years (5)			0.461***	0.488***
			(−3.166)	(−2.898)
Tertiary >16 years (5)			0.616	0.632
			(−0.686)	(−0.647)
Tertiary, all (5)	0.346***	0.366***		
	(−6.009)	(−5.551)		
Literacy (1 = 25 pts.)		0.972		0.970
		(−1.396)		(−1.437)
N	1,893	1,893	1,754	1,754
Pseudo R^2	0.263	0.264	0.293	0.294
Log likelihood	−1,523	−1,521	−1,357	−1,356

Note: Empty cells indicate values are not applicable.
*** $p<0.01$, ** $p<0.05$, * $p<0.1$.

Table 6.12 Logistic Regressions Predicting Mismatch, by Country—Vietnam
t-statistics in parentheses

		Baseline	Literacy scores	No literacy	All
Under-education					
Experience	10–29 years			1.603	1.797
				(0.922)	(1.139)
	30+ years			1.097	1.297
				(0.168)	(0.466)
	Female, no young kids			0.784	0.796
				(−0.864)	(−0.808)
	Female, young kids			0.678	0.687
				(−1.054)	(−1.014)
	Voluntary part-time			2.116*	2.025*
				(1.955)	(1.831)
	Health problem			0.769	0.747
				(−0.777)	(−0.854)

table continues next page

Table 6.12 Logistic Regressions Predicting Mismatch, by Country—Vietnam *(continued)*

		Baseline	Literacy scores	No literacy	All
	Public sector			0.915	0.919
				(−0.251)	(−0.237)
	Informal employee			0.718	0.733
				(−0.917)	(−0.855)
	Informal self-employed			0.610	0.607
				(−1.343)	(−1.349)
	Informal family			0.220*	0.215*
				(−1.863)	(−1.876)
	< Primary (ISCED = 0)	0.547	0.801	0.731	1.186
		(−1.440)	(−0.443)	(−0.649)	(0.307)
	Primary (ISCED = 1)	2.912***	3.458***	3.423***	4.328***
		(2.883)	(3.167)	(3.093)	(3.493)
	Low secondary (2)	2.877***	3.105***	3.212***	3.575***
		(3.007)	(3.182)	(3.216)	(3.459)
	Literacy (1 = 25 pts.)		1.082		1.114*
Over-education			(1.333)		(1.705)
Experience	10–29 years			0.852	0.832
				(−0.996)	(−1.141)
	30+ years			0.746	0.717
				(−1.427)	(−1.612)
	Female, no young kids			1.631***	1.633***
				(3.531)	(3.534)
	Female, young kids			1.305	1.304
				(1.611)	(1.603)
	Voluntary part-time			1.304	1.296
				(1.193)	(1.171)
	Health problem			1.138	1.133
				(0.802)	(0.777)
	Public sector			0.643***	0.637***
				(−2.836)	(−2.889)
	Informal employee			1.684***	1.651***
				(2.694)	(2.587)
	Informal self-employed			1.870***	1.824***
				(3.324)	(3.182)
	Informal family			1.910**	1.842*
				(1.996)	(1.876)
	Primary (ISCED = 1)	0.967	0.765	0.771	0.667*
		(−0.166)	(−1.241)	(−1.220)	(−1.785)
	Low secondary (2)	1.089	0.988	0.912	0.863
		(0.459)	(−0.0646)	(−0.480)	(−0.758)
	Tertiary <16 years (5)			1.692	1.741*
				(1.567)	(1.649)

table continues next page

Table 6.12 Logistic Regressions Predicting Mismatch, by Country—Vietnam *(continued)*

	Baseline	Literacy scores	No literacy	All
Tertiary 16 years (5)			0.154***	0.160***
			(−10.96)	(−10.62)
Tertiary >16 years (5)			0.0349***	0.0371***
			(−8.620)	(−8.443)
Tertiary, all (5)	0.149***	0.162***		
	(−13.27)	(−12.47)		
Literacy (1 = 25 pts.)		0.909***		0.939*
		(−2.946)		(−1.818)
N	2,183	2,183	2,130	2,130
Pseudo R^2	0.203	0.209	0.265	0.269
Log likelihood	−1,285	−1,277	−1,143	−1,138

Note: Empty cells indicate values are not applicable.
*** $p<0.01$, ** $p<0.05$, * $p<0.1$.

Table 6.13 Logistic Regressions Predicting Mismatch, by Country—Sri Lanka, Lao PDR, and Yunnan Province
t-statistics in parentheses

	Sri Lanka		Lao PDR		Yunnan Province	
	Baseline	No literacy	Baseline	No literacy	Baseline	No literacy
Under-education						
10–29 years experience		0.662		0.959		1.218
		(−0.694)		(−0.127)		(0.355)
30+ years experience		0.821		0.924		1.672
		(−0.308)		(−0.213)		(0.889)
Female, no young kids		1.360		0.794		1.054
		(0.748)		(−1.011)		(0.232)
Female, young kids		0.828		0.900		1.341
		(−0.282)		(−0.414)		(0.547)
Voluntary part-time		0.445		1.360		0.994
		(−1.491)		(1.011)		(−0.010)
Health problem		3.689***		1.190		1.627
		(2.816)		(0.602)		(1.492)
Public sector		1.546		1.869		1.581*
		(0.863)		(1.582)		(1.777)
Informal employee		1.894		0.333***		0.765
		(1.248)		(−2.636)		(−1.029)
Informal self-employed		1.254		0.321***		0.875
		(0.399)		(−2.719)		(−0.331)
Informal family		0.000		0.329*		0.796
		(−0.0145)		(−1.884)		(−0.427)
< Primary (ISCED = 0)	45.32***	128.0***	0.573*	1.631	31.56***	0.000
	(4.814)	(4.167)	(−1.918)	(1.308)	(4.227)	(0.000)

table continues next page

Table 6.13 Logistic Regressions Predicting Mismatch, by Country—Sri Lanka, Lao PDR, and Yunnan Province *(continued)*

	Sri Lanka		Lao PDR		Yunnan Province	
	Baseline	No literacy	Baseline	No literacy	Baseline	No literacy
Primary (ISCED = 1)	4.635***	5.842***	1.591	2.995***	6.663***	7.633***
	(3.760)	(3.483)	(1.491)	(2.968)	(6.312)	(5.494)
Low secondary (2)	0.409*	0.424	1.738	2.973***	1.810**	2.028**
	(−1.913)	(−1.643)	(1.586)	(2.775)	(2.329)	(2.507)
Over-education						
10–29 years experience		1.272		1.224		0.938
		(0.804)		(0.874)		(−0.348)
30+ years experience		2.013**		1.245		1.532*
		(2.002)		(0.734)		(1.763)
Female, no young kids		0.882		1.278		1.056
		(−0.509)		(1.276)		(0.392)
Female, young kids		0.942		1.649**		0.742
		(−0.190)		(2.266)		(−1.063)
Voluntary part-time		1.007		1.604*		1.769
		(0.0270)		(1.823)		(1.395)
Health problem		1.017		1.332		0.740
		(0.0570)		(1.026)		(−1.341)
Public sector		0.470**		0.263***		0.622***
		(−2.528)		(−3.817)		(−2.941)
Informal employee		3.579***		2.683***		1.548**
		(4.168)		(2.605)		(2.497)
Informal self-employed		3.768***		2.843***		4.157***
		(4.408)		(2.713)		(5.884)
Informal family		2.424		9.626***		2.464**
		(1.473)		(4.604)		(2.107)
Primary (ISCED = 1)	0.193***	0.0803***	0.937	0.672*	0.209***	0.0970***
	(−3.640)	(−5.201)	(−0.301)	(−1.690)	(−3.494)	(−4.937)
Low secondary (2)	0.257***	0.128***	1.686**	1.314	0.563***	0.376***
	(−6.055)	(−7.831)	(2.168)	(1.077)	(−3.410)	(−5.178)
Tertiary <16 years (5)		1.611		0.460*		n.a.
		(0.949)		(−1.909)		
Tertiary 16 years (5)		0.928		n.a.		3.514***
		(−0.172)				(6.468)
Tertiary >16 years (5)		0.0759**		0.186***		0.957
		(2.396)		(−4.523)		(−0.194)
Tertiary, all (5)	0.397***		0.0956***		1.322*	
	(−3.563)		(−9.208)		(1.904)	
N	579	560	1,283	1,172	1,268	1,247
Pseudo R^2	0.153	0.258	0.267	0.303	0.104	0.162
Log likelihood	−466.3	−393.2	−940.0	−819.1	−1,041	−953.7

Note: Empty cells indicate values are not applicable.
*** $p<0.01$, ** $p<0.05$, * $p<0.1$.

Table 6.14 Logistic Regressions Predicting Mismatch, by Country—Armenia and Georgia (Over-Education Only)
t-statistics in parentheses

	Armenia				Georgia			
	Baseline	Literacy	No literacy	All	Baseline	Literacy	No literacy	All
10–29 years			1.037	1.038			1.183	1.182
			(0.148)	(0.153)			(0.721)	(0.719)
30+ years			1.668*	1.705*			0.879	0.867
			(1.877)	(1.950)			(−0.452)	(−0.501)
Female, no young kids			0.764	0.757			0.681**	0.694**
			(−1.451)	(−1.497)			(−2.104)	(−1.995)
Female, young kids			0.952	0.947			0.585*	0.585*
			(−0.187)	(−0.209)			(−1.818)	(−1.818)
Voluntary part-time			1.123	1.124			0.746	0.743
			(0.492)	(0.492)			(−0.932)	(−0.945)
Health problem			0.888	0.885			1.345	1.353
			(−0.532)	(−0.546)			(1.289)	(1.314)
Public sector			0.591***	0.588***			0.573***	0.572***
			(−2.638)	(−2.663)			(−2.814)	(−2.820)
Informal employee			3.415***	3.409***			1.970***	1.953***
			(3.961)	(3.944)			(3.315)	(3.266)
Informal self-employed			1.748*	1.744*			3.219***	3.163***
			(1.901)	(1.894)			(4.111)	(4.035)
Informal family			4.435	4.502			5.153***	4.973**
			(1.574)	(1.575)			(2.608)	(2.548)
Tertiary <16 years			4.488***	4.430***			5.579***	5.658***
			(6.262)	(6.189)			(6.538)	(6.571)
Tertiary 16 years			0.773	0.746			0.761	0.797
			(−1.155)	(−1.295)			(−0.911)	(−0.745)
Tertiary >16 years			0.856	0.829			0.777	0.814
			(−0.498)	(−0.596)			(−1.130)	(−0.895)
Tertiary, all	0.844	0.860			0.911	1.060		
	(−0.988)	(−0.861)			(−0.494)	(0.300)		
Literacy		0.971		1.060		0.857***		0.957
(1 = 25 pts.)		(−0.509)		(0.910)		(−3.436)		(−0.886)
N	889	889	880	880	854	854	848	848
Pseudo R^2	0.000	0.001	0.133	0.134	0.000	0.012	0.168	0.169
Log likelihood	−530.5	−530.3	−457.8	−457.4	−526.4	−520.4	−436.1	−435.7

Note: Empty cells indicate values are not applicable.
*** p<0.01, ** p<0.05, * p<0.1.

at the 0.05 level or better out of the total number possible given the variation in country coverage described previously, as well as the absence of certain variables in some countries (for example, no informal employees in Ukraine). If the expected association between predictor and outcome is negative, a minus sign is prefixed to the count of significant coefficients. The number of significant coefficients with unexpected signs is shown in parentheses. Where only a count in

Table 6.15 Logistic Regressions Predicting Mismatch, by Country—Ukraine and FYR Macedonia (Over-Education Only)
t-statistics in parentheses

	Ukraine				Macedonia, FYR	
	Baseline	Literacy	No literacy	All	Baseline	No literacy
10–29 years			0.669*	0.663*		0.757
			(−1.915)	(−1.946)		(−1.543)
30+ years			0.969	0.919		0.545***
			(−0.133)	(−0.347)		(−2.838)
Female, no young kids			1.426*	1.478**		1.074
			(1.809)	(1.966)		(0.496)
Female, young kids			1.766**	1.756**		1.226
			(2.039)	(2.011)		(0.884)
Voluntary part-time			1.204	1.183		1.128
			(0.843)	(0.756)		(0.413)
Health problem			1.042	1.035		1.070
			(0.235)	(0.196)		(0.255)
Public sector			0.664**	0.664**		0.262***
			(−2.240)	(−2.220)		(−7.578)
Informal employee			na	na		2.259***
						(3.258)
Informal self-employed			1.802**	1.803**		2.374***
			(2.140)	(2.114)		(4.298)
Informal family			1.544	0.956		1.983
			(0.280)	(−0.0283)		(1.316)
Tertiary <16 years			2.847***	3.057***		4.959***
			(4.963)	(5.202)		(6.248)
Tertiary 16 years			0.679*	0.784	na	na
			(−1.903)	(−1.159)		
Tertiary >16 years			na	na		0.864
						(−0.890)
Tertiary, all	1.121	1.290			0.932	
	(0.708)	(1.512)			(−0.568)	
Literacy		0.853***		0.869***		
(1 = 25 pts.)		(−3.142)		(−2.614)		
N	893	887	870	864	1,496	1,427
Pseudo R^2	0.001	0.011	0.070	0.075	0.000	0.108
Log likelihood	−501.6	−491.5	−456.6	−449.7	−825.4	−713.2

Note: z-statistics in parentheses. Empty cells indicate values are not applicable.
*** p<0.01, ** p<0.05, * p<0.1.

parentheses is shown there are no significant coefficients with the expected signs, rather than a term indicating zero significant coefficients with expected signs. There are no strong expectations regarding the effects of primary and lower secondary education on the odds of being over-educated, so the numbers of positive and negative coefficients are presented without either appearing in parentheses.

(A version of these tables with country names rather than tallies summarizing results may be found in appendix C.)

In general, one expects coefficients for the same variables to be oppositely signed in the models predicting under- and over-education, because most forces facilitating upward mobility would not be expected to increase risks of downward mobility as well, and vice versa. Coefficients significant at the 0.05 level or better are shown in bold in tables 6.8 through 6.15, while those significant at the 0.10 level are marked with a single asterisk for convenience but neither shown in bold in that table nor included in the tallies in tables 6.6 and 6.7.

In most countries workers are more substitutable across jobs with different education requirements if the required level is below tertiary education. Baseline models predicting under-education summarized in table 6.6 indicate that workers with less than upper secondary education are upwardly mobile relative to being well-matched much more often than upper secondary school graduates, who serve as the reference category for both under- and over-education models. Recruitment of upper secondary graduates for jobs requiring tertiary education is less common than employment of workers with lower secondary education in jobs requiring upper secondary, and a similar tendency toward upward mobility affects those with primary education or less.

The boundary between jobs that do and do not require tertiary education appears less permeable in table 6.6, which accords with intuition and is visible in the row percentage charts in appendix A. By contrast, test scores contribute nothing to the explanation of under-education in the five countries for which such models can be estimated, either when added to the baseline model (column 2) or when added to the model with covariates (column 4). Not surprisingly, the magnitudes and significance of most covariates are relatively unchanged when literacy test scores are added to the initial covariate models that exclude them (column 3). From this evidence, it does not appear that the under-educated are drawn into higher-skilled jobs from the upper end of the achievement distribution within their (lower) level of formal education, contrary to the expectations illustrated in figure 2.2.

Evidence tends to be relatively weak for several of the other explanations represented by predictors in models 3 and 4. These models touch upon some of the alternative explanations for mismatch addressed in part 1 of this paper, as discussed next.

Transitory labor market frictions. More experienced workers would be expected to have a higher probability of under-education because they are more likely to have had the opportunity to work their way up job ladders, gradually acquiring necessary skills through experience. It is also possible that requirements for some jobs have been upgraded and while workers' level of education was sufficient when they were first hired the requirements have increased for recent hires. Neither explanation seems strongly supported. In only two of eight countries are workers who have been out of school more than 10 years more likely to be under-educated than workers who left school less than 10 years previously, though it is possible such effects are masked by offsetting effects for males and females.

Individual preferences. Indeed, given traditional gender attitudes, gender biases, and competing demands of household and job responsibilities, one would expect women to be much less able to substitute work experience for educational credentials in order to move upward. Nevertheless, only in Ghana are women, both with and without young children, less likely than men to report working in a job requiring more education than they have attained. Likewise, voluntary part-time work, which presumably indicates less focus on work, is negatively associated with under-education in only two of eight countries.

Health limitations. Chronic health problems do not predict under-education, in general.

Sector of employment. Informality is more consistently and negatively associated with under-education. This is consistent with the view that informality is an adaptation to constricted opportunities and is itself an example of constricted opportunities. Public sector employment does not appear to predict under-education. Other than the finding that the less-educated tend to have more opportunities for upward mobility than upper secondary graduates, it appears that employment in the formal sector is the only other variable that helps explain under-education relatively consistently.

The results for models predicting over-education, summarized in table 6.7, are generally stronger. Workers with tertiary education are less likely to be downwardly mobile than upper secondary graduates (column 1). This effect is particularly pronounced for tertiary graduates with more than 16 years of education, often somewhat less pronounced for those with 16 years of education, and frequently switches direction for tertiary graduates with less than 16 years of education. In other words, workers with the lowest levels of tertiary education often face greater risks of downward mobility than upper secondary graduates (column 3). These effects are generally robust to the inclusion of test scores in the models (column 4). Insofar as the literacy scores measure achievement effectively, the conclusion seems to be that degree type or *quantity* of education matters more than at least one standardized measure of competencies, achievement, or educational quality. Of course, a fuller battery of tests might produce stronger results, but the STEP assessment is one of the most concerted efforts to collect internationally comparable test scores for adults in developing countries.

The contrasts between other ISCED categories and upper secondary graduates are more complex. Given the possibly of greater substitutability of workers across jobs requiring lower levels of education, it is difficult to formulate strong expectations regarding direction of effects. In these cases it is possible for variables to have effects on upward and downward mobility that run in the same direction relative to upper secondary graduates. Therefore, neither tally appears in parentheses in table 6.7 when the same ISCED level has opposite effects across countries. The direction and robustness of the effects are quite mixed. Perhaps most interesting is that the odds of being over-educated relative to being well-matched tend to be lower for workers with a primary education compared to upper secondary workers, except in Ghana and Kenya, where the reverse is true across all four models. For Ghana, this appears to reflect the very large share of jobs that do not require even primary education (46 percent) (see figures 5.3 and 5.6).

The preceding should not be taken to mean that test scores do not predict over-education. Test scores are negatively associated with over-education in six of eight countries with data when they are added to the education-only baseline model (column 2). However, half of the scores are no longer significant once other predictors are added to the model (column 4), and effect sizes tend to be much smaller than those for education level and economic structure variables. To aid interpretation, test scores were transformed by dividing them by 25, which is the average difference between the scores of upper secondary and tertiary graduates. Therefore, coefficients for the reading assessment indicate the effects of differences that typically separate workers with these two levels of education.

For example, the coefficients for Ghana indicate the odds of being over-educated rather than well-matched decline by 9 percent for a unit difference in test scores controlling for education only; that is, the odds of over-education decline by a factor of 0.91 for each 25-point increase in test scores (table 6.10, column 2). The effect shrinks when the other predictors are added. Odds of over-education decline by 5.7 percent for each unit increase in test scores; that is, the odds are 0.943 as large for each 25-point score increase after adding controls (table 6.10, column 4).

Because the actual difference in scores for upper secondary and tertiary graduates in Ghana is closer to 50 points, accounting for a two-unit difference in the scaling used here gives a better indication of the protective power of improved reading associated with university relative to completed secondary school in Ghana. Fifty raw points or two units on the transformed scale is also approximately the standard deviation of test scores across all workers in many countries. Calculating the effects of a two-unit difference in reading scores means the coefficients in tables 6.8 through 6.15 must be squared because they represent the multiplicative effect of a one-unit change in the predictor on the odds of over-education. Squaring the coefficient for reading scores in the full model for Ghana implies an 11 percent reduction in the odds of over-education ($0.943^2 = 0.89$). By contrast, the upper secondary–tertiary test score gap is only half a unit (~13 points) in the Europe and Central Asia countries, so taking the square root of coefficients is necessary for simulating the effects of secondary-tertiary test score differences in those countries.

The effects of public sector employment and formality on the odds of over-education are much greater than the effects of test scores. For example, working in the public sector rather than the private sector in Ghana reduces the odds of over-education by 38 percent (that is, 1–0.62). The odds of over-education nearly double for employees working in the informal rather than the formal sector, and nearly triple for self-employed informal workers compared to those in the formal sector. Expressed another way, working in the formal sector reduces the odds of over-education by 50 percent and 66 percent relative to the most common types of informality. All of these effects are much greater than the 11 percent reduction associated with a two-unit (50 point) difference in test scores for Ghana.

The decreased odds of over-education for all tertiary relative to upper secondary graduates ($e^b = 0.64$) (table 6.10, column 2) and the increased odds associated with fewer years of education among tertiary graduates ($e^b = 1.68$) (column 4) also appear stronger than the effect of test scores. Of course, greater reading proficiency is one outcome of educational attainment, so coefficients for the latter partly incorporate the effects of the former. However, it is also important to note that the variation in test scores within education groups remains substantial (see figure 4.4), almost certainly ruling out restriction-of-range issues. Further, insofar as the chief concern regarding usually unobserved heterogeneity is possible test score effects after controlling for formal educational attainment, the models are correctly specified. Job type and tertiary degree type, both of which are easily observed in standard labor force surveys, are much more important in accounting for over-education than test scores, which are usually unobserved.

The results for almost all other countries are closely similar to those for Ghana. Coefficients for test scores are less likely to be significant when added to the baseline model than those for job type and education level, less likely to remain significant in the full model, and imply smaller effects when compared to those coefficients using any reasonable unit of test scores. Regardless of the model, unit differences in test scores are associated with odds of over-education that are 0.86–0.94 as large as otherwise, while public sector employment is associated with odds that are about 0.25 to 0.40 as large in four countries (Colombia, Kenya, Lao PDR, FYR Macedonia) and about 0.50–0.65 as large in seven countries (Armenia, Georgia, Ghana, Vietnam, Sri Lanka, Ukraine, Yunnan Province). Out of the 23 coefficients comparing informal employment and self-employment to jobs in the formal sector, 16 imply that formal jobs are associated with odds of over-education that are about 0.25 to 0.40 as large as those associated with informality and seven imply odds that are about 0.50 to 0.65 as large as those associated with informality.[1] The coefficients for all tertiary and varying years of education within tertiary show a similarly lopsided strength relative to the reading assessment.

The regression models for over-education among all workers confirm the impressions produced by the bivariate tables restricted to tertiary graduates in the previous section. Test scores play a role in explaining over-education. However, what appear more important are formal educational attainment, perhaps reflecting credentialism, signaling/screening, or specific kinds of knowledge in some unknown proportions, and structural labor market conditions reflected in the disadvantages of informal and private sector employment. Although no one would propose policies to grow the public sector in the same way growth of the formal sector is promoted, these results do shed new light on the attractiveness of public sector jobs to job-seekers in developing countries. Whatever other advantages it may hold in terms of pay, benefits, perks, and job security, public sector employment is strongly associated with jobs that are better matched to the education of workers than private sector jobs, as well. In any case, the strong association between over-education and informality in tandem with the weaker association with usually unobserved worker skill levels suggests that most observed mismatch is more genuine than apparent.

The regression results also shed light on the role of search-related and similar transient frictions, worker preferences, and worker health. Young workers are not more likely to be over-educated than prime-age (or well-experienced) workers. There is even some evidence they are *less* likely to be over-educated than workers with the most potential work experience (see table 6.7, columns 3 and 4), perhaps because the latter have more difficulty recovering after recent setbacks, as is known from studies in developed countries (Farber 2005, p.19; Gabriel, Gray, and Goregaokar 2013). Although longitudinal data are needed to draw firmer conclusions, there is no evidence from these data that over-education is characteristic of youthful inexperience and a transient life-cycle phenomenon. Panel data may show that these cross-sectional results mask frequent movement in and out of well-matched jobs as personal circumstances and labor market conditions wax and wane. However, such movement does not appear to be associated with labor market experience sufficiently strongly or simply to appear in this cross-sectional data. Nor is there evidence that over-education reflects primarily imperfect information and search costs falling disproportionately on recent labor market entrants, costs that could resolve themselves with time as people are re-sorted across jobs as they gain work experience.

There is some evidence that gender attitudes and biases contribute to over-education net of household responsibilities, since women without young children have higher odds of over-education than men in some countries. However, the contrasts with men are somewhat stronger for women with young children. By contrast, the direct measure of working part-time by choice is not generally associated with settling for jobs for which one is over-educated net of other predictors. Likewise, chronic health problems do not explain this form of downward mobility in any country.

These results do not settle the question of over-education entirely. Although accounting for usually unobserved worker skills does not alter the picture greatly, there remains the issue of unobserved job skill requirements. If the task content of jobs is tailored to reflect the different education levels of job-holders, mismatch may be more apparent than genuine.

Do Mismatched Tertiary Graduates Perform Tasks Reflecting Their *Education* or Their *Jobs*?

If a significant proportion of tertiary graduates work in jobs that appear to require less education, it is natural to ask whether the actual task content of these positions differs systematically from positions held by less educated workers who report their jobs require the same level of education. Just as there is a distribution of skills within broad categories of personal education, there may be a distribution of required skills among jobs grouped together based on broad categories of required education. If tertiary graduates perform high-skill tasks regardless of the job, then observed over-education may be more apparent than genuine. Finer measures of job skill requirements can shed light on this possibility and overcome the possible coarseness of the job-education categories.

Nevertheless, the question itself raises at least two important issues. The classification of jobs by required education is made by STEP respondents themselves rather than assigned by researchers based on the personal education of workers within occupations, as commonly practiced by studies using standard labor force surveys. Any theory of the cognitive processes by which people make judgments regarding objects recognizes that producing judgments involves some weighting of the object's relevant features, among other things. On this basis alone one would expect that respondents' answers to the questions on the tasks required for their jobs and the education required for their jobs would exhibit a certain level of consistency rather than pointing in very different directions. If tertiary graduates report that their jobs require only a secondary school education, there is presumably some underlying *reason* they do so, and the complexity of the tasks they perform on the job is likely one of the most important reasons. By contrast, researchers' classifying job education requirements typically have no job-specific information on work tasks to guide them, so the relationship between the analysts' choice of categories and the actual task content of the jobs is more of an open question than is the case with STEP's measurement strategy. Therefore, even before conducting analyses, one suspects some built-in association between responses to the items on required education and job tasks, based on plausible theories of the cognitive processes influencing workers' responses to both questions. Expectations that evidence on job task content will cast great doubt on the genuineness of reported over-education are probably unrealistic.

However, the likely dependency between global and facet-specific reports of job skill requirements raises the possibility of artifactual associations. Although motivations behind survey responding are complex, arguing against treating these associations as simply common-method variance is the fact that response biases usually work in the direction of self-enhancing, rather than self-lowering, responses (that is, over-claiming). Self-reports are well-known to produce consistently high estimates of job satisfaction (Handel 2005), for example, so one would not expect reports of job education requirements to be biased in the direction of frustrated hopes and downward mobility, but rather the reverse. Workers have no obvious reason to expose potentially awkward or embarrassing personal situations to questioners. They also know their own jobs better than almost anyone else. Both cognitive and motivational considerations suggest that any self-report implying under-achievement has an a priori claim to be taken seriously, rather than treated as methodological artifacts.

Because tertiary graduates who say their jobs require less than tertiary education probably hold jobs that *are* less skilled than those held by well-matched tertiary graduates, the next question is how much of a gap can be expected and how much counts as a great deal. Clearly, if there were no difference between the tasks performed by mismatched tertiary and well-matched upper secondary graduates there would be no question that over-education is genuine and severe. However, jobs can be expected to offer at least some scope for customization and adaptation according to the characteristics of their occupants, especially in the case of self-employment.

Therefore, just as one would not expect there to be *no* gap in the cognitive complexity of jobs held by well-matched and mismatched tertiary graduates, one would not expect it to be as large as the divide separating jobs of well-matched tertiary and secondary graduates. In terms of table 1.3, job complexity would follow the pattern, cell 5 < cell 8 < cell 9. If personal education and the inherent constraints embedded in a job (such as retail sales) were equally important, then the skill demands of jobs performed by mismatched tertiary workers might be midway between the skill levels of the two adjacent categories of well-matched workers. Alternatively, if one assumes that the combined effects of lower degree level and somewhat lower test scores made some workers with tertiary education an effectively intermediate category, then the skill level of their jobs would be somewhere near the midpoint between the other two groups. It turns out that the task content of jobs held by mismatched tertiary workers is not particularly close to this midpoint in general and much closer to work performed by well-matched secondary workers.

Tables 6.16 through 6.19 use the same definitions of low and high task complexity as tables 4.10 through 4.12, and also suppress values for rates of moderate task complexity, which can be easily calculated by subtracting the sum of the others from 100. Rates of task performance are shown for well-matched upper secondary workers, mismatched tertiary workers, and well-matched tertiary workers. There is generally a strong gradient in task performance, but rates for mismatched tertiary workers are usually close to those for well-matched secondary workers.

For example, table 6.16 shows the percentage of each group in Armenia that only reads short documents as a regular part of their jobs: 86 percent, 75 percent, and 35 percent. The percentage for mismatched tertiary workers is lower than for well-matched secondary workers, but not by a great deal, while the distance between both and well-matched tertiary workers is substantial. For mismatched tertiary workers, the difference in rates is 40 percentage points, and for well-matched upper secondary workers it is 51 percentage points. Consequently, as a group the downwardly mobile have slid 78 percent (= 40/51) of the distance separating the adjacent well-matched groups using this measure of job task content. When calculated for reading long documents at work the "gap ratio" for Armenia is quite similar in magnitude (83 percent). In fact, a gap ratio of about 75 percent is a reasonable summary for almost all countries and indicators of reading, writing, math, and problem-solving tasks performed on the job. Values differing meaningfully from this level are shaded in dark orange for gap ratios below 0.70 and light orange for values that are below 0.50. The latter are more consistent with the view that mismatch is more apparent than genuine but also quite uncommon empirically. Again, the job complexity of mismatched tertiary

Table 6.16 Rates of Reading Complexity, by Match Group and Country
percent

		Reading length				Reading type			
		3, 3	5, 3	5, 5	Gap ratio	3, 3	5, 3	5, 5	Gap ratio
Armenia	Low	86	75	35	0.779	65	64	20	0.973
	High	7	13	43	0.827	12	13	41	0.970
Bolivia	Low	78	65	21	0.773	55	44	9	0.775
	High	12	20	72	0.868	12	23	59	0.771
Colombia	Low	80	73	32	0.850	41	38	14	0.907
	High	12	17	52	0.871	25	32	51	0.753
Georgia	Low	85	86	38	> 1.0	77	75	25	0.964
	High	7	10	46	0.928	10	13	31	0.850
Ghana	Low	68	58	39	0.663	42	24	10	0.429
	High	18	35	48	0.427	23	54	56	0.065
Kenya	Low	72	63	18	0.841	42	26	2	0.592
	High	21	30	74	0.827	26	45	66	0.520
Lao PDR	Low	89	94	56	> 1.0	23	40	2	> 1.0
	High	3	1	17	> 1.0	15	22	68	0.870
Macedonia, FYR	Low	66	50	20	0.643	41	31	6	0.710
	High	22	36	68	0.688	36	46	71	0.727
Sri Lanka	Low	46	51	29	> 1.0	17	6	9	0.380
	High	32	42	47	0.382	60	65	69	0.457
Ukraine	Low	79	74	47	0.860	49	35	12	0.631
	High	11	15	39	0.839	32	39	72	0.836
Vietnam	Low	67	46	24	0.507	34	25	10	0.628
	High	16	39	60	0.471	30	35	57	0.807
Yunnan Province	Low	60	43	24	0.522	16	13	5	0.726
	High	24	36	60	0.670	46	54	64	0.575
Mean	Low	67	60	29	0.726	39	32	10	0.670
	High	14	23	48	0.677	25	34	54	0.631
Median	Low	72	63	29	0.779	41	31	9	0.710
	High	12	20	48	0.827	25	35	59	0.753

Source: World Bank STEP Skills Measurement Program.
Note: Groups are *well-matched upper secondary graduates* (ISCED = 3, job's ISCED = 3), *over-educated tertiary graduates (5,3)*, and *well-matched tertiary (5,5)*, where the first number in parentheses is the ISCED code for worker education and the second is the code for job-required education. The *gap ratio* is the difference in rates of job task performance between well-matched and mismatched tertiary graduates as a proportion of the gap between well-matched tertiary and well-matched upper secondary graduates, e.g., for rates of short document reading on the job in Armenia the gap ratio is (75–35)/(86–35) = 0.79.

graduates is more similar to that of their coworkers (well-matched upper secondary graduates) to the extent the gap ratio approaches 1.0, and more similar to that of their classmates (well-matched tertiary graduates) to the extent the gap ratio approaches zero.

Values for Kenya, Lao PDR, and Sri Lanka must be used with caution because cell sizes are quite small for tertiary graduates in those countries and are presented for the sake of completeness only. Some unusually low ratios, some of which are from these countries, are sufficient to affect the cross-country means

Table 6.17 Rates of Writing and Math Complexity, by Match Group and Country
percent

		Writing length				Math level			
		3, 3	5, 3	5, 5	Gap ratio	3, 3	5, 3	5, 5	Gap ratio
Armenia	Low	69	57	19	0.758	30	24	22	0.276
	High	8	16	44	0.773	6	9	19	0.761
Bolivia	Low	63	49	12	0.720	5	3	15	> 1.0
	High	5	16	61	0.810	6	18	35	0.598
Colombia	Low	67	64	35	0.905	16	16	11	0.940
	High	3	11	33	0.731	10	9	21	> 1.0
Georgia	Low	84	87	41	> 1.0	39	33	32	0.111
	High	1	5	30	0.851	4	6	11	0.649
Ghana	Low	43	27	17	0.375	10	9	14	> 1.0
	High	19	31	46	0.560	3	13	28	0.607
Kenya	Low	59	40	9	0.632	12	9	4	0.630
	High	10	27	61	0.680	3	8	39	0.848
Lao PDR	Low	38	74	15	—	3	4	3	—
	High	2	1	31	> 1.0	22	16	17	—
Macedonia, FYR	Low	61	47	12	0.729	24	16	24	—
	High	14	20	57	0.865	7	7	27	> 1.0
Sri Lanka	Low	42	57	26	> 1.0	18	14	15	0.355
	High	25	4	48	> 1.0	16	20	28	0.713
Ukraine	Low	72	60	21	0.768	17	19	13	> 1.0
	High	8	12	36	0.848	6	8	27	0.904
Vietnam	Low	59	37	20	0.431	5	16	13	0.354
	High	12	25	46	0.608	8	9	30	0.949
Yunnan Province	Low	24	21	4	0.845	16	12	17	—
	High	27	35	60	0.753	7	9	17	0.842
Mean	Low	52	48	18	0.742	15	13	14	0.567
	High	10	16	43	0.790	8	10	23	0.739

Source: World Bank STEP Skills Measurement Program.
Note: Gap ratios that are too anomalous to present are replaced with dashes and not used in calculating means. For other details, see note to table 6.16.

for the reading measures, so medians are also presented in this table. When gap ratios exceed 1.0, suggesting that mismatched tertiary workers are less skilled than well-matched secondary workers for some indicator, the symbol ">1.0" is used to avoid attributing too much significance to the actual value, which may well reflect sampling flukes in countries with few cases in these cells. In certain cases of math use on the job, particularly at the low level, there is too little variation between groups for gap ratios to be meaningful. The measure's discrimination is so low that very small changes in a group's rate can alter the size of the gap ratio dramatically. These rows are shaded gray in table 6.17.

All gap ratios for tables 6.16 through 6.18 are shown in compact form in table 6.19 for convenience. Of the 107 out of 120 values that are valid, 10 (9 percent) are less than 0.50, 9 (8.4 percent) are between 0.50 and 0.60, 14 (13 percent) are between 0.60 and 0.69, and 75 values (70 percent) are 0.70 or above. Average gap

Table 6.18 Rates of Problem-Solving Complexity, by Match Group and Country
percent

		Problem solving			
		3, 3	5, 3	5, 5	Gap ratio
Armenia	Low	57	67	41	> 1.0
	High	31	24	47	> 1.0
Bolivia	Low	45	38	19	0.735
	High	40	52	69	0.591
Colombia	Low	64	51	21	0.708
	High	26	34	64	0.791
Georgia	Low	84	82	55	0.925
	High	11	12	34	0.969
Ghana	Low	57	33	23	0.292
	High	34	51	70	0.531
Kenya	Low	43	34	16	0.654
	High	43	54	74	0.657
Lao PDR	Low	64	91	61	—
	High	11	1	14	—
Macedonia, FYR	Low	48	49	22	> 1.0
	High	46	46	69	> 1.0
Sri Lanka	Low	34	42	21	> 1.0
	High	46	53	67	0.680
Ukraine	Low	60	52	28	0.751
	High	25	36	57	0.647
Vietnam	Low	50	59	37	> 1.0
	High	39	27	54	> 1.0
Yunnan Province	Low	65	67	46	> 1.0
	High	22	15	39	> 1.0
Mean	Low	52	48	30	0.755
	High	29	34	51	0.739

Source: World Bank STEP Skills Measurement Program.
Note: Gap ratios that are too anomalous to present are replaced with dashes and not used in calculating means. For other details, see note to table 6.16.

ratios for most tasks and countries are about 0.75. These figures are not sensitive to alternative scales constructed from the task indicators, such as the percentages performing uniformly low-skill tasks (except math), just one high-skill task, or the numbers of low- and high-skill tasks workers perform. Only in Ghana do mismatched tertiary graduates look consistently like an intermediate category between the two well-matched groups, rather than more similar to the well-matched workers in their job education category.

Measured by what people actually do at work, tertiary workers in jobs requiring only upper secondary education perform more complex tasks than their well-matched coworkers with an upper secondary education, but the over-educated tertiary workers generally close only about one-quarter of the gap between their coworkers and their well-matched tertiary classmates. The character of their work is determined more by their job than by their own education level.

Table 6.19 Gap Ratios for All Task Measures and Means, by Country and Task

		Reading length	Reading type	Writing	Math	Problem solving	Country mean
Armenia	Low	0.779	0.973	0.758	0.276	> 1.0	0.878
	High	0.827	0.970	0.773	0.761	> 1.0	0.866
Bolivia	Low	0.773	0.775	0.720	> 1.0	0.735	0.801
	High	0.868	0.771	0.810	0.598	0.591	0.728
Colombia	Low	0.850	0.907	0.905	0.940	0.708	0.862
	High	0.871	0.753	0.731	> 1.0	0.791	0.829
Georgia	Low	> 1.0	0.964	> 1.0	0.111	0.925	0.972
	High	0.928	0.850	0.851	0.649	0.969	0.900
Ghana	Low	0.663	0.429	0.375	> 1.0	0.292	0.552
	High	0.427	0.065	0.560	0.607	0.531	0.438
Kenya	Low	0.841	0.592	0.632	0.630	0.654	0.680
	High	0.827	0.520	0.680	0.848	0.657	0.706
Lao PDR	Low	> 1.0	> 1.0	—	—	—	1.000
	High	> 1.0	0.870	> 1.0	—	—	0.957
Macedonia, FYR	Low	0.643	0.710	0.729	—	> 1.0	0.771
	High	0.688	0.727	0.865	> 1.0	> 1.0	0.856
Sri Lanka	Low	> 1.0	0.380	> 1.0	0.355	> 1.0	0.845
	High	0.382	0.457	> 1.0	0.713	0.680	0.646
Ukraine	Low	0.860	0.631	0.768	> 1.0	0.751	0.802
	High	0.839	0.836	0.848	0.904	0.647	0.815
Vietnam	Low	0.507	0.628	0.431	0.354	> 1.0	0.642
	High	0.471	0.807	0.608	0.949	> 1.0	0.767
Yunnan Province	Low	0.522	0.726	0.845	—	> 1.0	0.773
	High	0.670	0.575	0.753	0.842	> 1.0	0.768
Mean	Low	0.726	0.670	0.742	0.567	0.755	0.723
	High	0.677	0.631	0.790	0.739	0.739	0.715
Medians	Low	0.779	0.710	0.742	0.567	0.755	0.747
for reading	High	0.827	0.753	0.790	0.739	0.739	0.770

Source: World Bank STEP Skills Measurement Program.

The jobs of mismatched tertiary workers are much closer to those of their coworkers than those of their classmates. Measured over-education among tertiary graduates seems to involve considerable skill underutilization, and in this sense is mostly genuine rather than merely apparent. Given that even most tertiary jobs held by tertiary graduates involve unexpectedly low levels of reading, writing, and math complexity, this conclusion seems a relatively safe one, though the cognitive skill domain is large and this paper does not even exhaust all of the measures available in STEP.

Note

1. This includes the coefficient for informal self-employment in Armenia ($e^b = 1.7$), which is substantively large but significant at the 0.10 level.

References

Farber, Henry S. 2005. "What Do We Know about Job Loss in the United States? Evidence from the Displaced Workers Survey, 1984–2004." *Economic Perspectives* 29: 13–28.

Gabriel, Yiannis, David E. Gray, and Harshita Goregaokar. 2013. "Job Loss and Its Aftermath among Managers and Professionals: Wounded, Fragmented and Flexible." *Work, Employment and Society* 27: 56–72.

Handel, Michael J. 2005. "Trends in Perceived Job Quality, 1989 to 1998." *Work and Occupations* 32: 66–94.

CHAPTER 7

Conclusion

Low- and middle-income countries vary significantly from one another in national income, employment and job-generation education stocks and flows, institutions, and numerous other conditions that affect their productive potential and the extent to which it is realized. Nevertheless, significant proportions of workers in all countries report that the education required for their jobs does not match their own educational level, and this mostly reflects what has been called over-education rather than under-education. It appears that labor markets lag the education system in generating jobs that utilize fully the skills of those seeking employment.

Key findings. Most hypotheses that would render observed mismatch more apparent than genuine receive scant support from the preceding analyses. *Observed mismatch does not seem to be the result of transient life cycle factors.* However, further analyses may reveal that young workers face particular difficulties securing well-matched positions, such as lack of experience and networks, that are masked by other kinds of difficulties faced by prime-age and older workers, such as employer age preferences that hinder rematching after job loss. Indeed this problem may be quite common in low- and middle-income countries due to volatile market conditions. *Health limitations do not account for mismatch among the employed* either, and mismatch does not seem related to preferences for part-time work.

Another hypothetical explanation that receives limited support from this research concerns gender. *While gender predicts over-education in just under half the countries, the interpretation of these effects is ambiguous.* To the extent that gender effects reflect purely personal preferences by workers, they may be less serious than they appear at first sight, but to the extent that they reflect discrimination or even sociocultural norms, they represent genuine mismatch between persons and jobs. The low rate of labor force participation among women in Sri Lanka supports the view that gender disparities represent skill underutilization there, despite the absence of a gender effect among Sri Lankans who are employed.

Test scores are somewhat more consistently related to over-education, but the effect sizes are small. The effects are smaller than those relating to gender, and much smaller than those relating to public sector employment, informality, and years of formal education in the case of tertiary graduates, especially net of these covariates. Thus, differences across workers in achievement or school quality that are usually unobserved account for a modest share of over-education, particularly compared to the roles of formal attainment and structural characteristics of the labor market.

Finally, *the job task profiles found among over-educated tertiary graduates are much closer to the profiles of their coworkers who are well-matched secondary graduates than they are to their classmates, the well-matched tertiary graduates.* Even tertiary graduates in well-matched jobs do not seem to perform tasks that are especially demanding in an absolute sense (see tables 6.16 through 6.18). The balance of evidence suggests strongly that observed over-education is more genuine than apparent and that the biggest source of the problem is a general weakness in private sector formal job creation. At the same time, the roles played by attainment levels within tertiary education and by field of study deserve further research. Scores on STEP's test of general verbal skills may pick up variation in competencies within a specific field of study as well, but a general household survey like STEP (Skills Toward Employment and Productivity) cannot test for such diverse competencies and skill sets directly. Country education agencies and sector skills councils will need to devise such assessments to determine whether it is poor learning outcomes in specific fields of study that is driving mismatch, particularly for those with lower-level tertiary degrees. Likewise, both the descriptive and the analytical results for test scores provide concrete indication of the benefits of raising achievement levels, though it is also important to note test scores vary widely within education levels and test score distributions by education level overlap one another significantly. Test scores are not clustered tightly within education levels nor are they separated cleanly across education levels. Research provides no clear guidance regarding how much of this variation stems from problems with educational effectiveness as opposed to being "normal" or inevitable variation.

Although everyone agrees that improving the quality of education is a necessary and ongoing task, there seems little doubt that the productive potential of a significant proportion of persons desiring skilled work remains unrealized in developing countries. Slack job markets are a key driver, as is apparent from the prevalence of informal workers, particularly those creating their own jobs (the self-employed), as well as from the numbers of unemployed and nonworking discouraged workers in certain countries in Europe and Central Asia.

Caveats. An important qualification to this conclusion is that the STEP study, like any study, is unable to measure every relevant personal and job characteristic. The workers who appear to have more education than required for their jobs may be under-skilled in ways that are difficult to measure in a standard survey. Curricula may be shallow and lack relevance for the job market. Neither achievement within fields of study nor competencies in highly occupation-specific skills were measured by STEP, and indeed they would be difficult to measure in any general survey. There are also intangible, tacit skills and knowledge that can make a great difference to a worker's job performance but are nearly impossible to measure in a survey; this report also did not consider the role of noncognitive skills and personality characteristics on employment outcomes. Clearly, there is a role for education policy with respect to a number of these variables, though addressing others would be more challenging.

Likewise, STEP's job task measures do not cover every imaginable aspect of the work people perform. Few studies are able to eliminate bias due to omitted variables, and conclusions should be interpreted in this light. Nevertheless, there is a great deal of informality and self-employment in most STEP countries, both of which are strongly associated with over-education (see tables 4.8 and 6.4). Unless worker quality is so low that this is considered effective matching, these results seem to support the main conclusion that STEP countries have more problems generating jobs than graduates, even if there is much work to be done on the education side as well.

While everyone has long known that not all graduates work in jobs that match their education, the STEP surveys provide estimates of mismatch levels that can be used to understand the extent of mismatch, track progress over time through replication, and benchmark levels and trends internationally. The STEP suite of measures includes controls for usually unobserved characteristics of workers and jobs that address the doubts often expressed regarding the validity of more indirect methods for estimating mismatch rates. Combined with more standard labor force survey variables, STEP measures also shed light on the underlying drivers of education mismatch.

Although the search for additional innovative measures to address knowledge gaps must continue, the results in this STEP report represent important progress toward that goal and provide key indicators and benchmarks against which national progress, policy effectiveness, and development approaches can be monitored and evaluated.

Implications. The results have implications for broader policy orientations, as well. Although more and better education is a common prescription for development, education and training do not create or guarantee more and better jobs in themselves. High rates of self-employment and other forms of informality suggest that good jobs that utilize existing workforce skills are in short supply. This may reflect some combination of weak investment, unattractive business conditions, low levels of overall economic activity, and/or the quality of institutions and general social conditions. It is also important to recall that demand for labor is derived from the demand for products and services. Domestic demand will be relatively concentrated on relatively simple and inexpensive goods and services produced with low-cost methods, because this is what is affordable for other workers in similar circumstances. Low purchasing power is a significant source of informality, which is itself a source of mismatch. Generally higher living standards are necessary for people to be able to afford higher value-added goods and services produced with more skilled labor. However, higher living standards require that these kinds of jobs be plentiful in the first place, that is, countries need many high-skilled jobs to support the consumption of goods/services that are produced by high-skilled jobs.

Not surprisingly, an export orientation can be seen as one way out of this trap, because it relies mostly on external demand from countries that are already developed to support creation of more and better jobs domestically. That in turn may initiate the virtuous circle of workers in more skilled jobs demanding goods and services produced domestically by other workers in skilled jobs. It may be possible also to move up the value chain based on building up internal demand alone or in combination with trade involving other developing countries. However, perhaps more important is the possibility that such movement involving export-oriented manufacturing may not require notably high levels of education. For many developing countries, manufacturing jobs paying wages that are high relative to prevailing levels may be partly decoupled from traits acquired through schooling beyond general cognitive and literacy skills and reliable work habits. Many relatively high-wage jobs that are most easily within reach for many developing countries need not be high-skilled in terms of formal education and training.

Nothing in the preceding contradicts the development goal that all countries provide universal, high-quality upper secondary education to all young people, not only to impart job-relevant skills but to promote individual well-being and civic engagement as well as to provide a foundation for further socioeconomic advancement in subsequent generations. All countries need tertiary graduates for government functions, such as public administration and civil engineering, and for management of modern enterprises, among other tasks. However, tertiary education is significantly more costly and raises complex issues. Although many stakeholders place great hope in tertiary education, we still do not know the extent to which prior abundance of workers with higher education can prime the pump of occupational upgrading by attracting or enabling its own employment in well-matched jobs, as opposed to remaining unused or underutilized due to the low absorptive capacity of a labor market without an upgrading process that is already established. While it is possible that improved education in STEP countries can jump-start development on its own, the country conditions discussed in chapter 4 suggest most face multiple barriers to improved employment outcomes and improving education alone may not solve them to the extent assumed.

While many of these educational policy issues are beyond the scope of the present report, it should be clear that skills are only one ingredient in a complex mix of factors affecting the quality of employment, not a cure-all. Policy makers cannot assume that all employment problems can be addressed through education alone. The education system and job market are two related but distinct institutional spheres: although they must work in tandem, they may also be independent sources of difficulties. Job market woes can reflect job market problems and not problems with the education system. Any study of mismatch must address this question, that is, whether the main problem is a scarcity of qualified workers or, alternatively, a scarcity of good jobs, using direct and detailed measures of both workers and jobs.

The results of this study suggest that many countries are not reaping as much benefit from their investments in education as they might, because weak job creation leaves the skills of many workers underutilized. For individuals, over-education represents downward mobility relative to their expectations when they chose to enter noncompulsory education. Although weak job creation may partly reflect the level of workforce skills, it is clear that other variables are critical as well, such as government policy, capital availability, investment climate, and deficient demand.

A possible qualification to the preceding is that relatively high rates of over-education for tertiary graduates are common in higher-income countries as well. It is possible that the phenomenon of attainment outrunning opportunities is general and perhaps unavoidable. Additional, explicitly comparative research is needed to address this question. Nevertheless, the leakage of tertiary graduates from high-skill jobs is particularly worrisome for low- and middle-income countries that have more difficulty affording the investment costs and greater need for the benefits of high-skilled workers matched to high-skill jobs.

References

Allen, J. and R. van der Velden. 2001. "Educational Mismatches versus Skill Mismatches: Effects on Wages, Job Satisfaction, and On-the-Job Search." *Oxford Economic Papers* 53: 434–52.

Battu, H., C. Belfield, and P. Sloane. 2000. "How Well Can We Measure Graduate Over-Education and Its Effects?" *National Institute Economic Review* 171: 82–93.

Blau, Peter M., and Otis Dudley Duncan. 1967. *The American Occupational Structure*. New York: Wiley and Sons.

Büchel, Felix, Andries de Grip, and Antje Merten. 2003. *Overeducation in Europe: Current Issues in Theory and Policy*. Cheltenham, UK: Edward Elgar.

Cain, Pamela S., and Donald J. Treiman. 1981. "The *Dictionary of Occupational Titles* as a Source of Occupational Data." *American Sociological Review* 46: 253–78.

Carneiro, P., C. Crawford, and A. Goodman. 2007. "The Impact of Early Cognitive and Non-cognitive Skills on Later Outcomes." Discussion Paper 0092, Centre for the Economics of Education, London School of Economics, London.

CEDEFOP. 2015. "Skills, Qualifications and Jobs in the EU: The Making of a Perfect Match? Evidence from Cedefop's European Skills and Jobs Survey." CEDEFOP reference series 103, Publications Office of the European Union, Luxembourg. http://dx.doi.org/10.2801/606129.

Davidov, Eldad, Bart Meuleman, Jan Cieciuch, Peter Schmidt, and Jaak Billiet. 2014. "Measurement Equivalence in Cross-National Research." *Annual Review of Sociology* 40: 55–75.

de Grip, Andries, Hans Bosma, Dick Willems, and Martin van Boxtel. 2008. "Job-Worker Mismatch and Cognitive Decline." *Oxford Economic Papers* 60: 237–53.

Deaton, Angus. 2005. "Measuring Poverty in a Growing World (or Measuring Growth in a Poor World)." *Review of Economics and Statistics* 87 (1): 1–19.

Deaton, Angus, and Alan Heston. 2008. "Understanding PPPs and PPP-based National Accounts." Paper w14499, National Bureau of Economic Research, Cambridge, MA.

Duncan, G., and S. Hoffman. 1981. "The Incidence and Wage Effects of Overeducation." *Economics of Education Review* 1: 57–68.

European Social Survey. 2010. *ESS Round 5 Source Questionnaire*. London: Centre for Comparative Social Surveys, City University London.

Farber, Henry S. 2005. "What Do We Know about Job Loss in the United States? Evidence from the Displaced Workers Survey, 1984–2004." *Economic Perspectives* 29: 13–28.

Fernandez, Roberto M. 2001. "Skill-Biased Technological Change and Wage Inequality: Evidence from a Plant Retooling." *American Journal of Sociology* 107: 273–320.

Freeman, Richard B. 1976. *The Overeducated American*. New York: Academic Press.

Gabriel, Yiannis, David E. Gray, and Harshita Goregaokar. 2013. "Job Loss and Its Aftermath among Managers and Professionals: Wounded, Fragmented and Flexible." *Work, Employment and Society* 27: 56–72.

Green, Francis, and Yu Zhu. 2010. "Overqualification, Job Dissatisfaction, and Increasing Dispersion in the Returns to Graduate Education." *Oxford Economic Papers* 62: 740–63.

Guvenen, Faith, Burhan Kuruscu, Satoshi Tanaka, and David Wiczer. 2015. "Multidimensional Skills Mismatch." Federal Reserve Bank of Minneapolis Research Department Working Paper 729, Federal Reserve Bank of Minneapolis, Minneapolis, MN. https://www.minneapolisfed.org/research/wp/wp729.pdf

Handel, Michael J., ed. 2003a. *The Sociology of Organizations*. Thousand Oaks, CA: SAGE Publications.

———. 2003b. "Skills Mismatch in the Labor Market." *Annual Review of Sociology* 29: 135–65.

———. 2005a. "Trends in Perceived Job Quality, 1989 to 1998." *Work and Occupations* 32: 66–94.

———. 2005b. *Worker Skills and Job Requirements: Is There a Mismatch?* Washington, DC: Economic Policy Institute.

———. 2008. "Measuring Job Content: Skills, Technology, and Management Practices." Discussion Paper 1357-08, University of Wisconsin, Institute for Research on Poverty, Madison, WI.

———. 2015a. "Measuring Job Content: Skills, Technology, and Management Practices." In *Oxford Handbook of Skills and Training*, edited by John Buchanan, David Finegold, Ken Mayhew, and Chris Warhurst. Oxford: Oxford University Press.

———. 2015b. *Methodological Issues Related to the Occupational Requirements Survey*. Report to the Bureau of Labor Statistics. Washington, DC: Department of Labor. www.bls.gov/ncs/ors/handel_report_feb15.pdf

———. Forthcoming. "What Do People Do at Work? A Profile of U.S. Jobs from the Survey of Workplace Skills, Technology, and Management Practices (STAMP)." In *Job Tasks, Work Skills and the Labour Market*, edited by Francis Green and Mark Keese. Paris: Organisation for Economic Co-operation and Development (OECD).

Hartog, Joop. 2000. "Over-Education and Earnings: Where Are We, Where Should We Go?" *Economics of Education Review* 19: 131–47.

Harvey, Robert J. 1991. "Job Analysis." In *Handbook of Industrial and Organizational Psychology*, edited by Marvin D. Dunnette and Leaetta M. Hough, 71–163. Palo Alto, CA: Consulting Psychologists Press.

Hauser, Robert M., and Carol L. Roan. 2007. "Work Complexity and Cognitive Functioning at Midlife: Cross-Validating the Kohn-Schooler Hypothesis in an

American Cohort." Unpublished manuscript, Center for Demography and Ecology, University of Wisconsin-Madison, Madison, WI.

Heckman, J. J., J. Stixrud, and S. Urzua. 2006. "The Effects of Cognitive and Noncognitive Abilities on Labor Market Outcomes and Social Behavior." Paper w12006, National Bureau of Economic Research, Cambridge, MA.

Herrera, Javier, and Sébastien Merceron. 2013. "Underemployment and Job Mismatch in Sub-Saharan Africa." In *Urban Labor Markets in Sub-Saharan Africa*, edited by Philippe De Vreyer and François Roubaud, 83–107. Washington, DC: World Bank.

Jerven, Morten. 2013. "Poor Numbers: How We Are Misled by African Development Statistics and What to Do about It." Ithaca, NY: Cornell University Press.

Jones, Melanie K., Kostas G. Mavromaras, Peter J. Sloane, and Zhang Wei. 2014. "Disability and Job Mismatches in the Australian Labour Market." *Cambridge Journal of Economics* 38: 1221–46.

Juárez, Fatima, and Cecilia Gayet. 2014. "Transitions to Adulthood in Developing Countries." *Annual Review of Sociology* 40: 521–38.

Kalleberg, Arne L. 2006. *The Mismatched Worker*. New York: W. W. Norton & Company.

Kirsch, Irwin S., John de Jong, Dominique LaFontaine, Joy McQueen, Juliette Mendelovits, and Christian Monseur. 2002. *Reading for Change: Performance and Engagement across Countries—Results from PISA 2000*. Paris: Organisation for Economic Co-operation and Development.

Klare, George R. 1974–1975. "Assessing Readability." *Reading Research Quarterly* 10: 62–102.

Kohn, Melvin L., and Carmi Schooler. 1983. *Work and Personality: An Inquiry Into the Impact of Social Stratification*. Norwood, NJ: Ablex Pub. Corp.

La Porta, Rafael, and Andrei Shleifer. 2014. "Informality and Development. "*Journal of Economic Perspectives* 28 (3): 109–26.

Leuven, E., and H. Oosterbeek. 2011. "Overeducation and Mismatch in the Labor Market." In *Handbook of the Economics of Education*, edited by E. Hanushek and F. Welch, 283–326. Philadelphia: Elsevier Science.

Maier, Mark H., and Jennifer Imazeki. 2013. *The Data Game: Controversies in Social Science Statistics*. 4th ed. Armonk, NY: M.E. Sharpe.

Mbaye, Ahmadou Aly, Benjamin, Nancy Claire, and Stephen Golub. 2015. "How the Interplay Between Large and Small Informal Firms Affects Jobs in West Africa." World Bank *Jobs and Development* blog, retrieved March 4, 2015. http://blogs.worldbank.org/jobs/how-interplay-between-large-and-small-informal-firms-affects-jobs-west-africa.

Mehta, Aashish, Jesus Felipe, Pilipinas Quising, and Sheila Camingue. 2011. "Overeducation in Developing Economies: How Can We Test for It, and What Does It Mean?" *Economics of Education Review* 30: 1334–47.

Modestino, Alicia Sasser, Daniel Shoag, and Joshua Balance. 2015. "Upskilling: Do Employers Demand Greater Skill When Workers Are Plentiful?" Unpublished manuscript.

Mosenthal, Peter B, and Irwin S. Kirsch. 1998."A New Measure for Assessing Document Complexity: The PMOSE/IKIRSCH Document Readability Formula." *Journal of Adolescent and Adult Literacy* 41: 638–57.

Oreopoulos, Philip, and Kjell G. Salvanes. 2011. "Priceless: The Nonpecuniary Benefits of Schooling." *Journal of Economic Perspectives* 25: 159–84.

Organisation for Economic Co-operation and Development. 2013. *OECD Skills Outlook 2013—First Results from the Survey of Adult Skills*. Paris: Organisation for Economic Co-operation and Development.

Oswald, Frederick, John Campbell, Rod McCloy, David Rivkin, and Phil Lewis. 1999. "Stratifying Occupational Units by Specific Vocational Preparation (SVP)." Raleigh, NC: National Center for O*NET Development, Employment Security Commission.

Peterson, Norman G., Michael D. Mumford, Walter C. Borman, P. Richard Jeanneret, and Edwin A. Fleishman. 1999. *An Occupational Information System for the 21st Century: The Development of O*NET*. Washington, DC: American Psychological Association.

Portes, Alejandro and William Haller. 2005. "The Informal Economy." In *Handbook of Economic Sociology*, edited by Neil J. Smelser and Richard Swedberg, 403–25. Princeton, NJ: Princeton University Press.

Quinn, Michael A., and Stephen Rubb. 2006. "Mexico's Labor Market: The Importance of Education-Occupation Matching on Wages and Productivity in Developing Countries." *Economics of Education Review* 25: 147–56.

Quintini, Glenda. 2011. "Over-Qualified or Under-Skilled: A Review of Existing Literature." *OECD Social, Employment and Migration Working Papers*, 121, OECD Publishing. http://dx.doi.org/10.1787/5kg58j9d7b6d-en.

Ravallion, Martin. 2010. Comment. *American Economic Journal: Macroeconomics* 2 (4): 46–52.

Schooler, Carmi, Mesfin Samuel Mulatu, and Gary Oates. 1999. "The Continuing Effects of Substantively Complex Work on the Intellectual Functioning of Older Workers." *Psychology and Aging* 14: 483–506.

Scribner, Sylvia. 1986. "Thinking in Action: Some Characteristics of Practical Thought." In *Practical Intelligence: Nature and Origins of Competence in the Everyday World*, edited by Robert J. Sternberg and Richard K. Wagner, 13–30. London: Cambridge University Press.

Sloane, Peter J. 2003. "Much Ado about Nothing? What Does the Overeducation Literature Really Tell Us?" In *Overeducation in Europe*, edited by Felix Büchel, Andries de Grip, and Antje Merten, 11–48. Northampton, MA: Edward Elgar.

Smart, Emily L., Alan J. Gow, and Ian J. Deary. 2014. "Occupational Complexity and Lifetime Cognitive Abilities." *Neurology* 83: 2285–91.

Smith, J. and F. Welch. 1978. "The Overeducated American: A Review Article." RAND P-6253, RAND, Santa Monica, CA.

Stasz, Catherine. 2001. "Assessing Skills for Work: Two Perspectives." *Oxford Economic Papers* 53: 385–405.

Tsang, M. 1987. "The Impact of Underutilisation of Education on Productivity: A Case Study of the US Bell Companies." *Economics of Education Review* 6: 239–54.

U.S. Department of Labor. 1991. *Dictionary of Occupational Titles*. 4th ed. Revised. Washington, DC: U.S. Government Printing Office.

van Schuur, Wijbrandt H. 2011. *Ordinal Item Response Theory: Mokken Scale Analysis*. Thousand Oaks, CA: SAGE Publications.

Verhaest, D., and E. Omey. 2006. "The Impact of Overeducation and Its Measurement." *Social Indicators Research* 77: 419–48.

Verhofstadt, E., H. De Witte, and E. Omey. 2007. "The Impact of Education on Job Satisfaction in the First Job." *International Journal of Manpower* 28: 135–51.

APPENDIX A

Conditional Distributions of Worker and Required Education

Figure A.1 Lao PDR Row and Column Percentages

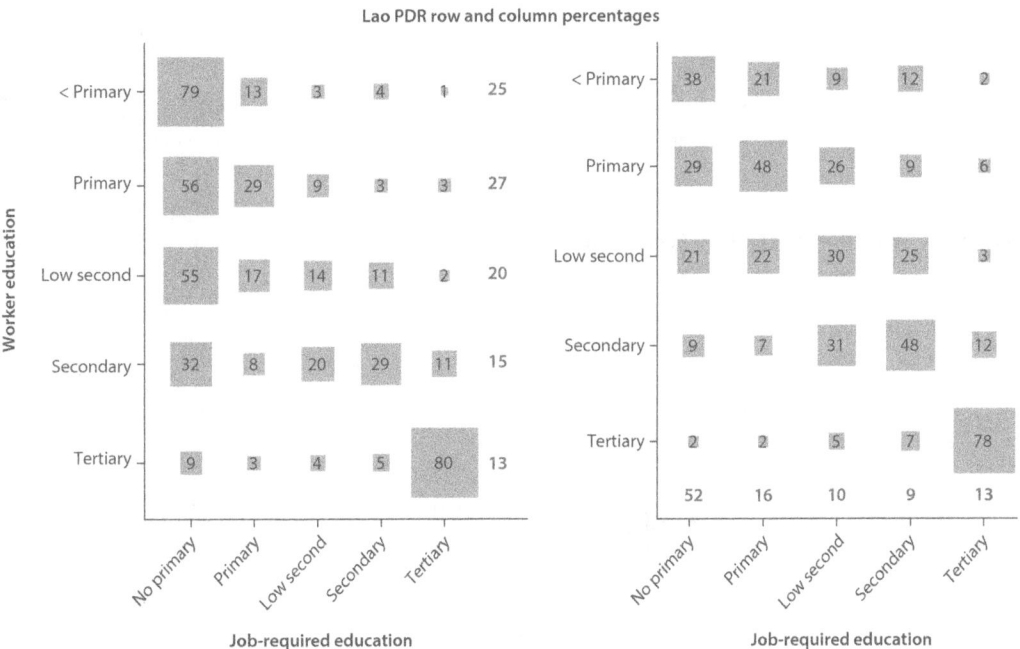

Note: Numbers in blue show the marginal distribution.

Figure A.2 Ghana Row and Column Percentages

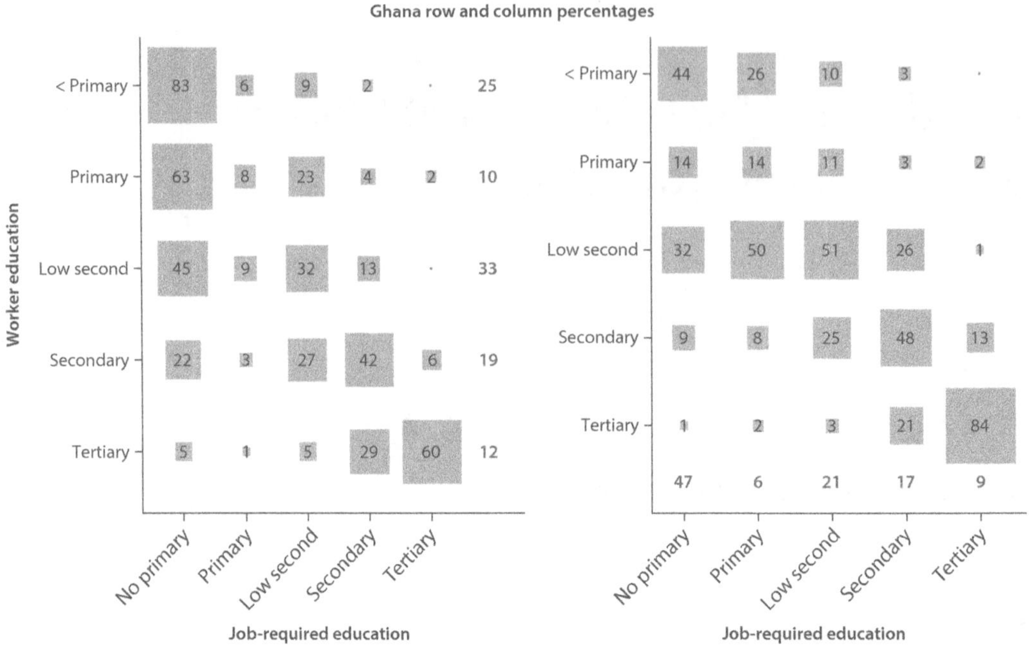

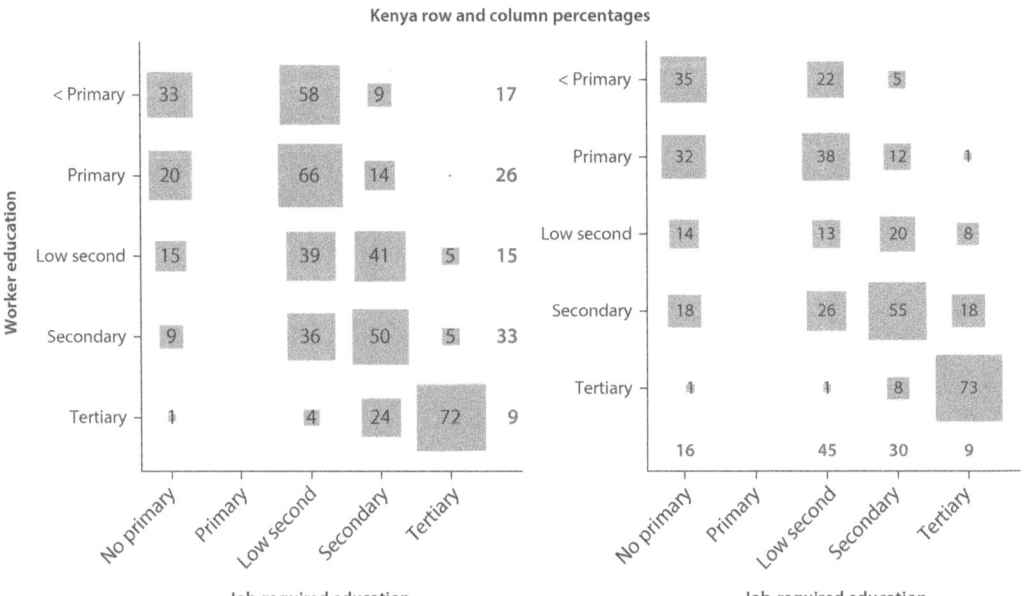

Note: Numbers in blue show the marginal distribution. Dark gray dots indicate figures that fall below 1 percent after rounding.

Figure A.3 Kenya Row and Column Percentages

Note: Numbers in blue show the marginal distribution. Dark gray dots indicate figures that fall below 1 percent after rounding.

Conditional Distributions of Worker and Required Education

Figure A.4 Bolivia Row and Column Percentages

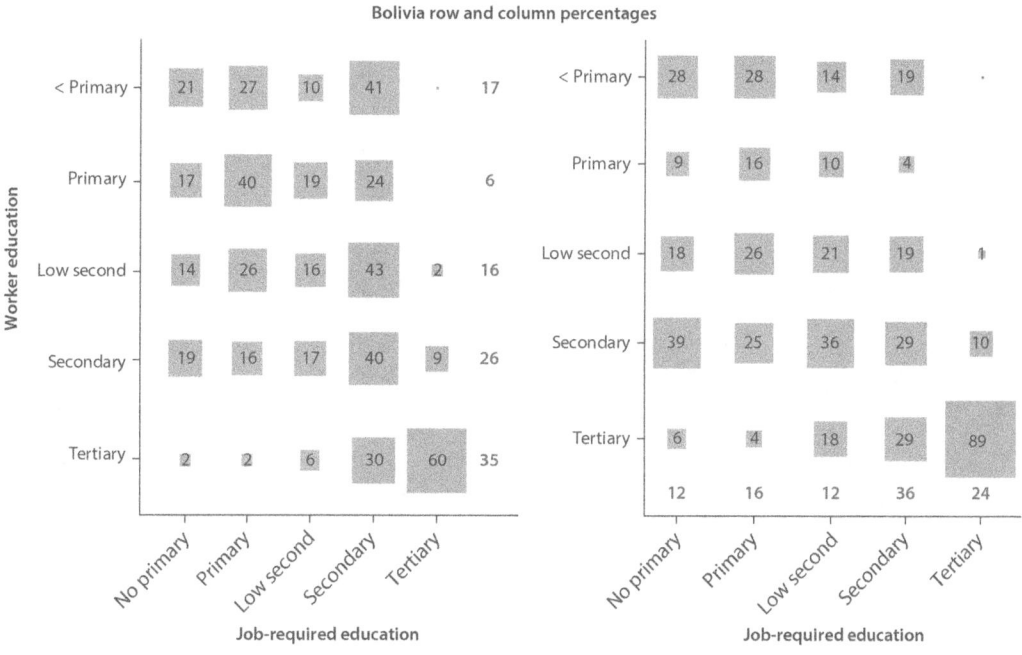

Note: Numbers in blue show the marginal distribution. Dark gray dots indicate figures that fall below 1 percent after rounding.

Figure A.5 Vietnam Row and Column Percentages

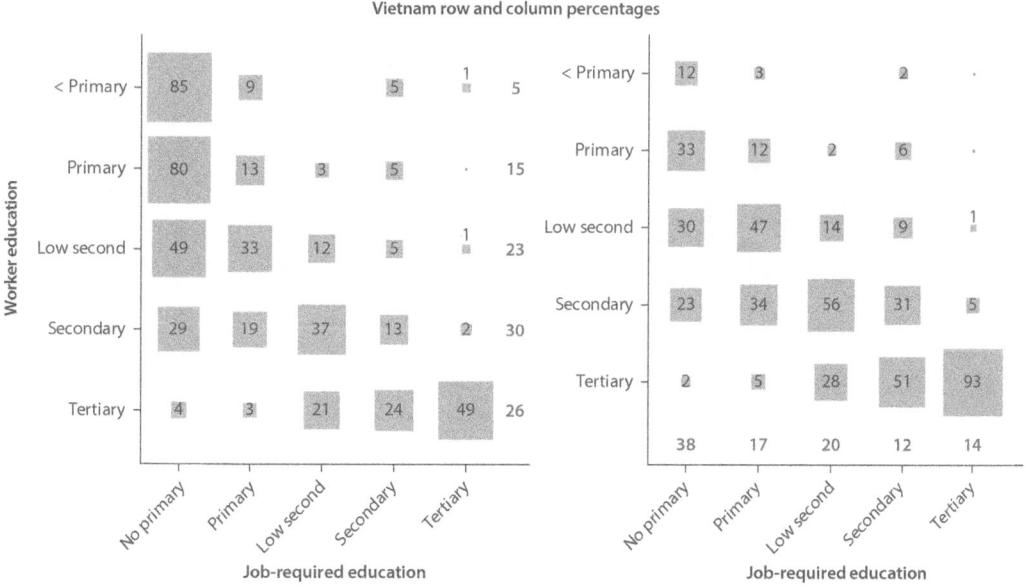

Note: Numbers in blue show the marginal distribution. Dark gray dots indicate figures that fall below 1 percent after rounding.

Figure A.6 Sri Lanka Row and Column Percentages

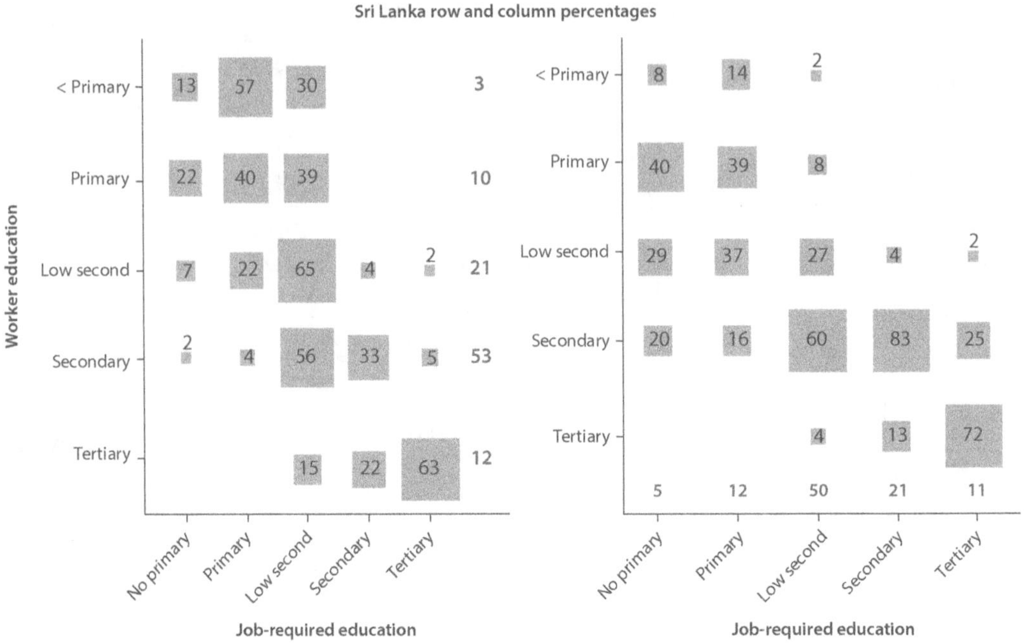

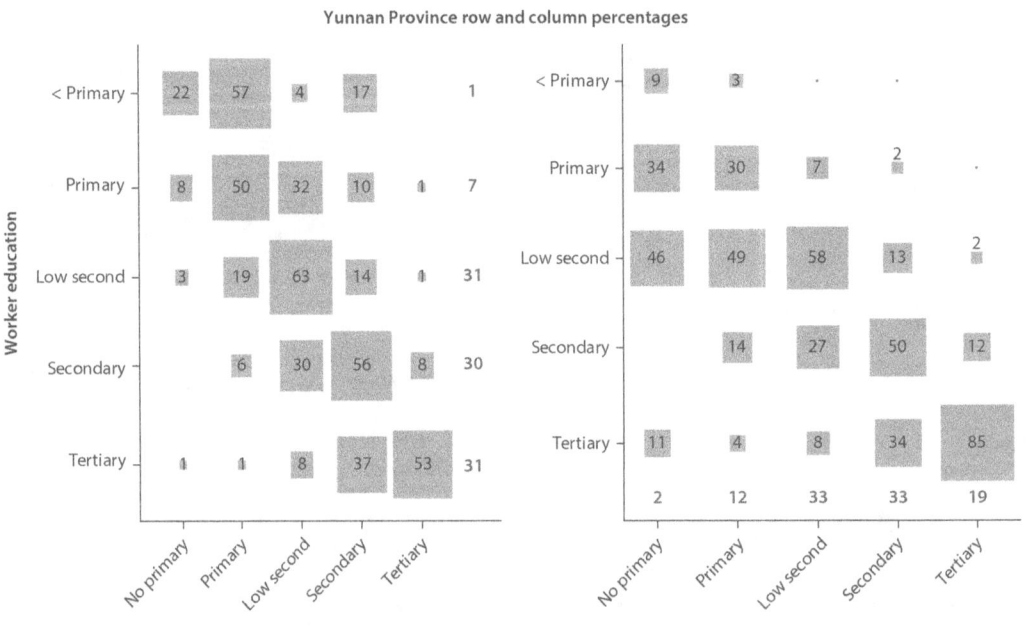

Note: Numbers in blue show the marginal distribution. Dark gray dots indicate figures that fall below 1 percent after rounding.

Figure A.7 Yunnan Province Row and Column Percentages

Note: Numbers in blue show the marginal distribution. Dark gray dots indicate figures that fall below 1 percent after rounding.

Conditional Distributions of Worker and Required Education 123

Figure A.8 Armenia Row and Column Percentages

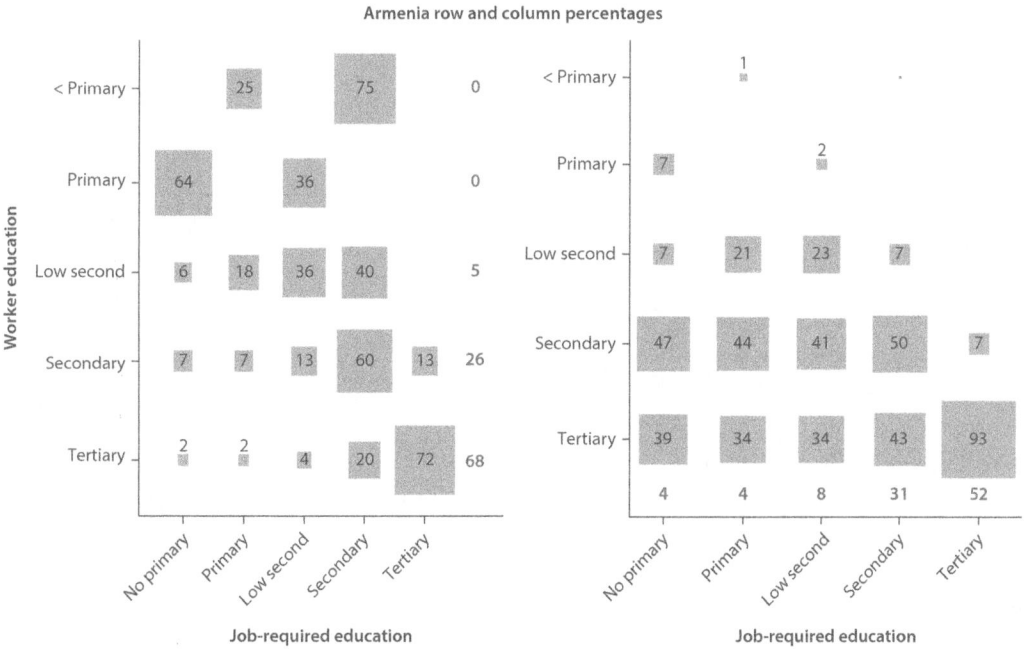

Note: Numbers in blue show the marginal distribution. Dark gray dots indicate figures that fall below 1 percent after rounding.

Figure A.9 Macedonia, FYR, Row and Column Percentages

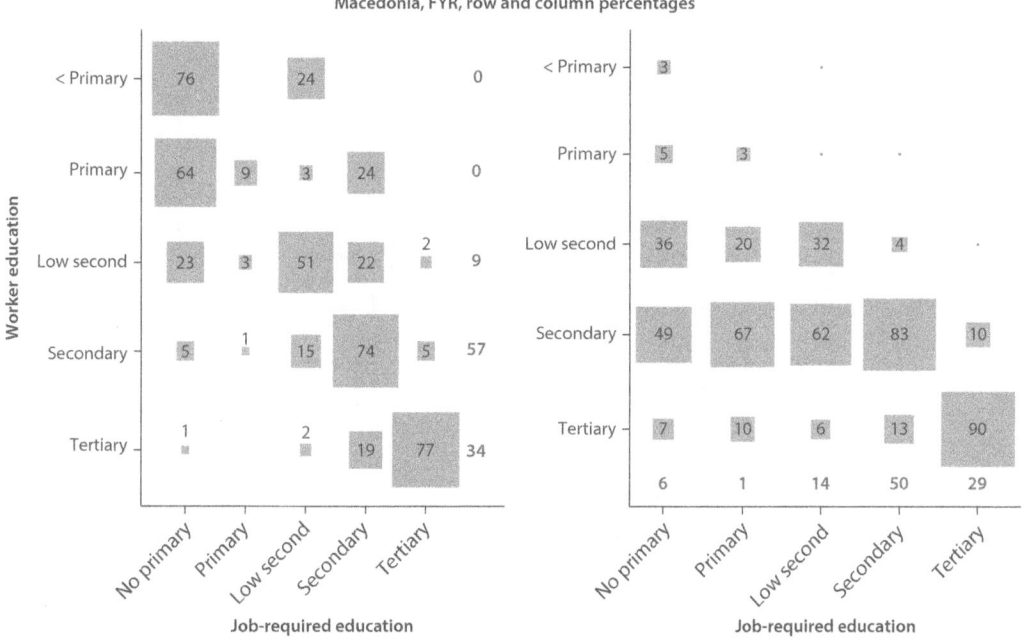

Note: Numbers in blue show the marginal distribution. Dark gray dots indicate figures that fall below 1 percent after rounding.

Accounting for Mismatch in Low- and Middle-Income Countries
http://dx.doi.org/10.1596/978-1-4648-0908-8

Figure A.10 Georgia Row and Column Percentages

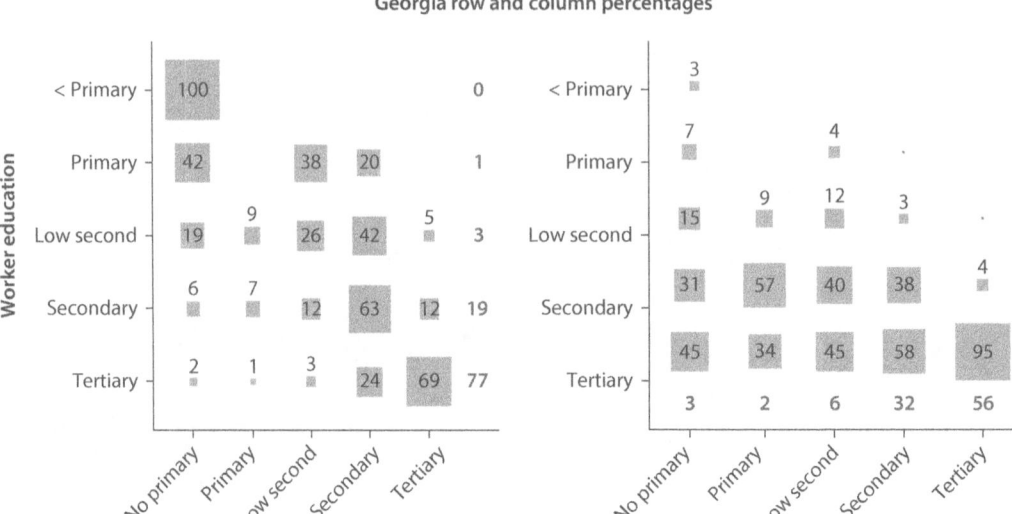

Note: Numbers in blue show the marginal distribution. Dark gray dots indicate figures that fall below 1 percent after rounding.

Figure A.11 Ukraine Row and Column Percentages

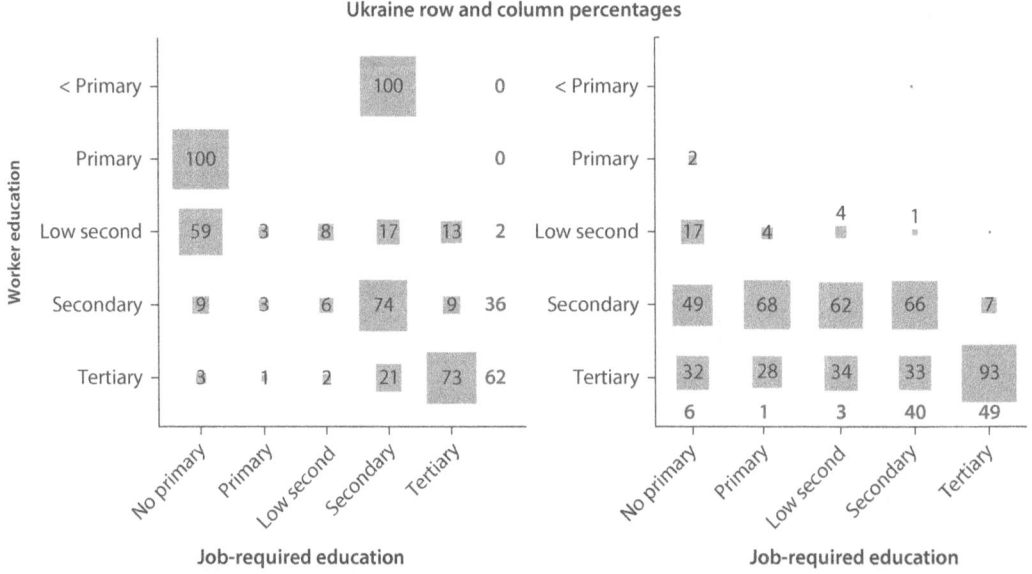

Note: Numbers in blue show the marginal distribution. Dark gray dots indicate figures that fall below 1 percent after rounding.

APPENDIX B

Conditional Distributions of Job Education by Worker Education for Workers with Less than Upper Secondary Education

Row percentages sum to ~100.

Figure B.1 Distribution of Job-Required Education for Workers with Less than Primary Education

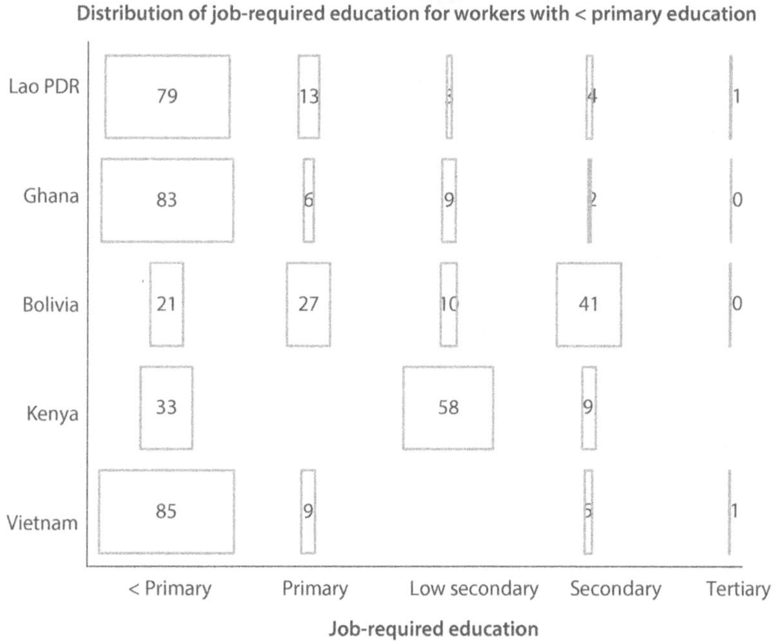

Distribution of job-required education for workers with < primary education

Country	< Primary	Primary	Low secondary	Secondary	Tertiary
Lao PDR	79	13	3	4	1
Ghana	83	6	9	2	0
Bolivia	21	27	10	41	0
Kenya	33		58	9	
Vietnam	85	9		5	1

Job-required education

Accounting for Mismatch in Low- and Middle-Income Countries
http://dx.doi.org/10.1596/978-1-4648-0908-8

Figure B.2 Distribution of Job-Required Education for Workers with Primary Education

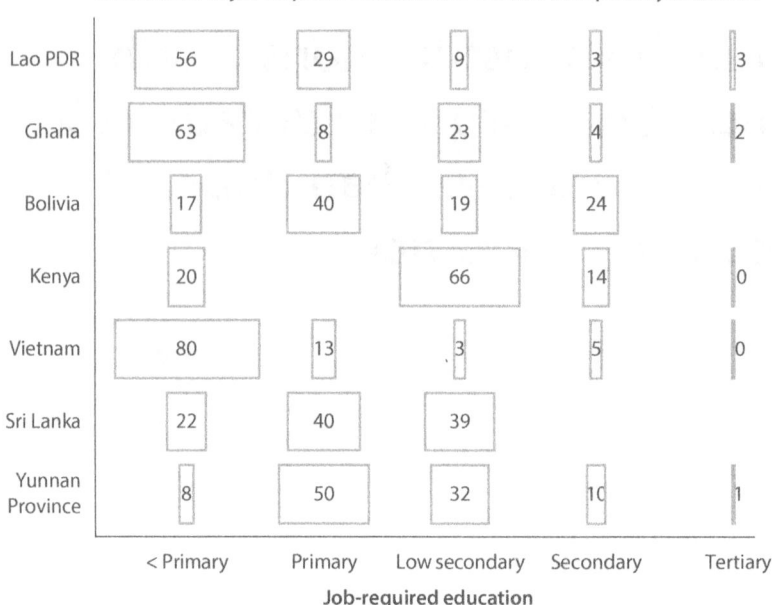

Figure B.3 Distribution of Job-Required Education for Workers with Low Secondary Education

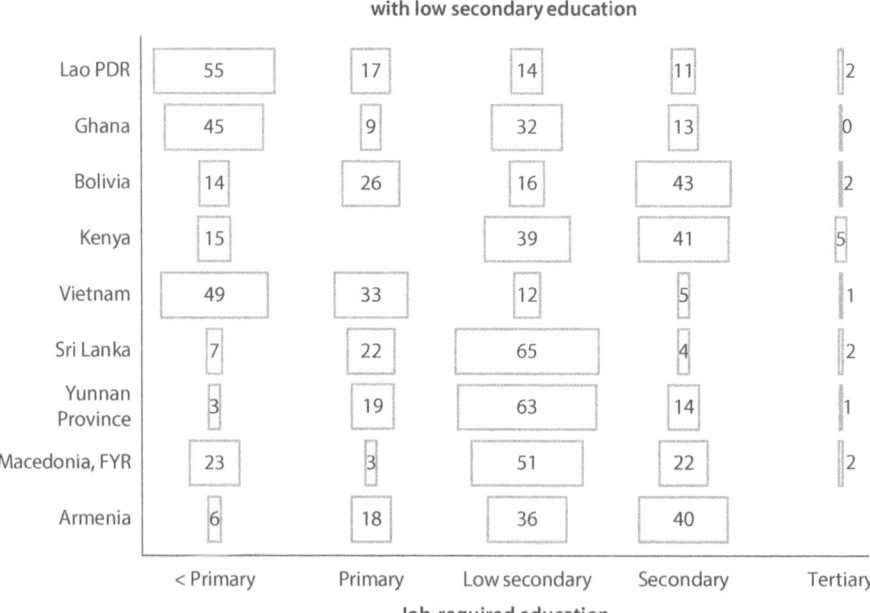

APPENDIX C

Summary of Logistic Regression Results with Country Labels

Table C.1 Summary of Logistic Regression Results with Country Labels

		Baseline	Literacy	No literacy	All
Under-education					
Experience	10–29 years			Bolivia, Ghana	Bolivia, Ghana
<10 years = 0					
	30+ years			Bolivia, Ghana	Bolivia, Ghana
Male = 0	Female, no young kids			Ghana	Ghana
	Female, young kids			Ghana	Ghana
	Voluntary part-time			Colombia, Ghana	Colombia, Ghana
	Health problem			(Sri Lanka)	
Private = 0	Public sector			Kenya	Kenya
Formal = 0	Informal employee			Bolivia, Colombia, Ghana, Kenya, Lao PDR	Bolivia, Colombia, Ghana, Kenya
	Informal self-employed			Bolivia, Kenya, Lao PDR	Bolivia, Kenya
	Informal family			Kenya	Kenya
ISCED	< Primary (ISCED 0)	Bolivia, Colombia, Kenya, Sri Lanka, Yunnan Province	Bolivia, Colombia, Kenya	Bolivia, Colombia, Ghana, Kenya	Bolivia, Colombia, Ghana, Kenya
Upper sec = 0					
ISCED 1	Primary	Bolivia, Colombia, Ghana, Kenya, Vietnam, Sri Lanka, Yunnan Province	Bolivia, Colombia, Ghana, Kenya, Vietnam, Yunnan Province	Bolivia, Colombia, Ghana, Kenya, Vietnam, Lao PDR	Bolivia, Colombia, Ghana, Kenya, Vietnam
ISCED 2	Low secondary	Bolivia, Colombia, Ghana, Kenya, Vietnam, Yunnan Province	Bolivia, Colombia, Ghana, Kenya, Vietnam, Yunnan Province	Bolivia, Colombia, Ghana, Kenya, Vietnam, Lao PDR	Bolivia, Colombia, Ghana, Kenya, Vietnam
	Literacy (1 = 25 pts.)				

table continues next page

Table C.1 **Summary of Logistic Regression Results with Country Labels** *(continued)*

		Baseline	Literacy	No literacy	All
Over-education					
Experience	10–29 years				
	30+ years			(Bolivia; Ghana; Sri Lanka; Macedonia, FYR)	(Ghana)
	Female, no young kids			Ghana, Vietnam, (Georgia)	Ghana, Vietnam, Ukraine, (Georgia)
	Female, young kids			Bolivia, Ghana, Kenya, Lao PDR, Ukraine	Bolivia, Ghana, Ukraine
	Voluntary part-time			Kenya	Kenya
	Health problem				
	Public sector			Colombia; Ghana; Kenya; Vietnam; Sri Lanka; Lao PDR; Yunnan Province; Armenia; Georgia; Ukraine; Macedonia, FYR	Colombia, Ghana, Kenya, Vietnam, Armenia, Georgia, Ukraine
	Informal employee			Bolivia; Colombia; Ghana; Kenya; Vietnam; Sri Lanka; Lao PDR; Yunnan Province, Armenia; Georgia; Macedonia, FYR	Bolivia, Colombia, Ghana, Kenya, Vietnam, Armenia, Georgia
	Informal self-employed			Bolivia; Colombia; Ghana; Kenya; Vietnam; Sri Lanka; Lao PDR; Yunnan Province; Georgia; Ukraine; Macedonia, FYR	Bolivia, Colombia, Ghana, Kenya, Vietnam, Georgia, Ukraine
	Informal family			Bolivia; Ghana; Vietnam; Lao PDR; Yunnan Province; Georgia	Bolivia, Ghana, Georgia
ISCED 1	Primary	Colombia, Ghana, Kenya, Sri Lanka, Yunnan Province	Bolivia, Colombia, Ghana, Kenya	Bolivia, Colombia, Ghana, Kenya, Sri Lanka, Yunnan Province	Bolivia, Colombia, Ghana, Kenya
ISCED 2	Low secondary	Bolivia; Colombia; Kenya; Sri Lanka; Lao PDR; Yunnan Province	Colombia, Kenya	Colombia, Kenya, Sri Lanka, Yunnan Province	Colombia, Kenya

table continues next page

Table C.1 Summary of Logistic Regression Results with Country Labels *(continued)*

		Baseline	Literacy	No literacy	All
ISCED 5	Tertiary <16 years			Bolivia; Colombia; Armenia; Georgia, Ukraine; Macedonia, FYR	Bolivia, Colombia, Armenia, Georgia, Ukraine
ISCED 5	Tertiary 16 years			Colombia, Kenya, Vietnam, Yunnan Province	Colombia, Ghana, Kenya, Vietnam
ISCED 5	Tertiary >16 years			Bolivia, Colombia, Vietnam, Sri Lanka, Lao PDR	Bolivia, Colombia, Vietnam
ISCED 5	Tertiary, all	Bolivia, Colombia, Ghana, Kenya, Vietnam, Sri Lanka, Lao PDR	Bolivia, Colombia, Ghana, Kenya, Vietnam		
	Literacy		Bolivia, Colombia, Ghana, Vietnam, Georgia, Ukraine		Bolivia, Ghana, Ukraine

Environmental Benefits Statement

The World Bank Group is committed to reducing its environmental footprint. In support of this commitment, the Publishing and Knowledge Division leverages electronic publishing options and print-on-demand technology, which is located in regional hubs worldwide. Together, these initiatives enable print runs to be lowered and shipping distances decreased, resulting in reduced paper consumption, chemical use, greenhouse gas emissions, and waste.

The Publishing and Knowledge Division follows the recommended standards for paper use set by the Green Press Initiative. The majority of our books are printed on Forest Stewardship Council (FSC)–certified paper, with nearly all containing 50–100 percent recycled content. The recycled fiber in our book paper is either unbleached or bleached using totally chlorine-free (TCF), processed chlorine-free (PCF), or enhanced elemental chlorine-free (EECF) processes.

More information about the Bank's environmental philosophy can be found at http://www.worldbank.org/corporateresponsibility.

www.ingramcontent.com/pod-product-compliance
Lightning Source LLC
Chambersburg PA
CBHW060315240426
43661CB00059B/2772